Roman & Greek Warfare

Roman & Greek Warfare

Tactics, Equipment, Weapons & Battles
of the Ancient Period

Warfare by Land and Sea

Eugene S. McCartney

Five Decisive Battles of the World

Edward Creasy

The Catapult and the Balista

Ralph Payne-Gallwey.

Roman & Greek Warfare
Tactics, Equipment, Weapons & Battles of the Ancient Period
Warfare by Land and Sea
by Eugene S. McCartney
Five Decisive Battles of the World
by Edward Creasy
The Catapult and the Balista
By Ralph Payne-Gallwey

FIRST EDITION

First published under the titles
Warfare by Land and Sea
Fifteen Decisive Battles of the World from Marathon to Waterloo
Appendix to the Book of the Crossbow and Ancient Projectile Engines

Leonaur is an imprint
of Oakpast Ltd

ISBN: 978-1-78282-162-5 (hardcover)
ISBN: 978-1-78282-163-2 (softcover)

http://www.leonaur.com

Contents

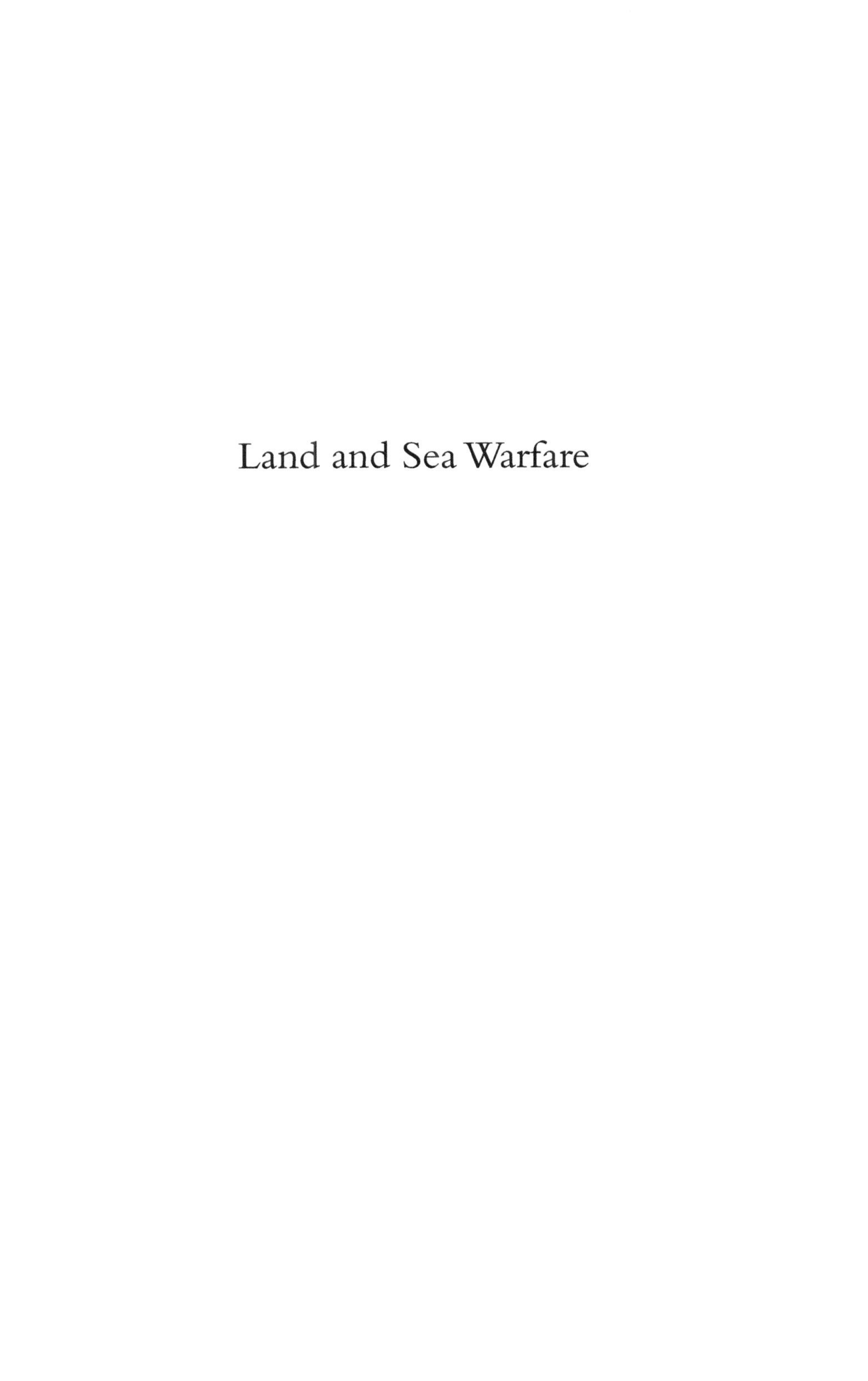

Land and Sea Warfare

SIEGE OPERATIONS

TURRIS AMBULATORIA "*Walking tower*" — TESTUDO ARIETARIA *Mantlet with ram suspended beneath it* — TESTUDO "*Tortoise*" *of shields (in center of picture.)* — ONAGER BALLISTA *Ancient Artillery*

Contents

To

The

Memory

of

My Parents

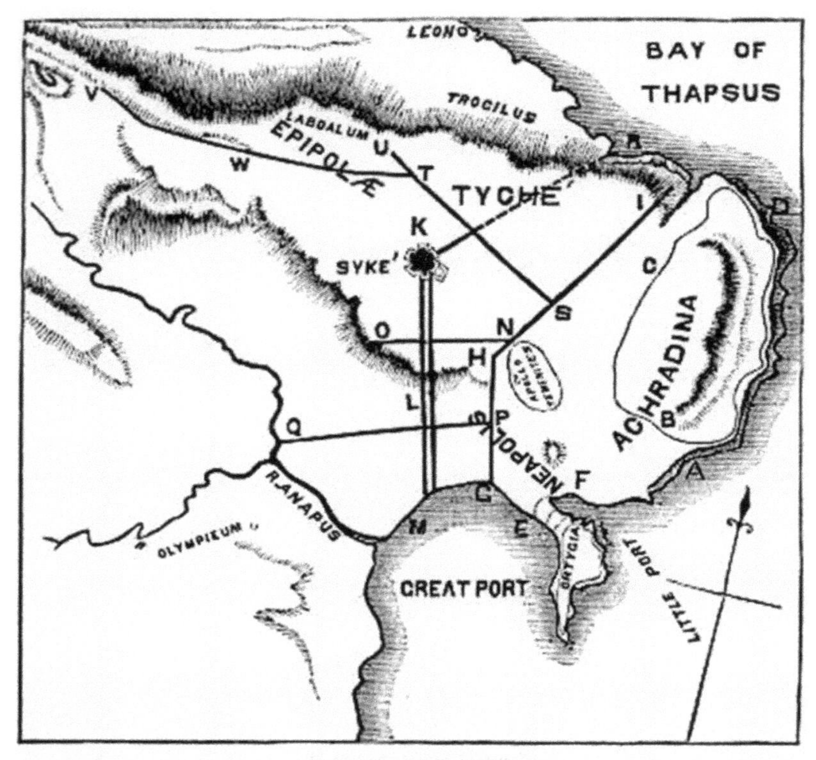

PLAN OF SYRACUSE.

A, B, C, D. Wall of the Outer City of Syracuse at time of the arrival of Nicias in Sicily.
E, F. Wall of Ortygia, or the Inner City of Syracuse, at the same time.
G, H, I. Additional fortification built by the Syracusans in the winter of 415–414 B.C.
K. Athenian fortification at Syke.
K, L, M. Southern portion of the Athenian circumvallation from Syke to the Great Harbor.
N, O. First counter-work erected by the Syracusans.
P, Q. Second counter-work constructed by the Syracusans.
K, R. Intended, but unfinished, circumvallation of the Athenians from the northern side of Syke to the outer sea at Trogilus.
S, T, U. Third Syracusan counter-wall.
V. Outer fort constructed by Gylippus.
V, W, T. Wall of junction between this outer fort and the third Syracusan counter-work.

Introduction

Some books need no preface, and I believe this work of Mr. McCartney is one of them. However, an expression of commendation, by one whose profession is military, of a work on a military subject by a layman, may not be amiss.

The author has presented us with a book that should be appreciated by those who have neither the time nor the opportunity to delve into ancient Grecian and Roman military history at length. A book of this kind, following on the heels of the World War, in which Germany, a super-military nation, presumably so erudite in the principles of war, failed to win, may seem to be a gratuitous offering; and a reader may well ask, "What is there to this science of war anyway?" Germany's failure cannot be credited to ignorance of the science of war, but may be attributed more to her failure to apply it as an art and to her error in figuring that the principles of war could be applied to respective situations and a certain specific result obtained. No set of principles, no matter how meticulously applied, will win a battle or a campaign, not unless "Dame Fortune" is 100 *per cent* on our side, and possibly not then. There must be something more than a knowledge of science. There must be the ability to apply these scientific principles, in which we must include a proper conception of what is known as " Command."

We are apt to refer to successful military leaders as lucky gamblers, and many of the best took the greatest chances. But these chances were only taken after all the preventable factors that might have contributed to failure had been eliminated in advance.

Since science is the sum of all knowledge on a given subject, we would not be actually true to that definition did we not familiarize ourselves with military history, even the most ancient, from which these principles are deduced. The author has shown how similar in the principles involved certain modern battles are to those fought by Alexander, Hannibal, and Julius Caesar. And one cannot but be impressed, in reading this book, with the sincerity of Napoleon when he delivered himself of his 78th war maxim:

> Read and re-read the campaigns of Alexander, Hannibal, Caesar, Gustavus Adolphus, Turenne, Eugene, and Frederick; take them for your model; that is the only way of becoming a great captain, and of obtaining the secrets of the art of war.

But in reading and studying the campaigns of these great commanders from a military viewpoint, one must only be a historian long enough to become informed of what occurred and then be a soldier in drawing lessons and applying them to concrete cases.

In this the author has excelled, for he gives us enough of the history to localize the event and show the application of the principle, and then deduces the principle and shows its application to a modern battle.

The author brings out the importance of leadership in connection with command. In the days of small armies that operated under the eye of the commander, it was not so difficult to play up this important element "leadership," but in the modern armies that number hundreds of thousands of men and hundreds of guns, it is quite difficult for the commander, particularly of the larger units, to get into personal touch with his men to the same extent that Hannibal and Alexander did. But, nevertheless, where opportunity offers itself, and that opportunity can often be made, even the highest commanders should, and in the World War generally did, make themselves acquainted personally with the troops in the front line.

The evolution of military organisation into its present form is but a development of the organisations of the ancient Grecian and Roman *phalanx* and *legion*; and it has only been in most recent times that the word "legion" has disappeared from the American organisations; while in our organisations it did not, strictly speaking, mean the same thing it did to the Roman, yet, nevertheless, we had in the Civil War such organisations as Hampton's Legion.

In taking up the principle of shock and fire, the author is but giving us a discussion of the principles of fire and movement, or the principle of movement. In ancient times, fire to cover movement in the attack, which culminated in the shock of physical contact, took the form of a standing barrage of arrows, javelins and other missiles, while the troops moved forward to get in personal contact with the enemy and to destroy him with the sword as we now do with the bayonet. This barrage now takes the form of projectiles from 75mm. and 155mm. artillery, machine guns, etc.

In Chapter 6, referring to the victory at Marathon, the writer gives us one sentence which should appeal to the armies of democracy:

> For the first time a free citizen-soldiery, inspired by lofty ideals and love of country, had turned back the lash-driven hordes of a military despotism.

In reading Chapter 6 one sees illustrated by their application so many of our modern strategical, tactical formations that one must be convinced that strategy and tactics have undergone very little change, particularly the former, and the latter only in so far as to adapt itself to modern weapons. In the World War it was some time before the Allies awoke to the fact that the principle of concentrating masses against the enemy at some one point was still as good as when Theban Epaminondas applied that principle at the Battle of Leuctra, 371 B.C. We soon learned to send our reinforcements in where they could get through, which was the enemy's weakest point, and not where they could not get through, which was the enemy's strongest point. The wedge at Arbela, and the overlapping and flank attacks on other occasions by Alexander read like a preliminary to campaigns of Napoleon, and I am not sure that Napoleon in forcing the crossing of the Danube near the Island of Labou had not in mind Alexander's crossing of the Hydaspes.

Surely, Hooker at Chancellorsville must have heard something about that crossing of Alexander. The question of instruction and discipline, so ably handled in Chapter 9, cannot but impress the readers with the source of the strength of the Roman soldier. Our preliminary drills with the bayonet and the grenade in our various instruction camps at the beginning of the World War could not but have impressed the Roman legionaries had they been about to see these activities, and the discipline that we tried to instil into our soldiers and in which we met with considerable success was only that form of discipline which Caesar found so necessary—that subconscious obedience to the will of the commander. Military hygiene, sanitation, castrametation, and subsistence were not unknown to Caesar, as shown in Chapter 9.

Had the spade been used at Shiloh by the Federal troops as assiduously as it was used by the Romans in protecting their camps, the Federal Army would not have come so near to an overwhelming defeat.

The Germans since the days of Von Schlieffen have been most profound in their study of the principle of the Battle of Cannae, and it was no fault of the Von Schlieffen plan which he intended should be carried out on "*Der Tag*," that the Battle of the Marne was a Teutonic failure. The Von Schlieffen plan in spirit was not carried out by the younger Moltke, for Von Schlieffen welcomed the French offensive into Lorraine, since it would facilitate a wide turning movement by his main striking arm through the plains of Belgium and Northern France.

One might discuss the points of this book at length in the preface, but it would be to no purpose, since the reader will find copious references and the specific illustrations from which he can extend his reading as far as he may see fit.

In conclusion, I might say that while having a full appreciation of the necessity for a knowledge of military history and a familiarity with the principles of war, the reader must never forget that the great difficulty is in arriving at a decision as to what shall be done, and then the greater difficulty is to get the orders executed. Marshal Foch has stated that the great difficulty in war is in the execution.

A poor plan well executed may be better in the long run than the most brilliant conception carried out in a half-hearted manner.

Colonel W. K. Naylor, U. S. A.

Author's Preface

In picturing the high efficiency attained by the ancients in military science, I shall call attention, not only to first instances of manoeuvres and to examples of direct influence, but also to certain analogies in modern warfare which are in some cases virtually a return to ancient practice, military atavism, so to speak.

It is with some misgiving that I introduce so many quotations into the text, yet my purpose is best served by letting military critics, ancient and modern, speak *ex cathedra*.

I have used the manual of Vegetius on Military Science more freely than does the average writer on things military. It is unfortunate that he does not indicate to whom he is indebted for the miscellaneous pieces of information which he brings together. Most of his material was taken from or based upon authors who wrote when Roman discipline was stricter, Roman training more exacting, and the military machine more efficient than in his day. More than any other writer he gives us an insight into the German-like thoroughness with which the Roman Army was trained. Those who desire a full readable account of the equipment, organisation, tactics and strategy of ancient armies will be able to find it in convenient form in Dodge's *Alexander*, *Hannibal* and *Caesar*, the first three volumes of the *Great Captains* series.

1. Permanency of Ancient Contributions

Can anyone be so indifferent or idle as not to care to know by what means, and under what kind of polity, almost the whole inhabited world was conquered and brought under the dominion of the single city of Rome, and that too within a period of not quite fifty-three years? [1]

This question is put by Polybius, a Greek, whose country at the end of those fifty-three years, 167 B.C., was part of the Roman dominion and who was himself practically a prisoner in Italy. We of the present generation marvel likewise at the achievements of Polybius's countrymen, which reached their climax in a material way in world empire under Alexander. It is not the province of this investigation to answer in full, even from the military side, the question put by Polybius, but rather to note advances made by the Greeks and Romans in the art of war while they were acquiring this power, and to record their lasting contributions, especially in tactics and strategy. War, even as conducted today, is to be included among the many activities of modern life which owe their first scientific development in Europe to Greece and Rome.

Greeks and Romans were not, of course, the first peoples in the world to have soldiers as distinguished from warriors. In the fourteenth century before Christ, in the Battle of Kadesh, fought in North Syria between the Hittites and the Egyptians under Ramses II, tactical and strategical ability of a high order was displayed, yet this is the only very early battle the manoeuvres of which can be ascertained in considerable detail. [2]

---

1. Polybius, I. i; E. S. Shuckburgh, *The Histories of Polybius*, Translated, 2 vols., London, 1889. I have used Shuckburgh's translation for all quotations from Polybius.
2. See J. A. Breasted, *The Battle of Kadesh*.

Not until 546 B.C. was there fought another engagement of whose formations and manoeuvres we have a detailed record. At the battle of Sardis in which Cyrus the Great vanquished Croesus, one of the great obstacles to the consolidation of the Persian Empire, we see the first skilful attempt to coordinate shock and fire tactics.

Cyrus says:

> The javelin-men I shall range behind those armed with corselets, and behind the javelin-men the archers; for how could any one place those in front who themselves confess that they can sustain no encounter hand to hand? But when they have those armed with corselets in front of them, they will stand; and the one line hurling their javelins, and the other discharging their arrows, over the heads of those ranged before them, will do execution upon the enemy; and as far as any one does harm to the enemy, it is plain that so far he relieves his fellow combatants.

These words Xenophon records for us in the *Cyropaedia*, [3] a work throughout which we find attributed to Cyrus and even to his opponents a marked appreciation of military formations and manoeuvres and principles.

Greece and Rome are the only ancient European nations that had soldiers with all that such a word implies in matters of organisation and coordination and discipline. The fighting men of other nations were merely warriors, men with as much strength and heroism and perhaps as much patriotism as the Greeks and Romans, yet for want of training unable to use these qualities to the greatest advantage.

Most of us have a mental picture of the ancient soldier clad in helmet, breast-plate, greaves and shield, and equipped for the offensive with javelin, spear or sword, and perhaps a dagger. We think of light-armed active men, consisting of slingers, archers or javelin-throwers, or even the cavalry as engaging in preliminary skirmishes, while behind them advance hoplites or legionaries. We see the heavy-armed men, protected by cavalry on the flanks, fighting grimly in ranks in a stand-up finish fight in which brawn and manual dexterity gain the day. Such, in its lowest terms, is a description of the equipment and method of the ancient soldier. It may pertinently be asked what contribution he could make to the science of warfare.

Tactical methods change with the change of weapons. The in-

3. *Cyropaedia*, VI. 3. 24. The translation is that of H. G. Dakyns, *The Works of Xenophon*, 4 vols.

vention of complicated mechanisms of destruction has made modern warfare an involved operation and in general has caused ancient methods to be discarded, so that in present-day military instruction they have only an historical interest. Tactical principles, however, are not so transitory.

Today, (1923), armies may fight in the open many miles apart with mountains intervening, or a few yards away in the depths of trenches, yet the salient so common in contemporary warfare is really a logical descendant of the ancient tactical formation of the *cuneus* or wedge, and conveys the same ominous threat. Another factor that makes for the modification of tactical theories is the national temperament. A Roman could hardly be expected to fight like a Greek, or an American like a German, in spite of the fact that one nation cannot disregard what another progressive one is doing. Changes will be inaugurated to allow for the evolution of the man as well as of the weapon. Still modern tactics are in many cases a development of ancient tactics, and, as far as Europe is concerned, the Greeks and Romans must be given credit for doing pioneer work.

In grand tactics, the immediate moves which bring about the clash of armies, we shall find modern analogies to ancient situations and even instances of indebtedness. In 1851 the great military critic Jomini, when asked whether recent improvements in firearms would cause any great modifications in the art of war, replied that:

> They would probably have an influence upon the details of tactics, but that in great strategical operations and the grand combinations of battles, victory would, now as ever, result from the application of principles which had led to the success of great generals in all ages; of Alexander and Caesar, as well as of Frederick and Napoleon.

Comparisons with the strategy of Frederick have in fact been made in a special study to explain and illustrate the strategy of Pericles. [4]

A decade before the Great War Marshal Foch quoted with approval the words of Von der Goltz to the effect that the principles of military art are everlasting, although it deals with factors that undergo a ceaseless evolution. Material and mechanical development will not nullify principles of strategy, although it will affect the application of

4. Delbrück, *Die Strategie des Perikles, erläutert durch die Strategie Friedrichs des Grossen.* Compare also the title of another work by Delbrück, *Die Perserkriege und Burgunderkriege.*

them. It is the practice of strategy that is elastic, and in this field, each age has its own peculiar problems to face and solve.

Not even the inventions of the last two or three decades have changed the fundamental principles of strategy. With the greatest of all wars in mind, a recent authority writes:

> While this war involved greater numbers of men on both sides than any previous war, weapons of greater destructive power and more rapid and sure means of transportation and communication, yet the general methods followed were like those of Thutmose III, Alexander, and the rest. We see the same endeavour to bring destructive forces to positions of strategic importance; the same endeavour to find the weak point, to make flank attacks, to feint at the line of communication or attack it; to feint at the line of retreat or attack it; the same endeavour to hold a force of the enemy with a part of one's own force while dealing an important blow with another part; the same endeavour to envelop and capture the enemy. [5]

Napoleon tells us that:

> Gustavus Adolphus, Turenne, and Frederick, as well as Alexander, Hannibal, and Caesar, have all acted upon the same principles. These have been—to keep their forces united; to leave no weak spot unguarded; to seize with rapidity on important points.

That antiquity still has military lessons to teach is shown by other words of Napoleon in which he urges the aspiring general to make war after the fashion of Alexander, Hannibal, Caesar, Gustavus Adolphus, Turenne, Prince Eugene, and Frederick the Great; to read and read again the history of their eighty-eight campaigns; to use them as a pattern, the sole means of becoming a great captain. Such study, he says, will be enlightening and through it one will learn to reject all maxims foreign to those of these great commanders.

In his schooldays, Napoleon is said to have sacrificed many a play hour to read works of history, particularly Polybius and Plutarch. An indication of the early ripening of his judgment is seen in his preference for Arrian's history of Alexander over that of Quintus Curtius. In his camp library were included classical authors treating of things military, such as Thucydides, Polybius, Plutarch, Arrian, Livy, Tacitus.

---

5. Rear-Admiral Bradley A. Fiske, *The Art of Fighting*.

Even though a general has come up from the ranks in time of war, his observation and experience cannot possibly be broad enough to enable him to meet every emergency. He can, however, fortify himself by reading, and to this extent is able to prepare for war in time of peace. Napoleon says:

> On the field of battle the happiest inspiration is often only a recollection.

It will be noticed that of Napoleon's seven great captains, there are three ancients, one a Greek, one a Roman, one neither Greek nor Roman, but a student of Greek military history and a teacher, though an unwilling one, of the Romans. In view of his relation to both great classical races, it seems imperative to include in this volume his contribution to the science of warfare.

Of the eighty-eight campaigns, from which Napoleon says a complete treatise of the art of war could be written, embracing all the principles of offensive and defensive warfare, thirty-eight were carried on by the three ancient generals, eight by Alexander, seventeen by Hannibal and thirteen by Caesar.

In Creasy's *Fifteen Decisive Battles of the World*, which ends with Waterloo, five conflicts are ancient. We may stop to mention them, although military authorities are not in entire accord with Creasy's judgment. The first one, Marathon, 490 B.C., decided not merely that the course of empire should go westward, but that the empire should be western. In 331 B.C. at the Battle of Arbela, or, as Plutarch prefers to call it, Gaugamela, Alexander ended forever the Persian peril. The defeat of the Athenians before Syracuse in 413 B.C. was decisive, according to Creasy, in removing the menace of Athens to the independent nations of the West. The disaster to Hasdrubal at the Metaurus in 207 B.C. made it clear that an Aryan rather than a Semitic civilization should dominate the world. At Teutoberg forest in 9 *A.D.*, a terrible defeat was administered to the Romans by the Germans under Arminius. Creasy writes:

> Had Arminius been supine or unsuccessful our Germanic ancestors would have been enslaved or exterminated in their original seats along the Eyder and the Elbe.

The island which is now the seat of a world empire would never have borne the name England.

In spite of the advances in methods of warfare made by other nations, the Greeks seem to have derived and formulated their military art almost entirely from their own experience in battle. Though it seems safe to assume that knowledge of machines of war was introduced from Persia, since, among other reasons, Cyrus the Great had used them in his campaigns, they were probably recommended to mainland Greeks by Asiatic Greeks who had had painful experiences with them. At all events, the study of the evolution of modern warfare begins with the Greeks.

If the study of strategy could be conveniently divorced from that of tactics, it would still be possible in large measure to make ancient examples of strategical principles the basis of modern instruction.

2. The Evolution of Generalship

The modern idea that the general is first and foremost the intellectual leader of the army is so well established that it is hard to realize that it is an evolution from an origin far different. The Greek word for general is *strategos*, 'one who leads the army;' the old Latin word is *praetor*, 'one who goes before.' From the etymologies one would suspect that the ideal general was the man qualified to set his army an example in courage and prowess. And such the history of war shows him to have been. It is not surprising that Plutarch should make the observation [1] that from the earliest times the soldiers thought that man best fitted to rule who was most valiant in feats of arms.

How strong the conception of physical leadership was will be recognized more clearly if we recall the names of a few of the many generals who were casualties on the field of battle. The Athenian Cleon was slain in retreating from the fight at Amphipolis (422 B.C.), and his victorious opponent, Brasidas, was fatally wounded; Cleombrotus was mortally wounded at Leuctra (371 B.C.); Epaminondas died shortly after the Battle of Mantinea (362 B.C.) from a spear wound he received in the breast while heading the charge, pike in hand; Philip was wounded at Chaeronea (338 B.C); Agis was slain at Megalopolis (331 B.C); at the third Battle of Mantinea (207 B.C.), Philopoemen completed his victory by personally slaying his opponent, Machanidas. The Persian prince Cyrus was killed at the head of his combined Persian and Greek Army.

In quelling a mutiny among his soldiers, Alexander boasted that he could show wound for wound with the bravest and still have some to spare. Plutarch [2] gives a long list of injuries inflicted upon Alexander by mace, scimitar, sword, arrow, dart and spear. In the attack on the

1. Demetrius.

2. Moralia.

city of the Malli Alexander personally led one of the storming parties. Impatient with the progress of events, he seized one of the first two scaling ladders to arrive and led the way up. When with only three companions he had reached the top of the wall, the ladders broke with the weight of the Macedonians hurrying to his assistance. Not heeding the entreaties of his men who implored him to jump down into their arms, Alexander with his companions leaped down on the inside. Fighting desperately, he had his corselet pierced by an arrow that penetrated a lung. When it seemed that nothing could save him, his men arrived and rescued him. Thanks to a good constitution and robust health, the young king recovered.

This hair-breadth escape emboldened Alexander's officers to protest against his risking his life in dare-devil feats, but it was neither his nature nor policy to direct engagements from a position in the rear. As one writer puts it:

> Napoleon used his sword once as generalissimo; Alexander was first in a breach, first in a charge, wounded a dozen times, himself the leader of every desperate expedition. Half of it was mad recklessness, the other was set purpose; professional armies were new as yet, and the machine needed animating with a personal feeling, if it were to submit to the labours which Alexander designed for its endurance.[3]

The killing of Alexander at either Issus or Arbela would have meant the destruction of the Macedonians, yet without the inspiration of his magnetic presence and prowess in the front line, it is hard to see how these battles could have been won. Armies were not yet ready for solely intellectual leadership.

If chivalry in war ever existed, it was among the Greeks, and in the days of the Trojan War, when champions fought openly and prided themselves upon taking no unfair advantage. Homeric notions about the proprieties of battle died hard. When the Spartan Archidamus saw a dart from a machine of war that had just been brought from Sicily, he exclaimed:

> Hercules, the valour of man is at an end.

On the eve of the Battle of Arbela, Alexander rejected the proposal to attack by night, declaring that he would not steal a victory.

The Athenians especially took pride in the display of valour. In the

3. Hogarth, in *The Journal of Philology*, XVII.

funeral speech of Pericles eulogizing those who had fallen in the first year of the Peloponnesian War, we find set forth with pride a policy that seems to us to be suicidal:

> In the study of war also we differ from our enemies in the following respects. We throw our city open to all, and never, by the expulsion of strangers, exclude anyone from either learning or observing things, by seeing which unconcealed any of our enemies might gain an advantage; for we trust not so much to preparations and stratagems, as to our own valour for daring deeds. [4]

Not even in Hellenistic days was there general recognition regarding the commander's proper part in a battle. In Polybius [5]we find a significant sentence *apropos* of the Battle of Mantinea in 207 B.C.:

> And now there occurred an undoubted instance of what some doubt, namely, that the issues in war are for the most part decided by the skill or want of skill of the commanders.

In making his plans for the battle, Philopoemen had shown wonderful foresight, and it was only his precautionary measures that enabled him to convert into victory an apparently overwhelming disaster.

Perhaps no Greek had a clearer conception of the intellectual side of generalship than Philopoemen. Of him Livy writes [6] that when he came to a place that was difficult of passage, he would, when alone, ask himself, or if accompanied, his companions, what measures should be taken if the enemy appeared in front, on the flank, or in the rear. These and other questions he used to ask.

Napoleon knew Livy well, and one of his maxims of war sounds strangely familiar:

> A general-in-chief should ask himself frequently in the day, 'What would I do if the enemy's army appeared now in my front, or on my right, or my left?' If he have any difficulty in answering these questions, his position is bad, and he should seek to remedy it.

The Romans, too, seem to have had a real Homeric code of fight-

---

4. Thuc, II. 39. The translation is that of H. Dale.
5. XI.
6. XXXV.

ing. With them, war was a sort of duel (*bellum<duellum*), a personal encounter in which the most valiant won. For the commander who stripped off the armour of the opposing commander-in-chief whom he had vanquished in single combat, there was the reward of the *spolia opima*, 'the richest spoils.' This honour was gained but three times, although champions at times represented the contesting armies, notably in the case of the Horatii and Curiatii. Titus Manlius Torquatus and Marcus Valerius Corvinus gained both fame and *cognomina* by defeating in single combat Gauls of huge stature. During the Spanish campaigns Scipio deliberated whether he should accept the challenge of a Gaul to single combat. Marcellus never declined a challenge and always succeeded in killing his opponents.

Among the Romans for centuries we find the idea of personal leadership very pronounced. In the Second Punic War, many Roman consuls met a tragic end. Flaminius, Aemilius Paulus, and Marcellus were among those who perished. Publius Cornelius Scipio, the father of the destined conqueror of Hannibal, was carried wounded from the Battle of the Ticinus (219 B.C.).

At one time the Romans seem to have looked upon strategy as base deceit or treachery. In connection with the story of the refusal of the Roman senate to treat with victorious Pyrrhus, we are told that the Romans placed their dependence on heroism, and not on ruses or plotting. Even Caesar, when he found it necessary to abandon the investment of Pompey's army at Dyrrachium, imperative as it was for him to steal a march upon his foe, still made it a point of honour (or pride?) to sound the signal for retreat by a blast of the trumpet. There is a significant passage in Livy, [7] in which the historian of Rome's greatness makes it a point of national pride that the Romans did not employ the stratagems of the Carthaginians, or the wiliness of the Greeks of that period, among whom, says our author contemptuously, it was more glorious to outwit a foe than to vanquish him with main strength.

Rome's arch enemies in this war well understood the province of the general. Polybius tells us that, at the Battle of the Metaurus, Hasdrubal regarded his personal safety as of the highest importance until all was lost. Then he faced his fate, and died a death worthy of the lion's brood, the sons of Barca.

Their first real insight into generalship was acquired by the Romans during the Second Punic War. When Hannibal was addressing

---

7. XLII.

the men who were to form an ambuscade for a flank attack upon the Romans at the Trebia (218 B.C.), he said:

You have an enemy blind to such arts of war.[8]

After their defeat in this engagement and the colossal disaster at Lake Trasimenus (217 B.C.), they began to sense the reason for continued Carthaginian success. Subsequent to the debacle at Cannae they had a wholesome respect for this new factor in warfare. Thereafter they paid it many a tacit compliment. Though they themselves had much better fighting material than the Carthaginians, time after time they allowed Hannibal with but a fraction of their own numbers to march without a fight up and down Italy and to pass by their armies almost unmolested. The Romans saw that they *must* take lessons from Hannibal. Under his instruction the Roman generals, especially Claudius Nero and the younger Scipio, began to execute movements they would never have dreamed of otherwise.

On one occasion during the African campaign against Metellus Scipio, Caesar was marking time at Ruspina while awaiting his veterans. His opponent, becoming emboldened, "advanced with his whole army and towered elephants" right up to Caesar's ramparts. Caesar, without leaving his tent, received reports of the moves of the enemy and gave directions how to meet them. " This is the first instance in ancient military books where a commanding general is described as managing a battle just as he would today." [9]

In an emergency, even Caesar did not hesitate to snatch a shield, and to direct the battle from the first ranks by precept and example. Unlike Alexander, however, Caesar was never a *beau sabreur*; he was the intellectual captain. In this connection one should remember that when Caesar began his real military career he was several years older than Alexander was at the end of his eventful life.

In the work of Onesander, who in 49 *A.D.* dedicated to a Roman consul a work on the duty of the general, we see a full realization of the proper functions of the commander. He says that the science of the general avails more than his strength, and that a general who fights as a common soldier is like a pilot who leaves his post to perform the duties of a common seaman. Plutarch expressed special admiration for Hannibal because, although he had been in so many battles that one wearied of counting them, he had never been wounded.

---

8. Livy, XXI.

9. Dodge, Caesar.

By the time of the famous siege of Jerusalem, it was generally recognized throughout the army that a general should not endanger his command by taking unnecessary personal risks, for the soldiers under Titus protested against his exposing himself. It is given as one of the maxims of war by Vegetius that a leader should not personally fight except in an emergency, or as a last resort.

Tactics and strategy had become increasingly complex so that the safety of the army depended on the safety of the general. The evolution of generalship was, then, a steady, natural, and inevitable growth. The realization that it was entirely beyond the province of a general to make a practice of fighting with weapons was a contribution chiefly of the Romans.

The lesson that antiquity teaches so clearly about the proper place for the commander has not always been heeded. Steele [10] severely criticizes the Union general at the First Battle of Bull Run because, instead of setting up his headquarters somewhere in the rear and directing his army as a whole, he was "at the very front, in the thick of the battle, scarcely exercising any influence on the action beyond the sound of his voice."

A lesson in sound generalship is available to all readers of Plutarch's *Life of Pelopidas*:[11]

> Therefore Timotheus was right, when Chares was once showing the Athenians some wounds he had received, and his shield pierced by a spear, in saying: 'But I, how greatly ashamed I was, at the siege of Samos, because a bolt fell near me; I thought I was behaving more like an impetuous youth than like a general in command of so large a force.'

10. *American Campaigns*, Washington, D. C, 1909; I.

11. II. 3; Translation, Perrin, in *The Loeb Classical Library,* New York, 1917.

3. The Phalanx and the Legion

Before noting further contributions of the Greeks and Romans, we shall stop to call attention to their tactical units, the *phalanx* and *legion*. The *phalanx* consisted of rows of hoplites, heavy-armed men, equipped for the offense with spear and sword and protected by shield, helmet, corselet and greaves. The hoplite was a spearman or pikeman whose heavy equipment restricted his effectiveness to level ground. As four-fifths of Greece is mountainous, it seems paradoxical that the hoplite was the mainstay of the Greek armies. The heavy arms and armour were designed to protect the open fields and arable valley lands, since possession of them gave an enemy control of the food-supply and consequent power to dictate peace. It will be recalled that winter campaigns were very infrequent.

Power was acquired by depth of ranks as well as by heavy weapons. The average depth of the *phalanx* was eight men, although it occasionally reached sixteen, even before the time of the Macedonians. As early as 424 B.C. at Delium the Theban *phalanx* had a depth of 25, while at Leuctra in 371 B.C. Epaminondas made his left wing about 50 ranks deep.

One ancient writer,[1] who consulted several sources of information, estimates the number of men in the phalanx at 16,384. With a depth of 16 men, this would make 1,024 files. Allowing the usual space of six feet to a man, *i.e.*, intervals of three feet, we see that the line would stretch out over half a mile in length. In close order of battle, this space might of course be reduced, as Polybius says. We hear of *phalanxes* of from 10,000 to 20,000 men. Naturally the *phalanx* was divided and sub-divided, as is the case with our own military division.

Polybius says:[2]

---

1. Aelianus, *De Instruendis Aciebus*.
2. XVIII.

Many considerations may easily convince us that, if only the *phalanx* has its proper formation and strength, nothing can resist it face to face or withstand its charge.

The spear, or *sarissa*, as the Macedonians called it, might be 21 feet long, or even 24 in Hellenistic times. Five or six rows of spearpoints would project beyond the front rank making an impenetrable barrier. The spears of the rear ranks rested upon the shoulders of men in front with their points directed upward. The formation looked like a huge porcupine with the quills pointing in one direction. The Roman consul, Lucius Aemilius, a seasoned veteran, confessed to friends at Rome that he had never seen anything more terrible and alarming than the Macedonian *phalanx* of Perseus.

We need not, however, suppose that the *phalanx* of Alexander was equipped with a spear of such length. The 24-foot *sarissa* mentioned by Polybius is possibly due to lack of imagination and tactical ability on the part of the generals, with perhaps some deterioration in the quality of the troops.

The Roman *legion* derives its name from the *legio*. the 'gathering' of the clans. Their fighting at first must have lacked orderly formation and intelligent direction. According to one account, the early Romans were utterly astounded when they found their opponents, the Tyrrheni (Etruscans), organising the attack and forming compact ranks. They showed their military bent by going and doing likewise.

The legion is a descendant of the Doric *phalanx*, which found its way into Latium by way of Magna Graecia. The Romans adopted and adapted it, making it far more mobile and flexible. Change in the phalanx was inevitable. Without cavalry as an efficient complementary arm, the formation of the *legion* had to be opened so that it alone might take the initiative; otherwise the *phalanx* formation was doomed to stagnation, as in Hellenistic Macedon. The history of these changes is lost, but it has been suggested that innovations were made by Camillus in order to meet the initial impact of the Gauls, who used long swords, by allowing fresh troops to advance between the contestants in the front line. Mountain wars against the Samnites may have caused other changes. By the time of the wars with Pyrrhus, the *manipular legion*, which is built around small bodies of men, was highly developed.

Theoretically, the legion was supposed to have 6,000 men. The century, the smallest division, consisted of 100 men commanded by a *centurion.* Two *centuries* made a company or *maniple.* Three *maniples* constituted a *cohort* and ten *cohorts* a *legion.* Polybius tells us that the *legion* of his day numbered 4,200 men, in times of emergency, 5,000.

The *legion* had three ranks, the second of which was designed to relieve or replace those in the front rank. The *triarii,* or men in the third rank, acted as reserves to those in front of them, although they are not reserves in our sense of the word.

The *legionary* was armed in much the same fashion as the *hoplite.* He was, however, a swordsman, and not a spearman. The spear, as a weapon for close fighting, had been replaced by a short, pointed, broad sword with two edges, which he was wont to use for thrusting and not for slashing. As a rule, the spear was hurled before the lines clashed.

Through adaptation and remodelling, the Italianisation of the *phalanx* was so complete that its foreign extraction passed unnoticed. The best type of *legion* never met the best type of *phalanx,* nor were conditions and generalship equal when *phalanx* and legion did meet. At Heraclea in 280 B.C., they battled for the first time. Here, after seven indecisive clashes, it was Pyrrhus's "Lucanian oxen" (elephants), aided by Thessalian horse, that beat the Romans. At Cynocephalae in 197 B.C., the *phalanx* under Philip V, after gaining an initial success over the *legion* under Flaminius, lost the day because of its inability to manoeuvre over broken ground.

It is really unfair to compare the best *phalanx* and the best *legion.* They were intended for different purposes. The Romans depended entirely upon the *legionaries* for victory; in set battles, the *phalanx* of Philip and Alexander was expected to hold or to engage the opposing infantry while cavalry manoeuvres were being executed. Cavalry was the striking arm. The *phalanx* of Alexander does not seem to have been at the mercy of uneven ground. It was flexible too. At Arbela it surprised the Persians by opening up to let the scythe-bearing chariots through.

The *legion* was, however, more flexible than the *phalanx.* Once the spears had been put in position, the *phalanx* could not be readily divided. The *legion* could act as a unit or in parts, and *maniples* and *cohorts* could be readily detached from it, even during an engagement.

Unlike the *phalanx,* the *legion* could defend itself from an attack in the rear. At Cynocephalae, one wing of the *phalanx* carried all before it until it was assailed from behind. Then it was easily defeated, since "the nature of the *phalanx* is such that the men cannot face round singly and defend themselves."[3] In the battle with the Helvetii in 58 B.C.,[4] an attack was made upon the Romans from the rear. The third line simply faced about and met the new peril.

Some flattering tributes were paid by Rome's enemies to the organisation and equipment of the Roman *legion*. Mommsen thus sums up the changes that were visible in the *phalanx* of the victor of Heraclea, when he faced the Romans at Ausculum (279 B.C.):

> Pyrrhus, perceiving with the sharp eye of a soldier the advantages of the Roman *manipular* organisation, had on the wings substituted for the long front of his *phalanxes* an arrangement by companies with intervals between them in imitation of the *cohorts*.

The equipment of the *legion* was equally good. Hannibal fitted out many of his soldiers with weapons taken from slain *legionaries*.

The clash of the *legion* aided by horse against Alexander's formation would have been a sight for Mars. With pardonable patriotism, Livy thought the Romans would have been able to defeat Alexander if he had invaded Italy. Polybius, who saw and judged with the discernment of a soldier, had no doubt of the superiority of the *legion* over the *phalanx*.[5]

The *legion* and, to a smaller extent, the *phalanx* also, with their divisions and subdivisions, capable of manoeuvring in harmony or in detachments, have proved models of efficiency. Whatever the names these smaller units may take today, and whatever their numbers may be, no modern army would dare to disregard the lessons of minute organisation first taught so supremely well by Greeks and Romans.

---

3. Polyb., XVIII.
4. Caes., *B. G.*, I.5. For an extended comparison of the *phalanx* and the *legion*, see Polybius, XVIII.

4. Army Organisation: The Growth of Its Branches

The complex organisation of an army with the coordination of its many arms is the result of a long process of evolution. Because of the mountainous character of their country, the Greeks in their earliest encounters among themselves placed almost their sole dependence on the *hoplite*, the heavy-armed man. Even the horseman was a mounted infantryman. They had no cavalry at Marathon. They employed it at the beginning of the Peloponnesian War, but not to decide the shock of battle. Nicias anticipated for the siege of Syracuse the need of an efficient cavalry force, since he did not wish to be shut out from the interior of Sicily by the numerous Syracusan horsemen. It remained for Alexander, however, to bring out the latent power of cavalry.

At the outbreak of the Peloponnesian War, light-armed troops were held in disdain. [1] In the mountains of Aetolia, however, Athenian forces under Demosthenes were completely defeated by agile light-armed archers, [2] who refused to come to close quarters. Light-armed men from countries which had no heavy-armed men were found to be far superior to the light-armed forces of more progressive nations which emphasized the *hoplite* force. Before five years of this war had elapsed, it was perfectly clear that slingers, archers, and especially *peltasts* were a necessary complement of an efficient army.

The heavy-armed Spartans who were trapped by the Athenians on the rough island of Sphacteria (425 B.C.) managed to defend themselves from the *hoplites*. They succumbed only when they were assailed from a higher position in the rear by light-armed men fighting them from a distance with arrows. [3]

1. Thuc, III.
2. *Ibid.*
3. Thuc, IV.

The first decade of the fourth century saw the equipment, training and organisation of the *peltasts*, or light-armed men, vastly improved under the Athenian Iphicrates. [4] In 390 B.C, with *peltasts* supported by *hoplites*, he attacked without hesitation a body of 600 Spartan *hoplites* near Lechaeum (the port of Corinth). His men assailed the Spartans at long range with their javelins, always retiring before attacks and picking off enemies in the disorder following their futile charges. With skirmishing tactics they wearied the Spartans and would have annihilated them, had it not been for the timely arrival of their horsemen.

This engagement exercised a profound influence upon Greece, making it clear that an army needed the auxiliary branches of the service. It demonstrated that *peltasts* and horsemen were essential to both the efficiency and security of *hoplites*.

Armies were, then, becoming more complex with the advent of the fourth century. Reading aright the lessons of the Peloponnesian War, Dionysius I of Syracuse, who organised an army having eighty thousand infantry, strove for greater cooperation of the various arms. As a modern historian phrases it, he was "the first of the Greeks to combine effectively a variety of troops, as heavy-armed, light-armed, cavalry, and artillery." [5] We shall note in the next chapter his contribution to the mechanism of warfare.

Philip was the great innovator in army organisation. As early as 342 B.C. we find the orator Demosthenes noting with alarm the unprecedented warlike preparations being made by Philip and calling attention to the Macedonian peril. He says in effect:

> Formerly, the Lacedaemonians as well as the other Greeks did nothing more than invade each other's territory, during the four or five summer months, with their native force of citizen hoplites: in winter they stayed at home. But now we see Philip in constant action, winter as well as summer, attacking all around him, not merely with Macedonian hoplites, but with cavalry, light infantry, bowmen, foreigners of all descriptions and siege-batteries.[6]

We shall see how he developed artillery and laid the foundation for scientific siege-craft. Attention will be directed likewise to the part cavalry played in his army. In view of Philip's passion to invade Per-

4. Xen., *Hell*, IV.
5. Botsford, *A History of Greece*.
6. See George Grote, *A History of Greece*, London, 1851-56; XII.

sia, it is a warranted assumption that the experiences of Xenophon's Ten Thousand in that land had something to do with the increased complexity and greater coordination of the Macedonian armies, although in Greece itself a tendency in that direction had already become manifest. Xenophon's *hoplite* was infinitely superior to any Persian infantryman, but he was severely dealt with by the Persian cavalry in the plains, and fared badly at times at the hands of the light-armed mountaineer. When the Greeks again entered Persian dominions, they were prepared for all kinds of warfare.

> This scientific organisation of military force, on a large scale and with all the varieties of arming and equipment made to co-operate for one end, is the great fact of Macedonian history. [7]

With Philip war had become the business of the specialist.

Before Philip's time no army, not even the Spartan, was kept constantly under arms. Although there had been before his day professional soldiers, *i.e.,* mercenaries, even in the Greek armies, and though Greeks themselves had served as mercenaries, yet he was the first leader to institute a professional standing army imbued with a national spirit and instantly and permanently operative.

Philip's untimely death left unfulfilled his hope of invading Persia, but to his genius as an organiser must go much of the credit for Alexander's achievements. Alexander inherited his father's organising ability as well as an organised army. With his improvements and additions Greek military efficiency had reached its acme.

The Romans instituted a standing army in dependently of Greek influence. According to Livy, the protracted siege ofVeii, which lasted ten years (406-396), caused the Romans for the first time to engage in winter campaigning, and, incidentally, to inaugurate the custom of paying soldiers. Here too was a standing professional army, but it lacked the modern aspects of complex organisation and intensive training which characterized Philip's. It was not until the Second Punic War that the Roman Army attained a complexity and a system of coordination at all comparable with the Macedonian. To the Greeks must be given the credit of priority in this field.

---

7. Grote, *Op. cit.*, XII.

5. Shock and Fire: The Development of Artillery

The two cardinal means of bringing force to bear upon an opponent are shock and fire. Today, with the discoveries and inventions of modern science at command, fire is in the ascendant. In antiquity the reverse was the case. No body of men ever crashed through an opposing line with greater power and momentum than did the deep-ranked *phalanx*.

In the Great War, the Germans especially trained 'shock' troops who were used to form a 'spearhead' in assaults. This formation is virtually a return to the wedge of antiquity. One ancient writer tells us that the Thracians borrowed this formation from the Scythians. Philip of Macedon used it so effectively that its invention was attributed to him. [1] Alexander employed it with good results, notably, at Arbela. It was used by the Romans, too, who in camp slang sometimes called it the 'hog's head.'

Shock tactics were not, however, used to the exclusion of fire in antiquity. We find ancient analogues to our small arms in hand-thrown missiles, leaden bullets for the sling, the javelin and spear. The Romans were in the habit of hurling the *pila* before the shock and of resorting to their swords after the clash of the lines. The combination of spear and sword corresponds to our use of the rifle with the bayonet attached.

The Roman method of fighting reminds one of the tactical ideas of "Stonewall" Jackson, an outstanding infantry commander of the Civil War:

---

1. The "Leuctrian wedge" was somewhat different, being formed by the "refusing" of the entire line in sections. It is hardly probable that there was a *phalangite* serving as the apex of a body of men.

> There ought not to be much firing at all. My idea is that the best mode of fighting is to reserve your fire till the enemy get—or you get him—to close quarters. Then deliver one deadly, deliberate fire and—charge![2]

His tactics were Roman with the exception of the modification due to the substitution of explosives.

Among the Greeks especially we find a device that secured the same effect as the rifling of a gun. This was a detachable thong some eighteen inches long, which was wound tightly around the shaft in such a way as to leave a loop for the insertion of a finger or two. As the missile was thrown, the unwinding of the thong imparted a rotary motion to it and gave it greater steadiness, carriage, and penetrating power. The advantage of the thong has been demonstrated by experiments carried out for the Emperor Napoleon. It was found that a javelin which could be thrown only twenty meters without it could be hurled four times as far with it. [3]

Of Europeans, the Greeks and Romans first started to make war mechanical and they seem to have developed the warfare of machinery as far as was possible without the aid of explosives. The first of these machines of war was the ram, which was nothing more than a beam or trunk of a tree with one end fitted with metal, shaped at times like a prow, or even like a ram's head.

The first Athenian, and presumably the first Greek, to employ this device, was Pericles, who used it in the siege of Samos (440-439). [4] He was not, however, the inventor, since it had long been in use by older civilizations.

The beam of the *aries*, or ram, which resembled the mast of a ship, was often as much as 80, 100, or even 120 feet long. It could, therefore, reach across an intervening ditch or moat, and at the same time be operated from a position of comparative security. The Jewish historian Josephus tells us that there was no tower so strong or wall so broad that it could resist more than the first assaults. Demolition was only a question of time.

At the siege of Rhodes in 305 B.C., Demetrius, who acquired from the investment the epithet Poliorcetes, 'Besieger,' had two rams 120 cubits long. They were suspended from sheds and the moving and operation of them required the services of a thousand men. With them

2. G. F. R. Henderson, *Stonewall Jackson.*
3. See E. Norman Gardiner, *Greek Athletic Sports and Festivals.*
4. Diod. Sic, XII.

he battered down sections of wall containing stones four feet long.[5] A ram that the Romans used against Carthage (149 B.C.) was so large that 6,000 men were needed to bring it into action.[6] These monstrous devices demolished fortifications as inevitably as a 'Big Bertha' crushes modern defences.

For missiles, too, mechanical forces were utilized. The new power that was brought into play was the elasticity of torsion derived from immense coils of tightly twisted sinews, strands of horse-hair, or cordage. The credit of invention must go to the Sicilian Greeks. Diodorus, the Sicilian, who is doubtless proud of the achievements of his countrymen, tells us [7] that the catapult was invented in Syracuse about 400 B.C. under the patronage of Dionysius.

The catapult and *ballista* had three main parts: a stout standard, a track or groove for the missile, and the twisted skeins for creating motive force. The common ammunition of the catapult was arrows, of the *ballista*, stones. The term *ballista* was used only by the Romans, but the machine indicated by it is the same as the Greek 'stone-thrower.' The missile track of the *ballista* appears to have rested on the ground at an angle of 45 °. Naturally the lighter missiles of the catapult were shot at a lower trajectory.

These machines designed to increase the range and destructiveness of missiles are worthy of our utmost respect. Vitruvius speaks of ballistae intended to throw stones weighing from 2, 4, 6, 10, and 20 lbs. up to 360 lbs.

The engine which threw missiles with the highest trajectory, the *onager*, 'wild ass,' did not have a groove, but hurled stones from the end of a spoon-like holder in the end of a long wooden arm. Because of its high-angle fire, this machine is the nearest approach to the modern howitzer.[8] Its range could be in creased by the use of a sling attached to the end of this arm. It has been found that a modern model which will throw an 8-lb. stone from 350 to 360 yards will, when aided by a sling, cast it from 450 to 460 yards, and when the skein is twisted to its limit of tension, to nearly 500 yards. [9]

One Greek writer tells us that some engines could throw stones,

---

5. *Ibid.*, XX.
6. Appian, VIII.
7. XIV.
8. In Vegetius, II. 25, however, *onagri* are referred to as shooting arrows also. Lydus, *De Mag.*, I. 46, speaks of a vulgar use of the word *onager* in the sense of catapult.
9. Sir R. Payne-Gallwey, *The Projectile-Throwing Engines of the Ancients.*

the weight of which he does not specify, 700 or 800 yards. We are fortunate in having the testimony of an eyewitness of the performances of some of the Roman machines. In *The Jewish War* Josephus states[10] that at the siege of Jotapata by Vespasian the stones made a casualty of every man in their path, no matter how deep the ranks. In the same work, he says practically the same thing about their power at the siege of Jerusalem by Titus. Some stones the Romans shot weighed a talent (57¾ lbs.) and carried 1200 feet or more. Demetrius made a protracted bombardment of Rhodes with stones weighing a talent.

So powerful were missiles from artillery that, at the siege of Massilia, Caesar's men constructed sheds or *mantlets* (*porticus*) with beams a foot thick.[11]

In describing a battle fought near Cremona between the armies of Vitellius and Vespasian in 69 *A.D.*, Tacitus[12] tells us that a huge *ballista* of the Fifteenth Legion would have destroyed the opposing battle line, if it had not been put out of commission by two soldiers, who braved death to destroy its mechanism.

During the siege of Syracuse (214-212 B.C.), Marcellus prepared upon a raft a huge contrivance to attack the walls from the sea. The great mathematician, Archimedes, took counter-measures. While the device was still a great distance away, it was struck by stones of ten talents in weight. The third one, which fell with a terrible crash, broke the platform on which the machine stood, loosening its bolts, and tearing asunder its supports. It has been questioned whether the Attic talent is meant here, but in general the figures of the ancients about the performances of their machines are to be regarded as trustworthy.

Modern reconstructions of Greek and Roman artillery, although falling far below the perfection of the ancient devices, have made remarkable records.

> Small engines, with arms about 2 ft. in length and skeins of cord about 4 in. in diameter . . . will send a stone ball, 1lb. in weight, from 300 to 500 yards.

Some of these devices can:

> Cast arrows, or rather feathered javelins, of from 5 to 6 lbs. weight, to a range of from 450 to 500 yards.[13]

---

10. III. 7. 23; V. 6. 3.
11. *B. C*, II. 2.
12. *Hist.*, III. 23.
13. Sir Payne-Gallwey, *Op. cit.*

Strange to say, the ancients thought about the possibility of inventing a machine-gun. One was in fact contrived by a certain Dionysius of Alexandria. It fired a succession of arrows supplied by a magazine or hopper. This ancient counterpart of the *mitrailleuse* was called *polybolos*, 'repeater-thrower.'[14]

Caesar interrupts his story of the siege of Avaricum long enough to express his admiration for the bravery of the Gauls. We shall use the passage to show that the Romans had a quick-firing engine:

> A certain Gaul, before the gate of the town, was hurling into the fire over against a turret lumps of grease and pitch that were handed to him. He was pierced by a dart from a 'scorpion' in the right side and fell dead. One of the party next him stepped over his prostrate body and went on with the same work; and when this second man had been killed in the same fashion by a scorpion-shot, a third succeeded, and to the third a fourth; and that spot was not left bare of defenders until . . . a stop had been put to the fighting.[15]

Like the other pieces of artillery, this 'scorpion' presumably derived its power from the recoil of tightly twisted cordage.

In lieu of the explosive power of gas, the ancients endeavoured to use compressed air. Ctesibius, an Alexandrian engineer of the third century B.C., found a means of gearing to the bow-arms of the catapult pistons working in carefully wrought cylinders.[16]

Among the Greeks of the fifth century B.C. the defence in siege operations was infinitely superior to the offense. In this period successful sieges were rare, and were not conducted with a great deal of imagination or skill. The Spartan siege of Plataea early in the Peloponnesian War is remarkable for the vastness of its operations rather than for its cleverness. It was the old passive method of blockade by contravallation.

In the next century great improvements were made in siege machines by the Syracusan tyrant, Dionysius I, and by Philip of Macedon. Such a stock of engines and projectiles as they used had never before been seen. War had taken a big step toward industrialization. So many craftsmen were summoned to Syracuse by Dionysius that it seemed

---

14. Philon, *De Telorum Construction*, in Thévenot, *Veteres Mathematici*, Paris, 1693.

15. *B. G.*, VII. 25, Translation, H. J. Edwards, in *The Loeb Classical Library*, New York, 1917.

16. Philon, IV. 78. 33; cf. H. Diels, *Antike Technik*, Leipzig and Berlin, 1920.

"as if the best engineers from all over the world had been brought together in one place." [17] He used engines of war in great numbers at the siege of Motye, [18] a Carthaginian city on an island just off the western corner of Sicily.

The new era in siege-craft is really ushered in with Philip's investment of Perinthus and Byzantium in 340 B.C. [19] Perinthus, a promontory terminating in abrupt cliffs toward the Propontis, was unassailable by sea. A high wall stretching across a neck of land seemed to give it equal security by land. Philip did not, in fact, manage to take it, but in the endeavour he used devices and machines in a way in which they had not been employed before. From towers 120 feet high, loftier than the walls, he galled the defenders. Sappers undermined fortifications and rams battered down stretches of them, so that the besieged had to build a new wall. Artillery killed many upon the ramparts, but the defenders returned the fire with machines borrowed from Byzantium.[20] This is among the first artillery duels, if it is not the very first. After a siege of considerable duration, Philip had to abandon the attempt.

Philip was, then, the first to organise and equip an effective siege-train. Alexander was not slow in putting this new means of warfare to good use and in elevating siege-craft to a science.

We are fortunate in having some evidence as to the part played by artillery in the defence and capture of cities. When New Carthage was taken (210 B.C.) by the Romans, there were found in it 120 large catapults and 281 small ones, and 23 large *bastillae* and 52 small ones. [21] At the siege of Jotapata, Vespasian had 160 pieces; [22] in the defence of Jerusalem, the Jews had 300 catapults and 40 *ballistae*. [23]

In 149 B.C., as part of their plan for the disarmament of Carthage, Roman consuls forced the surrender of 2,000 catapults. [24] One authority [25] gives the number as 3,000. It is very probable, however, that many of these machines were part of the reserve supplies of Carthaginian armies and that they were taken from arsenals.

When Sulla was investing the Piraeus his siege-train was so great

---

17. Diod. Sic, XIV.
18. *Ibid.*
19. Athenaeus, *De Machinis*, in Thévenot, *Op. cit.*
20. Diod. Sic, XVI.
21. Livy, XXVI.
22. Josephus, *The Jewish War*, III.
23. Josephus, *op. cit.*, V.
24. Polyb., XXXVI.
25. Strabo, XVII.

that the operation of the siege-engines called for the daily employment of 10,000 pairs of mules. [26] In an expedition against the Parthians Antony had prepared siege engines enough to fill 300 wagons. [27]

The use of artillery was not, however, confined to siege operations. It is a remarkable thing that the first extension of its use, so far as we can tell, was to constitute a land-battery against ships. In 397 B.C, the Carthaginian Himilco attempted to raise the siege of Motye off Sicily. When he was trying to force the narrow entrance to the harbour, catapults on shore killed many men. This innovation with its element of surprise created great consternation in the attacking force. [28]

Artillery was put to another noteworthy use when Rhodes was besieged by the celebrated Demetrius Poliorcetes. During this operation the defenders placed three machines on ships near the entrance of the smaller harbour to cooperate with a land battery of two pieces in an effort to prevent disembarkation. [29]

Alexander was the first general on record to use artillery to protect the crossing of a river. In his youthful campaign in Illyria he was withdrawing his men across a river when an attack was made by the Illyrians. He ordered engineers to shoot missiles from their pieces as far as possible. With the aid of some archers, who waded to mid-stream and shot their arrows, he covered the retreat so effectively that not a man was lost. [30] The first instance on record of the employment of artillery to cover a crossing in the face of the enemy was at the Tanais River, which Alexander's men forded to do battle against the Scythians. A champion of the enemy on the other side, having no idea of the range of the machines, approached too near and was killed. His countrymen in fear retired so far that the Macedonians crossed without much trouble.[31] On another occasion Alexander used artillery to assist in repulsing sallies made by the Indians from the citadel of Aornus. [32]

Alexander had batteries sufficiently light to be transported on the backs of animals or even of men, so that they could be used in mountain warfare. At times only the more delicate mechanism would be carried with him, since the heavier parts could be quickly constructed on the spot.

26. Plut., *Sulla*, 12.
27. Plut., *Anton.*, 38.
28. Diod. Sic, XIV.
29. Diod. Sic, XX.
30. Arrian, I.
31. Arrian, IV.
32. *Ibid.*

By the time of the third Battle of Mantinea, 207 B.C, between the Achaean League and Sparta, the use of artillery had become customary. As the Spartan lines deployed, catapults were placed at intervals in front of the whole force with the idea of gaining an initial advantage.[33]

How well artillery had been assimilated into the Roman Army and coordinated with other branches of the service in Caesar's day, is illustrated by his line of battle against the Bellovaci in 51 B.C. His line was drawn up in such fashion that his engines could be used against the wedges of the enemy. [34]

During the Civil War when Caesar was trying to hem in Pompey at Dyrrachium, his Ninth Legion seized an elevation and started to fortify and organise it. Pompey's men took a position on a neighbouring hill and by means of concentrated artillery fire forced Caesar's *legionaries* to withdraw. This is the first known instance of the employment of field artillery to prevent the construction of field fortifications. [35] How effective these engines had come to be is shown by the fact that in subsequent operations care was taken to keep out of range.

The Romans had very serviceable gun-carriages (*carroballistae*), as we see from the sculptures on Trajan's Column. During at least part of the Empire, a *legion* was supposed to have fifty-five of them. They were used both in the field and in the defence of camps. In addition each *legion* had ten *onagri*, 'wild asses.' [36] Gibbon observes that the use of artillery in the field became more prevalent as personal valour and military skill declined with the Roman Empire.

Artillery was developed with reference to siege operations, but it was used in the field to such an extent that the history of the evolution of artillery tactics in Europe must begin with the innovations of the Greeks and Romans. Even a casual reading of Sir Payne-Gallwey, *The Projectile-Throwing Engines of the Ancients*, will inspire great respect for their achievements. The performances of models of his own construction have been so good that they dispel all doubt as to the dependability of ancient statements about range and power.

The same authority tells us that it is certain that if this type of engine:

Had survived in its perfect state the introduction of cannon

33. Polyb., XI.
34. *B. G.*, VIII.
35. *B. C*, III.
36. Veg., II.

would have been considerably delayed, for the effects in warfare of the early cannon were for a long period decidedly inferior to those of the best projectile engines of the ancients.

In form and appearance the modern gun-carriage would seem to be a fairly accurate counterpart of the ancient *carroballista*, or field-piece mounted on wheels.

6. Greek Contributions to Tactics and Strategy

In European tactics and strategy the Greeks did pioneer work. With that directness of vision that characterizes their race, they were able, when confronted with new situations, to see the correct solution. Each advance was only a stepping-stone to further improvement.

At Marathon, the first great battle of which we read in Greek history, we see manifested a considerable degree of tactical skill. Afraid of having his position turned, Miltiades thinned his centre, made his flanks many ranks deep, and rested them upon two marshes or brooks which ran down to the sea. This use of natural obstacles may well have been an innovation in Greek military tactics. In that case the mother of the invention was the necessity, on the part of the Greeks, of neutralizing their marked numerical inferiority. [1]

Grundy, however, in The Great Persian War, attributes the thinning of the centre to a deliberate intention to let the Persians force their way in so that the Greek wings when victorious might attack them in flank. He claims that in the enthusiasm of victory the Greek wings could not have been restrained from pursuit if their officers had not received previous instructions about the assault upon the centre. If this deduction is correct, the tactics of Marathon resemble those of Cannae and Tannenberg.

Herodotus [2] tells us that the Athenians were the first Greeks to his knowledge to charge the enemy on the run. This now seems like the only possible method of attack when forces are at close quarters, yet many things that seem simple today required a military genius to inaugurate them. Even in the Peloponnesian War the Spartans were still

1. Dodge, *Alexander*.
2. VI.

advancing to the attack with the greatest deliberation, with measured tread keeping time to the music of many flute-players. [3]

It is of course folly to suppose that the Athenians at Marathon, clad in their heavy armour, ran the entire distance of almost a mile. As was the case with Alexander's hoplites at the battle of Issus, they may not have started to run until they were coming within range of the Persian missiles, although at Pharsalus Caesar's *legionaries* did so when at quite a distance from Pompey's men. They stopped, however, of their own initiative to get their breath when the Pompeians failed to imitate their manoeuvre as they expected. In Plutarch's *Life of Pompey* we find Caesar stating that the impetuous rush to meet the opposing forces keys up the morale more than anything else, and that with the shouting and the excitement the courage is increased.

Whatever may be the significance of Marathon in military history, it had other results far more reaching, for it broadcasted into the world ideas that were destined to gather momentum as did the on-rushing Athenians. For the first time a free citizen-soldiery, inspired by lofty ideals and love of country, had turned back the lash-driven hordes of a military despotism. It was an ominous day for autocrats, for the train of events that it set in motion has greater power today than ever before. As if to set the seal of legitimacy upon the newborn ideas, the Greeks again vanquished the Persians, mastering their fleet at Salamis in 480 B.C. and beating back their army from Plataea in 479.

From Thermopylae onward, the conflicts of Greeks and Persians showed rather high appreciation of strategical principles. The Greeks were equipped with heavy armour for close fighting; the Persians, coming from a land where stretches of open country permitted more manoeuvring and the use of cavalry, wished to avoid the Greek method. The Persians were also expert archers, and, with a little drill, could have laid down a barrage. At Thermopylae a Spartan was informed that when the barbarians let fly their shafts, they obscured the light of the sun. [4] Undaunted, he replied: "We shall fight them in the shade and not in the sun."

> In every case throughout the war in which reverse or disaster fell on either party, it was due to its having been forced, either by the nature of the position or by some tactical error of its

3. Thuc, V.

4. This statement may well be taken at its face value. It is said that at the siege of Jotapata by Vespasian the arrows flew so fast that they shut off the light of the sun. (Josephus, *The Jewish War*, III. 7. 27; see also Plin., *Nat. Hist.*, XVI. 159.)

own, into adopting that method of combat for which it was least adapted.[5]

The formation of the hollow square, which has not long been discarded, has a remote pedigree. In a campaign into Illyricum in 424 B.C., Brasidas, a Spartan general, found himself deserted by his Macedonian allies. With but a handful of men against a host, he had to effect his retreat. On the march the hoplites were formed in a hollow square, with the light-armed troops and baggage in the center for protection.[6] This seems to be the first Greek use of the formation. [7] In his initial engagement with the Syracusans, Nicias, the Athenian general, drew up half of his forces as reserves in an oblong. [8]

Xenophon developed farther the tactics of the hollow square. When the Ten Thousand were making their retreat under fire, he suggested [9] that they form a square, so that they might place the baggage and camp followers on the inside and at the same time be prepared for attack from any quarter. With the help of a specially organised body of 200 slingers and a troop of fifty horse, the Greeks managed to ward off the enemy's slingers, bowmen, and horsemen.

Strange to say, less than three generations after the experience of Brasidas in Illyria, the Illyrians themselves formed in a square as a defence against Philip's cavalry. [10] This formation was used by Alexander too.

We find Jomini, in his *Art of War,* [11] recommending squares to oppose the enemy in plains, when he has a superiority in cavalry. The same writer says that:

> In the Turkish wars, squares were almost exclusively used because hostilities were carried on in the vast plains of Bessarabia, Moldavia, or Wallachia, and the Turks had an immense force of cavalry.
>
> The English squares at Waterloo were only in two ranks, and, notwithstanding the heroic efforts of the French cavalry, only one battalion was broken.

5. Grundy, *The Great Persian War.*
6. Thuc, IV.
7. For an instance of much earlier employment of the square by Egyptians, see Xen., *Cyropaedia*, VI.
8. Thuc, VI.
9. *Anab.*, III.
10. Diod. *Sic*, XVI.
11. *The Art of War* by Antoine Henri Jomini also published by Leonaur.

> At the battle of the Pyramids Napoleon advanced in *échelon* of five divisional squares, centre refused, the faces being six ranks deep, with the baggage in the centre of each square, and with an interval of effective cannon range between squares.[12]

The withholding of troops from battle to act as reserves is one of the most cardinal principles of contemporary warfare. The waning months of the World War saw the commanders of titanic armies juggling their forces in an effort to use up their opponent's reserves. The value of reserves, however, has not always been so obvious. It seems to have been the idea of the generals of the fifth century B.C. to get as much weight and momentum as possible into the initial impact. With that end in view, the whole available force was utilised.

At the end of the century, however, during the wearisome Peloponnesian War (431-404), special situations began to suggest to the generals the advisability of keeping some men out of the first encounter. When the Spartan Brasidas was making an enforced retreat from Illyria, he had picked men to dash out to whatever point might be assailed. [13] These men were not reserves in the true sense of the word, since they were to engage just as soon as they could. In Nicias's first engagement under the walls of Syracuse, he placed half his army near the encampment with orders to go to the aid of any part of the army that might be most distressed. [14] Nicias carried the idea much farther than did Brasidas. This is the only instance of a genuine reserve force of which Thucydides [15] speaks.

When Xenophon was leading the Ten Thousand toward the Black Sea, he had to be on the *qui vive* constantly to guard against surprises and ambuscades, for which the broken character of the country afforded abundant opportunity. In the country of the Bithynians, there flashed upon him the brilliant idea of detaching men from the rest of the army for emergency use. He took the three rear companies of about 200 men each and made of them three separate commands.[16]

Of this innovation Dodge, in his *Alexander*, writes:

> And Xenophon is, moreover, the first who established in rear of the *phalanx* a reserve from which he could at will feed parts

---

12. *The Evolution of Tactics.*
13. Thuc, IV.
14. Thuc, VI.
15. *Thucydides' Peloponnesian War* by Thucydides also published by Leonaur.
16. *Anab.*, VI.

of the line. This was a superb first conception. Something like reserves had been theretofore known; but nothing so nearly approaching our modern idea.

The men that Nicias kept out of battle were drawn up in a hollow square or oblong so that they lacked the freedom and mobility of Xenophon's reserves.

Naturally Alexander appreciated to the full the value of reserves. In Hellenistic times, too, Greek generals withheld some soldiers from the initial clash. At the Battle of Sellasia, for instance, which was fought in 222 B.C. between the Argive Antigonus and the Spartan Cleomenes, Antigonus had as many as 2,000 men in reserve. [17]

The vulnerability of the flank was early recognized in ancient warfare, but the problem of turning it was not easy of solution. The Persian method of swinging in, somewhat in the manner of a hinge, the wing of a vastly longer line of battle necessitated a great superiority of men, or a consequent weakening of the centre. Croesus's dispositions at Sardis were intended to outflank Cyrus the Great on both wings. At the very beginning of the fourth century, we find Darius at the Battle of Cunaxa planning to overlap the exposed wing of Cyrus the Younger.

Greek generals put their best troops on the wings with the idea, not of assailing the enemy in flank, but of attacking opposing wings and rolling up the line. Perhaps the most striking deviation from the stereotyped hoplite tactics of the Peloponnesian War is seen in the engagement near Olpae, 426 B.C., in which allied Amphilochians, Acarnanians and Athenians fought against Peloponnesians.

The Athenian Demosthenes shared the command with the allied generals.

> Fearing that he would be surrounded by the Peloponnesians, who were more numerous and extended beyond his own line, he placed *hoplites* and light-armed troops, numbering altogether four hundred, in a deep lane overgrown with brushwood, intending them to lie in wait until the moment of conflict, when they were to rush out from the rear on the line of the enemy where it overlapped.[18]

These tactics gained a signal victory. Two years later at Delium we find horsemen, instead of *hoplites*, employed to make an assault upon

17. Thuc, II.

18. Thuc, III. For another instance of overlapping, see Thuc, V.

the rear.[19]

In summarizing the strictly hoplite tactics of the Peloponnesian War, an astute critic of that great conflict writes:

> The hoplite *phalanx* was regarded as peculiarly vulnerable on either flank. The first care of a general seems to have been to make his front at least equal in length to that of the enemy.[20] As to the offensive, the indisposition to risk the flank attack may have been due to the fact that a body of hoplite troops engaged in making such an attack would be liable to expose its own flanks, since it must, under such circumstances, be detached from the rest of the line. That was a risk which a Greek general of the fifth century would not undertake, and one, it may be, that his soldiers would not face.[21]

The establishment of the principle of the flank attack by manoeuvre, instead of by overlapping, was to come in the next century.

Many military innovations followed in the wake of the efforts of Cyrus the Younger to wrest the throne from his brother, Artaxerxes. In 401 B.C. far within the Persian empire this young prince with a force of 100,000 barbarians leavened by his Greeks engaged a force of 900,000 men. The Greek mercenaries proved victorious in their sector, but found after the battle that Cyrus had been killed and that their Asiatic allies had deserted them. Leaderless, abandoned, in the heart of a hostile country, they were in a perilous plight. In this crisis they spurned the king's demand for surrender and decided to force their way back to Greece. Thus began the famous retreat of the "Ten Thousand."

The Persian king offered a truce, agreeing to furnish supplies if the Greeks would depart peaceably. The offer was accepted, but soon thereafter five Greek generals and twenty captains were lured into a parley with Tissaphernes, a Persian general, and treacherously put to death. In this emergency, an Athenian named Xenophon advised energetic action, and, along with Chirisophus, a Spartan, was put in command. Under his leadership there followed a daring running fight to the Euxine Sea, as resourceful a retreat as history records. Foiling spies, evading ambuscades, dislodging savage foemen from command-

19. Thuc, IV.

20. There was a tendency on the part of the soldiers themselves to shift to the right to prevent their shieldless side from being exposed to the enemy. See Thuc, V.

21. Grundy, *Thucydides and the History of his Age.*

ing heights, crossing rivers in the face of vigorous opposition, devising new tactical manoeuvres to meet emergencies, encountering snow six feet deep, and suffering from extreme hunger and exposure, this resourceful handful of men gradually worked their perilous way northward until, catching sight of the Euxine, the 10,000 survivors gave voice to one of the thrilling cries of the ages, "The sea! The sea!"

Of Xenophon's feat in extricating his army, Dodge, in his *Alexander*, writes:

> Nothing like this famous retreat is known in the world's history. Xenophon is the father of the system of retreat, the originator of all that appertains to the science of rear-guard fighting. He reduced its management to a perfect method. More originality in tactics has come from the *Anabasis* than from any dozen other books. Every system of war looks to this as to the fountain-head when it comes to rearward movements, as it looks to Alexander for a pattern of resistless and intelligent advance. . . . On this retreat also was first shown the necessary, if cruel, means of arresting a pursuing enemy by the systematic devastation of the country traversed and the destruction of its villages to deprive him of food and shelter.

During the march through the country of the Carduchi, the nimble light-armed mountaineers caused Xenophon's men great annoyance by their persistent skirmishing tactics. Apropos of this type of fighting, there is an interesting paragraph in a description of the siege of Louisbourg in 1758.[22]

> Wolfe had a large corps of light infantry, picked for their marksmanship from various regiments, and trained, so far as a week or two at Halifax could train them, in tactics that became familiar enough later on, but were regarded at the time as a strange innovation on the part of the vigorous and eccentric brigadier. It was merely a matter of advancing in loose formation, and using all the inequalities of the ground for protection, coupled with a light and easy costume for the men, namely, a short jacket, small round hat, and a kind of light woollen trouser, cut moderately tight. A story goes that an officer who was regarded as somewhat learned among his fellows remarked to Wolfe that his new corps reminded him of the Carduchi alluded to by Xenophon.

22. A. G. Bradley, *The Fight with France for North America*, republished by Leonaur as *A History of the French & Indian War.*

'That is exactly where I got the idea,' replied Wolfe; 'only these people never read anything, and consequently believe the idea to be a novel one.'

Only a year prior to the outbreak of the World War a French soldier, Colonel Arthur Boucher, wrote an historical and military commentary on the *Anabasis: L'Anabase de Xénophon.* He states that it is one of the best and most exact military books that the centuries have transmitted to us and that it still has lessons for military men to ponder over and apply. He regards Xenophon as a model in working up the morale of soldiers. One suspects that Marshal Foch had Xenophon in mind when he drew his distinction between active and passive obedience. Certainly no army has displayed active obedience to a higher degree than Xenophon's "Ten Thousand," and no author suggests more ways and means to obtain it than does Xenophon in his *Cyropaedia.*

Until the Battle of Leuctra, 371 B.C., which was fought between the Thebans and Spartans, it had been customary for generals to draw up their lines of battle in parallel formation. In this engagement the Theban Epaminondas wrote his name indelibly upon the scroll of master tacticians. He had about six thousand dispirited men, while the Spartans numbered some eleven thousand in the best of morale. The Theban offset this immense advantage by tactical resourcefulness. He drew up his men in oblique order with perhaps eight ranks in the centre and on the right. His advanced left wing he made some fifty men deep, thus forming a narrow column of attack. It is not certain that the 'refused' part of the line advanced in true echelon order, but there is no doubt that this was the first time that a battle line assaulted in oblique order with a deliberate concentration on one flank.

The new formation gained the day and it won the Battle of Mantinea, too, in 362 B.C., since the allied armies opposed to the Thebans had not yet mastered the details of the order.

A generation later we find a student of Theban tactics, Alexander, employing the oblique line to good advantage, but it reached its supreme development in the hands of Frederick the Great,[23] who at the Battle of Leuthen made a perfect echelon formation, and became celebrated for his brilliant and precise execution of this order of attack.

The massing of forces by the Theban general inaugurates a new epoch in military tactics. Before the battle of Leuctra, it was the custom to put the best troops on the right. Epaminondas, however, con-

23. *Frederick the Great & the Seven Years' War* by F.W. Longman also published by Leonaur.

centrated his own strength on his left, feeling that the right was the vital point of the enemy. It will be recalled that the obtaining of a superiority in numbers at the decisive point is the key to Napoleon's strategy.

> To Napoleon the offensive implied concentrated masses hurled at the right spot; and from the start he acted on the idea of concentration.[24]

In the military career of Epaminondas, there occurs, also, the first illustration of an attempt to draw an enemy from a menacing position by attacking his capital. In 362 B.C., when his opponents were at Mantinea ready to offer the Thebans battle, he slipped away by night with the intention of taking Sparta. The Spartan army had, however, learned of the movement a little too soon, and reached home just in time to prevent the city from being taken.

The great military figure of Greece and one of the outstanding military geniuses of all ages is the youthful Alexander. As a boy, he learned the Theban theory of war; his apprenticeship he served in subduing Greece and neighbouring barbarian tribes; as a master soldier he led a victorious army from one end of the Persian Empire to the other.

This heroic youth did his great work in his twenties. There seemed to be no limit to his powers, either mental or physical, as there was none to his ambition. We have already noted his unparalleled bravery. As conspicuous as his bravery was his intellectual leadership. The innovations of his predecessors he improved upon, and he made new contributions through his own resourcefulness.

Though the army organisation of his father Philip was superior to any that Greece had ever seen, he managed to improve it. He likewise made good use of the tactical and strategic contributions of his predecessors. In his early campaigns across the Danube he used the square

---

24. Dodge, *Napoleon I*, the complete Dodge set republished in six illustrated volumes by Leonaur as *Warfare in the Age of Napoleon*:—1). The Revolutionary Wars Against the First Coalition in Northern Europe and the Italian Campaign, 1789-1797—2). The Egyptian and Syrian Campaigns & the Wars of the Second and Third Coalitions, 1798-1805—3). The Retreat from Moscow, the Peninsular Campaign and the War of the Sixth Coalition, 1812-1813—4). The Battle of Austerlitz, the War of the Fourth Coalition and the Early Peninsular Campaigns, 1805-1809—5). The War of the Fifth Coalition, the Peninsular Campaign and the Invasion of Russia, 1809-1812 and 6). The South of France Campaign, the Campaign of 1814 and the Campaign to the Battle of Waterloo 1813-1815.

in the fashion of Brasidas and Xenophon. As we have seen, the wedge was not original with him. The value of reserves he appreciated even more fully than did Xenophon. It is said that he *established* the principle of a flank attack although he was not actually the first to use it.

The tactics that were to make Macedonia supreme were tried out by Philip in a conflict with the Illyrians. Here he engaged the whole barbarian line and held it, while he had his cavalry ride around and fall upon the flanks of the enemy.[25] This battle displayed a proper coordination of infantry and cavalry and was a harbinger of future victories. In one of his youthful engagements, that against the Triballi, Alexander employed the same methods.[26] Philip seems to have evolved this method of fighting independently, although at the battle of Delium, as we have seen, the Theban Pagondas used almost the same tactics.

Of Alexander's use of the wedge Dodge, in his *Alexander*, writes:

> Macdonald's column at Wagram was scarcely comparable to Alexander's wedge at Arbela. For this was the first of its kind.

The oblique march is a distinctive method of outflanking an army. Alexander employed it most successfully at Arbela. The Macedonians demonstrated that flanking was possible by manoeuvring. This was a great improvement upon the Persian and fifth-century Greek methods of swinging in the overlapping portion of a line of battle.

At present when whole nations are under arms, instead of being represented by two or three hundred thousand champions, it is almost impossible for large forces to get in the rear of the enemy. Modern enveloping movements are practically a return on a grand scale to the ancient method of turning the flank by drawing in the overlapping section of a line.

That an army has a strategic flank, the turning of which will cut it off from its line of retreat, is said to be a modern discovery. Both Marlborough and Wellington have been credited with it. Colonel Dodge, however, in his *Alexander*, assigns this innovation to the Macedonian. At the Battle of Issus, 333 B.C, Darius had taken up a defensive position upon the banks of the Pinarus River. His right wing rested upon the sea and his left was somewhat 'refused,' because of a bend in the stream.

Alexander picked out the left of the centre as the weakest point, and upon it he directed his first attack. Here he gained an initial suc-

---

25. Diod. *Sic*, XVI.

26. Arrian, I.

cess that enabled him to menace the line of retreat of the Persians. It may possibly be argued that Alexander directed the onset upon the left for the simple reason that it was the only side that gave him a chance to manoeuvre. We shall, however, find the same tactics ascribed to Hannibal and to the Scipio who was destined to defeat him.

We may stop long enough to give an extended illustration of Alexander's tactics and strategy. Perhaps military history affords no better example of the use of the feint to effect the passage of a river in the face of opposition. In his invasion of Persia, Alexander had not planned to go beyond the eastern limits of the kingdom of Darius, but on reaching that point he found a pretext for venturing into the unknown land of India. Taxiles, the king of the region between the Indus and the Hydaspes Rivers, surrendered to Alexander on condition that the invader should help him against Porus, king of the land to the east of the Hydaspes.

On reaching this stream the Macedonian found on the other side a powerful and resolute king whose well-equipped forces numbered, according to Curtius, thirty thousand men with eighty-five elephants and three hundred chariots. According to another estimate Porus had more than fifty thousand infantry, three thousand cavalry, more than a thousand chariots and one hundred and thirty elephants.

In addition, allies were expected whom it was necessary for Alexander to anticipate.

Though four *stades* wide, the river was swift and deep and nowhere could fords be seen. Wherever a crossing was even remotely possible, there Porus had stationed guards. Alexander could not cross by force and so the contest resolved itself into one of wits. To create the impression that he was going to await the subsidence of the waters, swollen by the melting of the mountain snows and seasonal rains, Alexander began to ravage the neighbouring country and to bring large quantities of supplies to the bank of the river. He inaugurated a deliberate policy of making feints at crossing. He sent boats, which he brought from the Indus, up and down stream to distract the enemy. He had his men stuffing animal skins with hay, as if he were going to have them float across on them, as Xenophon's men had done on their famous retreat. Bodies of infantry and horsemen were always making their appearance at different places, so that Porus was never allowed to rest from counter-measures.

At night small detachments of horse would gather at various places, raising the war-cry and making din enough for a large force, so that

Porus had to lead out large contingents toward the place where the noise was greatest and keep them there in all sorts of weather. After this experience had been repeated on numberless occasions, Porus began to relax his vigilance and to remain in camp when he heard the yelling. Porus was lulled to greater security by rumours that Alexander was waiting for the waters to subside, a piece of news that Alexander had carefully allowed to leak out.

About 17 miles from the Macedonian camp, in the bend of the river, was a wooded headland and out in the stream an overgrown island, both of which would serve to shield the movements of an army. Here the invader determined to cross. Between that spot and the camp he had patrols stationed. For many nights the sentries had been calling to one another and lighting fires. Alexander was now ready. His preparation had been as much psychological as logical.

Leaving a force confronting Porus, Alexander went to the chosen place, bent upon crossing under cover of the darkness by means of stuffed skins, rafts and boats. A heavy storm came up which at first threatened to prevent the attempt, but in the end it proved advantageous in drowning the inevitable noise of the preparations. Toward dawn the tempest died down and the Macedonians managed to embark without being detected by the sentinels of Porus.

Through unfamiliarity with the region, they landed on another large island instead of the opposite bank. There was no time to take the boats around. From the island the men waded to the other side in water which reached above their breasts, and of the horses only the heads protruded.

On receiving news of the crossing, Porus, thinking that the forces were those of allies, sent forward only a small detachment under his son and this was beaten. Once across, the matchless Macedonian horse and *phalanx* could be depended upon to complete the victory.

> This was the greatest day of Alexander's life, if we take together the splendour and difficulty of the military achievement, and the generous treatment of his conquered opponent.[27]

It would almost seem that Colonel Dodge is extravagant in declaring that Alexander's strategy and manoeuvres in effecting the passage of this stream have "furnished the world with a manual of all which is most valuable in the passage of rivers in the face of the enemy." Hannibal employed quite similar tactics in outwitting the Gauls on the

27. Grote, *Op. cit.*, XII.

Rhone.[28]

While I have been unable to find any definite acknowledgments of indebtedness to Alexander's tactics at the Hydaspes, there have been many crossings of the same general character although without the elaborate psychological preparation. A military man has called my attention to the fact that at the first battle of Bull Run:

> Beauregard's plan was exactly the same as that of Porus, with exactly the same result; the place where the river line was really crossed was undefended. Due to the fact that McDowell was not Alexander, Beauregard escaped from the defeat that he nearly met.

The boats that Alexander used on the Hydaspes had been employed in a pontoon bridge on the Indus, from which they were brought in sections.[29] In his *Deeds of Alexander the Great* Curtius informs us that they had been used previously in the passage of several rivers. Alexander seems to have made an innovation in constructing pontoons which could be taken apart, transported and reassembled. The first really great pontoon bridges known to history are Of course the ones constructed over the Hellespont for the enormous army of Xerxes.[30]

In siege-craft, too, Alexander was greater than his father. Before advancing into the Persian Empire he had to reduce the sea-coast cities on the Eastern Mediterranean. The investment of Tyre is one of the most famous sieges in the annals of mankind, if indeed it is not the most famous. In the heart of Persia, and especially on the eastern confines of the kingdom, Alexander had to subdue apparently inexpugnable hill-top fortresses, so that the mere report of their capture inspired the utmost fear in the neighbouring tribes. No man was ever more fertile in ruses so essential for the art of besieging.

At the time of the Battle of Marathon technical tactics and strategy did not exist; at the death of Alexander a firm foundation had been laid for the formulation of their laws.

The period of the great Greek contributions to military science is delimited by the wars with Persia, the war in which the Great King with an enormous host was driven back from the diminutive land of

---

28. Livy, XXI. Compare also the feint of Xenoetas at the Tigris, Polyb., V.

29. Diodorus Siculus, XVII., says that Alexander crossed the Indus on a bridge of boats. Arrian, V., is, however, not so sure, but this feeling is probably due to the failure of his authorities to specify the character of the bridge.

30. See Grote, *op. cit.*, V.

Greece, and the war in which the Great Captain in the character of adventurer, explorer, avenger, statesman and civilizer led victorious armies throughout the length and breadth of the land of the ancient invader.

> On the one side was a race with a war experience greater beyond comparison than that of any other contemporary nation; on the other, a people whose quickness of intellect rendered it peculiarly capable of supplying the defects of experience by appreciation of the exigencies of the situation.[31]

31. Grundy, *The Great Persian War.*

7. Greek Cavalry

In very early times, the Athenians used horses as a quick means of conveying foot-soldiers. The first horsemen were simply mounted infantrymen. They seem to have been the first dragoons. The idea that a man could fight more effectively on horseback was of slow growth. On one occasion during the Peloponnesian War, a contingent of five hundred Boeotian horse was accompanied by an equal number of men trained to fight on foot. [1] In his youthful campaign in Illyria, Alexander gave orders, in anticipation of an engagement with a detachment of the enemy, for half of his horse to dismount and fight on foot. [2]

It would seem that the ancient cavalryman with his javelin or lance was almost as well equipped as is the modern horseman. Frederick the Great forbade the use of firearms since he wished his men to rely upon the charge at full speed, sword in hand. At the beginning of the Great War, Uhlans were still using long lances and the Cossacks were equipped with a similar weapon.

At Marathon, the first great battle in Greek history, neither the Athenians nor their Plataean allies had cavalry. During the entire fifth century in fact the cavalry branch of the Greek armies was not highly developed. The reason is obvious. About four-fifths of the country is mountainous and ill-adapted to horse-breeding. As a result Thessalians with their broad plains were the only nation that laid great stress on cavalry. Lack of pasturage, then, caused the Greeks in general to depend at first almost solely upon infantry.

There were, however, among the Greeks men who were especially skilled in horsemanship. Xenophon tells us that the majesty of men is best disclosed in the graceful handling of animals. It is said that there

1. Thuc, V.

2. Arrian, I.

is nothing so perfect in equestrianism as the riders on the frieze of the Parthenon. The Greeks themselves are the best exemplification of their mythical creations, the centaurs, in which rider and horse are one being.

The Persians developed cavalry earlier than did the Greeks. After his defeat at Salamis in 480 B.C, Xerxes withdrew from Greece leaving Mardonius in command of a large army. In the following year the Greek forces operating against the Persians in Boeotia were receiving reinforcements and provisions by way of the passes of Cithaeron that led to Plataea. One night Mardonius sent a force of horsemen to get in the rear of the Greeks and strike at their communications. They came upon a convoy of 500 beasts carrying supplies from the Peloponnesus. This they attacked and succeeded in killing or capturing the escort and the beasts. [3]

> This is probably as early a record as there is of cavalry being detached in this way to operate upon the enemy's rear.[4]

The struggle with the Persians probably showed the Greeks the necessity of developing the cavalry arm. At all events, in the next great conflict, the Peloponnesian War, we find cavalry employed in lines of battle, especially to protect the flanks. It has been estimated that prior to the time of Alexander the cavalry never averaged more than a fifteenth or a twelfth of the infantry.

It was the irony of fate that the Greeks had to display their greatest efficiency in cavalry hundreds of miles from home. In preparation for the invasion of the Persian Empire, Alexander greatly increased the number of horsemen. Cavalry was the choice arm of the Persians, who had vast level stretches over which it could act. They relied on it so much that at the Battle of the Granicus they made the fatal mistake of using it in their effort to prevent the Macedonian crossing. At Arbela Alexander had 40,000 infantry and 7,000 horse. [5]

Alexander's dashing, impetuous temperament naturally inclined him to the cavalry service. With it he was apt to open battles, and with it at the catastrophe of the drama he was wont to appear like a *deus ex machina.* He taught his cavalry above all things to attack, never to await attack. He inaugurated in fact the impetuous method of attack.

---

3. Herod., IX.
4. Denison, *History of Cavalry.*
5. Arrian, III.
6. See Grundy, *Thucydides and the History of his Age.*

He is the first European to make a practice of using the cavalry as the striking arm while the infantry, in this case the *phalanx*, made a solid rigid resisting power. [6]

Of Arbela Denison [7] writes:

> There is no battle in history in which a better appreciation is shown of the cavalry service, nor a better use made of it, as well in action as in the pursuit.
>
> In the use of cavalry Alexander stands without a peer. No one ever hurled his cavalry upon the enemy with such precision, momentum or effect. Its charge was always well-timed; it always won. No one ever headed horse with such god-like boldness, or fought it to the bottom as he did. Had Alexander not been one of the world's great captains, he would have been the typical *beau sabreur* of the world's history.[8]

The use of cavalry by Philip for a vigorous pursuit after the battle of Chaeronea marked a new departure in Greek warfare. One of Napoleon's maxims was as follows:

> It is the business of cavalry to follow up the victory, and to prevent the beaten enemy from rallying.

We may note in general:

> That in the wars of Alexander, as well as long previously, light cavalry were used for outpost duties, that scouts were used for reconnoitring, and patrols and sentries and videttes seem to have been employed very much upon the same general principles as are in use at the present day.[9]

The greatest modern advocate of the cavalry arm was Frederick the Great. He is said to have found in the celerity and *élan* of the Macedonian attack a model for his own horsemen. He too taught that the offensive was the only proper sphere of action for cavalry. Like Alexander, he made the cavalry a striking arm. It is estimated that of the twenty-two great battles that he fought, his cavalry won at least fifteen.[10]

---

7. *Op. cit.*
8. Dodge, *Alexander.*
9. Denison.
10. See Denison.

8. The Martial Spirit of Rome

The Romans had their own explanation of the way in which their genius was directed into military channels. One day when Romulus was holding a review of the army, a great storm arose accompanied by loud crashing of thunder. The king was veiled in a dense cloud and snatched from the gaze of the assembled people. During the mourning of the people, who now looked upon him as a god, king and father, rumours began to spread that his body had been torn apart by the city fathers. At this juncture an influential Roman stepped forward and thus addressed the people:

> Romulus, my fellow citizens, the father of this city, at dawn today suddenly descended from heaven and revealed himself to me. When filled with awe I stood in reverent attitude, invoking heaven's consent to look upon him face to face, he exclaimed, 'Go, tell the Romans that it is the will of the gods that my Rome shall be the capital of the world; therefore let them cultivate the art of war and realize and tell posterity that no human power can resist the Romans by arms.' With these words he departed on high.[1]

Roman citizens were called *quirites*. One of the suggestions for its etymology is that it means "spearmen." The *legionaries* of Caesar's day were swordsmen, but their ancestors were spearmen. The *quirites* of early Rome were spearmen in fact, if not by etymology. In the old litanies it was upon the *pilumnus poplus* (=*populus*), "spear-armed body of warriors," that the blessing of Mars was invoked.[2]

A clear etymological indication of the martial proclivities of the

---

1. Livy, I.
2. Th. Mommsen, *The History of Rome*; I. 90. The translation is that of W. P. Dickson, New York, 1900.

PLATE II

Roman Legionaries on the March

From Cichorius, *Die Reliefs der Traianssäule*

Romans is seen in the word *virtus*, 'manhood.' The most obvious way to show one's manhood was by courage in battle and hence the word came to mean bravery, 'spunk,' 'grit.' Roman writers and speakers never tired of extolling heroism and heroic ancestors.

How dominant the martial spirit was in the Romans is well shown by an incident in Caesar's campaigns in Gaul. At Vesontio, when he was endeavouring to allay fear of the Germans under Ariovistus, he practically asserted that the terms 'Romans' and 'soldiers' were synonymous.

> Whenever anyone declares that it is not incumbent upon us to war, he might as well state that it is not necessary for us to amass wealth, or to rule others, or to be freemen, or to be Romans.[3]

Cicero[4] practically says that the Roman soldier looked upon his shield, sword, and helmet, as being just as much parts of his body as were his shoulders, his limbs, or his hands. Josephus [5] tells us that weapons were, so to speak, a part of the physical constitution of the Roman soldiers and hence they never had any respite from martial exercises.

We learn from Livy that at the Battle of Lake Trasimenus the Romans fought with such spirit that they failed to notice an earthquake as severe as those which waste great sections of Italian cities, or divert rushing streams from their courses, or dash the sea up into the rivers, or crumble mighty mountains. This is the incident referred to by Byron:

> *And such the shock of battle on this day*
> *And such the frenzy, whose convulsion blinds*
> *To all save carnage, that, beneath the fray,*
> *An earthquake rolled unheedingly away.*

The very language of the Romans reflects their martial character. Quintilian[6] harps upon the fact that Caesar spoke in the same manner that he fought. His diction was that of a military man. [7] The organisation of an involved Latin sentence, with its respect for rank and superiority, is military in character.

---

3. Dio Cass., XXXVIII.
4. *T. D.*, II.
5. *Op. cit.*, III.
6. *Inst.*, X.
7. Plut., *Caes.*

> An unmistakable note of discipline and subordination manifests itself in the orderly way in which the Romans carry out the sequence of their tenses, all dependent tenses being subordinated to the main clause; and it again comes out in the preference shown by Latin for dependent speech, in which sentence after sentence, and clause after clause, are set under the strict *régime* of a single governing verb, as soldiers under that of a general.... Just as soldiers in a regiment keep their eyes fixed on their commander, all the pronouns in *oratio obliqua* ('indirect discourse') which have reference to the speaker, look back to him.[8]

The Latin marshals its sentences like soldiers and—

> ....periods succeed each other with dignity and in well-marked cadence—spirited and irresistible like the Roman *legionary*. Their entire colouring recalls to us the picture of his weather-beaten face, and their stately march reminds us of his proud and masterful bearing. In fact, this well-matched pair, warrior and language, have stepped forth from their home in full consciousness of victory, and have overcome the world between them.[9]

But seldom among the Romans did "*grimvisaged war smooth his wrinkled brow*." The temple of Janus, whose open gates indicated symbolically that the god had taken the field with the armies, was closed but three times. Livy [10] well sums up the military character of the Romans:

> *Ea est Romana gens, quae victa quiescere nesciat,*
> Such is the temper of the Roman nation that it knows not how to remain at peace, vanquished though it be.

It was a boast of the Romans that, though defeated in many a battle, they never lost a war.[11] For them, *Vivere est militare*, "Life is a battle," was true literally as well as figuratively.

It is not strange, therefore, that among the most famous lines in Latin literature, is the passage in the *Aeneid* glorifying the martial spirit:

> *Let others melt and mould the breathing bronze*

---

8. O. Weise, *Language and Character of the Roman People*. The translation is that of Strong and Campbell, London, 1909.
9. Weise, *Op. cit.*
10. IX.
11. F. Marx, *C. Lucilii Carmina*, Leipzig, 1904; I. 42; cf. Livy, IX..

To forms more fair,—aye! out of marble bring
Features that live; let them plead causes well;
Or trace with pointed wand the cycled heaven,
And hail the constellations as they rise;
But thou, O Roman, learn with sovereign sway
To rule the nations. Thy great art shall be
To keep the world in lasting peace, to spare
The humbled foe, and crush to earth the proud. [12]

12. Aen., VI. 847 ff., Translation by Th. C. Williams, Boston and New York, 1908.

9. Roman Drill and Discipline

That the Romans clearly understood the source of their strength is readily understood from one of the introductory sentences in Vegetius I:

> We see that the Roman people have conquered the world by nothing other than drill in arms, camp discipline, and experience in campaigning.

The Gauls surpassed them in numbers, the Germans in height, the Spaniards in strength, the Carthaginians in craftiness and resources, the Greeks in the sharpness of their wits, yet the Romans were able to beat them all because of the thorough and rigorous training they gave their recruits, their meticulous attention to the smallest details, and the business-like manner in which they provided materials of war. Results that the Greeks achieved by inspiration, the Romans gained by laboured effort. They made war as much a business as an art.

The Romans were very modern in leaving Vegetius has left us a fairly comprehensive account of the training of a Roman army. Great care was taken in the selection of material for soldiers. Enlistment officers were to see to it that recruits had alert eyes, a head carried erect, a well-developed breast, a moderate girth, muscular shoulders, strong arms, rather long fingers and sinewy legs. When these requirements were complied with, no emphasis was laid on height, since it was regarded as important for the soldier to be strongly built rather than tall. Tall men were in demand, however, for the front cohorts of the legion or for cavalry detachments upon the wings.[1] Men who had led an active life were preferred. While nothing so formal as an intelligence test was given, an effort was made to get recruits who were mentally alert as well as physically sound.[2]

---

1. Veg., I.
2. *Ibid.*

One might suppose that the specialized bayonet drill of the last war has no counterpart in antiquity, but one is surprised at the thorough training given the ancient soldier in the use of the sword, which is after all much like our bayonet in that it was short and was regularly employed for thrusting and not for slashing. The 'rookie' (*tiro*) was given a wicker shield and a wooden foil, both of them twice as heavy as those used in battle. A wooden stake, projecting six feet from the ground and set so firmly in it that it would not yield, was his imaginary enemy. This he vigorously attacked, aiming at the head, as it were, or ribs, or legs, or hough, yielding ground and leaping forward as against a real opponent, and assailing it with every manner of attack. Special stress was laid on teaching the rookie to attack in such a way as not to expose himself to a counter-thrust. To this drill he was subjected both morning and afternoon. [3] Gladiators too were taught in this fashion and Vegetius knew of no champion swordsman who had not been so trained.

Since a slashing blow was often parried or stopped by bones without resulting in death, thrusting was taught as being more deadly. In addition, the thrust is more insidious and does not expose the right arm and side as does the sweeping blow. The wooden weapons were made extra heavy so that when the *tiro* got real weapons he would leap to the attack with greater alacrity, feeling that he had been freed from a heavy burden.[4] From this brief description it can be seen that the Roman omitted nothing that would tend to make a more efficient swordsman.

The recruit was taught marksmanship by throwing missiles at a stake. [5] Bowmen and slingers used to set as a target bunches of twigs or straw at a distance of 600 feet. Slingers were drilled to whirl the sling around the head only once before throwing the missile. Perhaps this was intended not merely to secure greater rapidity of fire, but also to reduce casualties. [6] During the American Civil War many soldiers were wounded while they had their arms raised in using the ramrod. In anticipation of emergencies, the ancient soldier was taught to throw with the hand alone stones weighing a pound. [7] This would seem to be an ancient prototype for the grenade.

3. Veg. I.
4. *Ibid.*
5. *Ibid.*
6. *Ibid.*, II.
7. *Loc. cit.*

The *legionary* was drilled in cutting down trees, carrying burdens, leaping over trenches, swimming in the sea or in streams, walking at double pace or running under arms and encumbered with baggage, so that daily practice in times of peace might anticipate the needs of war. Training was maintained in stormy weather even if a shelter had to be improvised with a roof of reeds or sedge-grass. On days when snow and rain ceased, drill was held in the open. Even veterans had to take some drill daily for a veteran out of condition was looked upon as a recruit. An effort was made to inspire confidence in the soldier by thoroughly familiarizing him with all the conditions of battle that could be anticipated. In a battle, knowledge and experience avail more than strength, says Vegetius, and a soldier without training in arms is not different from a barbarian. [8]

Marches were taken over every kind of country and every effort was made to harden the soldier's muscles and constitution. In order to give the recruit a thorough training, sham battles were fought on the Campus Martius, and no pains were spared in reproducing the conditions of actual warfare. As Josephus admirably puts it, their drills were bloodless battles and their battles bloody drills. [9]

The Romans were keenly alive to the necessity of guarding the health of the soldiers. It is only increased scientific knowledge that makes modern armies more careful. Vegetius [10] tells us that the health of the army should be maintained by all possible precautions, that is by careful selection of camping sites, attention to the water, to the seasons, by medical care and by exercise. The soldiers should not be compelled to stay in pestilential places near disease-breeding swamps, nor in arid regions without shade-trees, fields, and hills, nor should they be without tents in summer; they should not set out on the march so late in the day as to become ill from the heat of the sun and the fatigue of the route, but rather they should start the march before daybreak and stop in the heat of the day; nor should they in a severe winter march in snows or frosts by night; they should not have to suffer from lack of fuel or clothing; for a soldier who has to shiver is hard to treat and is not in condition to make a campaign.

The army should not use contaminated water nor swamp water;

---

8. *Loc. cit.*

9. This reminds one of the statement in Plutarch, Lycurgus, 22, that the Spartans were the only men in the world to whom war brought a respite in the training for war.

10. Veg., III.

for impure water, just like poison, causes diseases among the drinkers. Military men have concluded that the daily exercise in arms does more to maintain the health of the army than do the doctors. For this reason they wanted the soldiers to drill under shelter on inclement days, outside on clear days. In like manner they ordered the horsemen to train both themselves and their horses diligently not only on level ground but also on steep places, amid trenches and very difficult paths, so that they might not encounter any unfamiliar problem in actual battle. From this one can see how the army must ever be getting more instruction in the use of arms, since inuring them to exertion can bring both health in camp and victory in battle. If in the summer or fall the army has to stay rather long in the same place, very dangerous diseases may arise from contaminated water and from the tainted atmosphere. This can be prevented only by a frequent change of camping grounds.

The little manual of Vegetius is extremely interesting in showing the German type of thoroughness and attention to detail that existed in the Roman army.

The veteran soldier of Caesar's day had become such an automaton of efficiency that he could in an emergency comport himself as well as if he were officered by others. On one occasion in particular the ability of Roman soldiers to act for themselves was of great value to them since it offset the advantage the Belgae derived from a surprise attack. [11] As Vegetius says, soldiers do without alarm in battle that which they have been in the habit of doing in sham-battles on the drill-ground.

As the Battle of Pharsalia was about to start, Pompey ordered his men to remain still in order to allow Caesar's legions to exhaust themselves by running twice as far as they had expected, yet when the seasoned veterans of Caesar saw this move, of their own accord they stopped midway to regain their breath. [12]

At the present time in America we are indiscriminately calling every soldier who was enlisted in the World War a veteran. In antiquity it was not so easy to get such a distinction. In Hirtius's postscript to the Gallic War [13] we find this significant sentence:

> Three veteran legions conspicuous for valour, the 7th, 8th and 9th, he had with him; the 11th, composed of picked young men

11. Caes., *B. G.*, II. 20.
12. *Ibid.*, *B. C*, III.
13. VIII.

> of the greatest promise, which, though in its eighth campaign, had not acquired the same reputation for experience and bravery.

Eight years of fighting, twice the duration of the World War, and still suffering by comparison!

The martial strain, then, was dominant in Roman character and the great lesson that the Roman had to learn (*discere*) was discipline (*disciplina*). The Romans accomplished much by bravery, but even more by discipline. The earliest fighters of Rome were warriors; by the time of the Punic Wars they were well-drilled soldiers. The first fighting force was a *legio*, a gathering of the clans; the last was an *exercitus*, a body of men who had been trained. The great contributions of Rome to military science were organisation, discipline, attention to details, far-sighted preparation, the realization that battles could be won before they were fought.

10. The Spade in the Roman Army

In view of the developments of the World War, it is a very remarkable thing that the use of the spade was so fundamental in Roman warfare. High-angle fire and powerful explosives have put the modern soldier in the trench, whereas for ancient conditions of warfare, with the comparatively low trajectory of missiles, the embankment or rampart made of material excavated from the trenches afforded sufficient protection. 'Digging in' was a regular part of the day's task for the legionary. A Roman army on the march entrenched every night.

Under some conditions Napoleon recommended similar action, as we learn from one of his maxims:

> In a war of march and manoeuvre, if you would avoid a battle with a superior army, it is necessary to entrench every night, and occupy a good position. Those natural positions which are ordinarily met with are not sufficient to protect an army against superior numbers without recourse to art.

Napoleon's conqueror, as well as Napoleon himself, gleaned lessons of military value from Caesar. In *Reminiscences and Table Talk of Samuel Rogers*[1] there is preserved for us an acknowledgment of indebtedness by the Duke of Wellington: "Had Caesar's *Commentaries* with me in India, and learnt much from them, fortifying my camp every night as he did."

According to one ancient authority, [2] the trench of an ordinary encampment should be 9 feet wide and 7 deep if there seemed to be no immediate danger. When there was a menace from the enemy, the width should be increased to 12 feet and the depth to 9. The excavated material thrown out at the side increased the total depth several

1. London, 1903.
2. Veg., I..

PLATE III

Roman Legionaries " Digging in" and Fortifying

From Cichorius, *Die Reliefs der Traianssäule*

feet. Caesar [3] mentions a trench 15 feet wide from which was made a rampart 10 feet high and 10 feet wide. For a permanent camp, the width of the trench should be 9, 11, or 13 feet, and, in case a large force of the enemy was near, 17 feet.[4]

Even these measurements were exceeded. Colonel Stoffel, who has done so much for our knowledge of Caesar's campaigns in Gaul, speaks of finding in the trenches around the site of ancient Gergovia coins and other remains of Roman occupation as far down as 15 feet. [5] At Alesia there was a trench or moat 20 feet wide. Trenches were used, then, not only to protect camps, but to besiege cities, so that Varro could rightly say that the Roman conquered by sitting still.

The largest trench of antiquity was, perhaps, the one constructed by Crassus during the servile uprising to shut up Spartacus and his followers within the peninsula forming the toe of Italy. From sea to sea across the neck of land over 34 (English) miles broad he ran an entrenchment fifteen feet deep and fifteen feet in breadth. [6]

It is worth while to stop to note the methods employed by the French officer in locating Caesar's entrenchments. Wherever from literary evidence and on a *priori* reasons he suspected Caesar's lines might have run, he dug trial transverse trenches, so that they would cut across any old trenches. The intersections of trenches were readily recognized by the clear V-shaped profiles made by the lines of contact between the undisturbed and the made earth.

In the use of the spade and the creation of obstacles, the siege of Alesia by Caesar [7] is the most memorable in antiquity. This great natural stronghold of the Gauls was situated on the summit of a hill so high that it was inexpugnable except by siege. At its foot on the northern and southern sides ran two streams. As the space between the brooks on the west gave the inhabitants the best opportunity to attack, Caesar built across it an immense trench twenty feet wide with vertical sides instead of the more usual tapering ones.

Farther back from the town were two other trenches fifteen feet wide and fifteen feet deep, one of which continued its course around the town as part of a line of contravallation eleven miles in extent. Outside of this was constructed a rampart surmounted by a palisade, the total height of which was twelve feet. From the rampart projected

---

3. *B. C*, III. 63.
4. Veg., III.
5. See T. Rice Holmes, *Caesar's Conquest of Gaul.*
6. Plut, *Crassus*.7. *B. G.*, VII.

breastworks consisting of a tangle of stout branches. At frequent intervals wooden towers were erected.

To guard against sallies from the besieged he built in front of the town a series of trenches five feet deep. According to the interpretation of our best authority on Caesar:

> Five rows of strong boughs were fixed in each, with one end protruding above ground, sharpened and with the branches projecting so as to form a kind of abatis.

These branches were dubbed in camp slang *cippi*, 'boundary posts,' from their resemblance to surveyors' markers. [8]

In front of all these defences there were arranged in checkerboard fashion cone-like holes into which were set sharp stakes projecting not more than four finger-breadths. The holes were concealed with brush. There were eight rows of these pits, which the soldiers dubbed *lilia*, 'lilies,' because of the way they spread out from a point. Almost identical with them are the wolf-holes constructed before Ypres[9] by the Germans in 1914. The system of fortification ended with barbed pieces of iron, called *stimuli*, 'goads,' in soldier argot, which were set in pieces of wood implanted in the earth.

In anticipation of an attempt by the countrymen of Vercingetorix to raise the siege, Caesar constructed a circumvallation with the same defences, but in reverse order. This was fourteen miles long.

At Dyrrachium in the Civil War, Caesar used earthworks to enclose Pompey's men and the Pompeians constructed defensive works against them. Both sides exerted their ingenuity to the utmost. Caesar tells us [10] that this was a new and untried method of warfare and comments especially on the number of redoubts and the extent of the fortifications. Dodge [11] pays his respects to these operations:

> It was on the terrain thus enclosed that there were constructed the most remarkable fortifications in antiquity.

In giving a summary of the development of the art of fortification, a pamphlet prepared since the close of the Great War under the direction of a major general of the United States Army says:

---

8. It has been suggested that the soldiers were comparing the *cippi* to gravestones.
9. *Ypres, 1914 - The German Perspective of the Early Battles of the First World War* - by Otto Schwink also published by Leonaur.
10. *B. C*, III.
11. *Caesar.*

From the description Caesar gives of the defences he erected (*e.g.*, at Alesia and Dyrrachium), it is evident that he was thoroughly familiar with all the essential principles of fortification, and with the function and use of obstacles we now know, except the wire entanglement. [12]

The maze of barbed-wire of the recent war is but an improvement upon the palisades and brushwood entanglements of the Romans. Stakes and branches were at times so closely interlaced and so firmly secured that it was impossible to insert the hand and pull them away. The Greek Polybius,[13] struck by the great contrast between the efficiency of the Roman devices and those of his own countrymen, concludes that of all the military arts of the Romans their method of palisading and intertwining branches is the one most worthy of admiration and imitation.

Spade work, especially when assisted by stakes and branches, was, therefore, just as effective in antiquity as it is today. Even Hannibal had to desist from the attempt to break through the defences made by Marcellus before Capua. He had as much respect for fortified positions as had the British regulars, later on, after they had charged against the hastily constructed Colonial earthworks and entrenchments at Bunker Hill. In the civil wars, Roman generals regarded fortified positions as all but unassailable. Caesar refrained from attacking the camp of Scipio in the African campaign.

Sapping and mining are other ancient forms of warfare to which modern armies have resorted. In antiquity they were restricted to siege operations. Alexander had with him on his Persian expedition men who were especially skilled in these arts.

If we may believe Roman tradition, the city ofVeii was taken after a ten-year siege by a tunnel which admitted the Romans to the heart of the citadel. Undermining walls beneath the protection of *mantlets* or moving towers was a regular part of siege operations. Countermining too was practised.

The best illustration, perhaps, of these tactics is seen in the siege of the Greek city of Massilia by Caesar's forces under Trebonius in the Civil War. When some thirty mines were being driven forward toward the walls:

The people of Marseilles, distrusting the entire moat in front

12. *Pamphlet on the Evolution of the Art of Fortification.*
13. XVIII.

> of their wall, lowered it by digging it deeper. Thus all the mines found their outlet in the moat. In places where the moat could not be dug, they constructed, within the walls, a basin of enormous length and breadth, like a fish pond, in front of the place where the mines were being pushed, and filled it from wells and from the port. And so, when the passages of the mine were suddenly opened, the immense mass of water let in undermined the supports, and all who were within were overpowered by the mass of water and the caving in of the mine. [14]

From the illustrations already given, it is clear that the Roman used the spade to good advantage. Behind his trench and other obstacles, the Roman legionary felt even more secure than did the modern soldier in the Great War. Even hastily constructed entrenchments were looked upon with wholesome respect by attacking generals.

---

14. Vitruvius, X. 16. 11, Translation, M. H. Morgan, Cambridge, Mass., 1914.

11. Roman Contributions to Tactics and Strategy

The Latins who settled on the hills of Rome seem to have differed from the neighbouring tribes of central Italy chiefly in their capacity to assimilate. Their army was at first merely a *legio*, a gathering of the clans, and their first warlike activities were simply forays. In spite of the far-reaching reorganisation of the Roman military system said to have been instituted by Servius Tullius, the sixth king of Rome, raids seem to have characterized their warfare from the time of Romulus to the siege of Veii.

In Livy's description of the battle with the Gauls at the Allia in 390 B.C., the Romans are represented as being familiar with tactics infinitely superior to any they used until the middle of the Second Punic War. He says that the Romans stationed reserves on a piece of rising ground, and that Brennus feared it was the Roman purpose to use these after the lines had clashed to make an attack upon the flank and rear. [1] If the Romans at that time knew as much as this, then Roman generalship soon went into a Rip Van Winkle dormancy from which it did not awake for over 175 years.

An incident in Roman legendary history provided a German, at a time in the Great War when Germany had only three big avowed enemies, with an illustration that enabled him to drive home a point in strategy. Helfferich thought:

> Germany ought to dispose of her enemies, like the last of the three Horatii, who in the story defeated the three Curiatii who were attacking him, separating them by a clever retreat.[2]

1. Livy, V.

2. A. P. F. von Tirpitz, *My Memoirs*, New York, 1919; II. 161. The reader will doubtless recall this story which is told in Livy's most delightful vein. (Continued next page).

Perhaps the only striking tactical manoeuvre made by a Roman general during the First Punic War was executed just outside of the walls of Panormus (Palermo) in 251 B.C.[3] The consul Caecilius lured the Carthaginians up to the very walls by means of skirmishers. At a propitious time he led his maniples from the gate opposite the enemy's left and charged them diagonally on the flank. This move reminds one of Alexander's oblique march upon the Persian flank at Arbela. One suspects, however, that this alignment was forced upon Caecilius by the character of the terrain rather than evolved by any superior tactical skill.

The outstanding military achievement of the Romans prior to the Second Punic War was the organisation of their " division," so to speak, the *legion*. The Roman *legionary* was then the best fighting material in the world and he had the best equipment. Generalship had not, however, kept pace with him, thanks to lack of imagination and the belief that main strength and discipline were the only deciding factors in battles. We have already noted Hannibal's contempt of Roman generalship just prior to the battle of the Trebia.

In discussing Roman tactics and strategy, it would be not only unfair, but impossible to disregard Hannibal, the Carthaginian patriot, whom Livy excoriates, but for whom he cannot entirely conceal his admiration. We have already had occasion to note that it was Hannibal who opened the eyes of the Romans to the real meaning of generalship. In conformity with their policy of adopting whatever superior equipment they found in the hands of foreigners, the Romans after Cannae assimilated what they could of Hannibal's tactics.

It would seem that until the Second Punic War (218-201 B.C.) the Carthaginians knew even less of tactics and strategy than did the Romans. In 255 B.C. a Roman army of occupation had utterly defeated and cowed the Carthaginians. So sure was Regulus of his ability to capture Carthage that he undertook to dictate a ruthless peace. In sheer despair the Carthaginians refused. At this juncture, there was brought to Carthage a soldier of fortune, Xanthippus, a Spartan. He

---

Alban and Roman armies had agreed to settle the question of supremacy by the outcome of a battle between champions. As it chanced, each army had a family of three brothers who were triplets, the Curiatii (Albans) and Horatii (Romans). These were selected to represent their nations. At the first encounter of these youths, two Horatii fell, while all the Albans were wounded. The surviving Horatius took to flight, but when the injured Albans became separated in the pursuit, he turned and vanquished them one at a time.

3. Polyb., I.

showed the Carthaginians that their defeat was due to blundering generalship. With more skilful tactical dispositions under his leadership, the Carthaginians inflicted a crushing defeat upon the Romans.

Yet only forty years after their wretched exhibition of generalship, a commander of Carthaginian extraction was roaming at large in Italy, unable to find a Roman army that would meet him in the open field. There is every reason to believe that he too profited by Greek lessons.

When Hannibal was making his final preparations to march against Italy, he took measures to protect Africa from an attack by way of Sicily, and to ensure the loyalty of Spain. Accordingly he sent Spaniards to guard Africa and Africans to garrison Spain, so that there would not be too much cooperation between garrison and people. In the same way during the period of the greatest expansion of the Roman Empire, recruits from one part of the Empire would be stationed in another in order to prevent undue sympathy between garrisons and inhabitants. One is reminded of the case of Switzerland in the Great War. It is said that she sent French-speaking soldiers to guard the German frontier and German-speaking troops to protect the Italian border.

At the Rhone in 219 B.C., Hannibal found his passage blocked by the Gauls on the farther bank. He sent a detachment a day's journey up stream with instructions to cross by night and to attack the Gauls from the rear while he himself essayed a crossing in front. [4] This method is suggestive of Alexander's tactics at the Hydaspes, though it may be only a coincidence.

Hannibal understood as clearly as did Alexander the necessity of securing his communications. This was no easy thing to do in Gaul, on account of the numbers and fickleness of the inhabitants, yet Livy[5] says that he left no unconquered tribes behind him.

In the fall of 219, after an unprecedented conquest of the snowy barriers of the Alps, Hannibal took up such a position near Placentia, to which the consul Scipio had retired, that he severed Scipio's communications with Tiberius Sempronius, the other consul, who was hurrying up with assistance. It has been denied by a French military critic that Hannibal intended to separate the armies of the Romans and then beat them one at a time. If such was his purpose, to effect strategical penetration, clearly Polybius, an extremely astute military writer, did not understand the significance of the move.

4. Polyb., III.; Livy, XXI.

5. XXI.

Napoleon, however, seems to have had no doubt of the meaning of the Carthaginian manoeuvre. Of his strategy in 1796 in taking up a central position between his opponents in Northern Italy, he says:

> I was in a position more favourable than Hannibal's. The two consuls had a common interest, to cover Rome; the two generals that I was attacking had each a particular interest that dominated them: Beaulieu that of covering Milan; Colli that of covering Piedmont.

Dodge [6] characterizes Hannibal's move as "crisp and masterly," and sees in Napoleon's words an acknowledgment of the source of inspiration for this stroke.

At the Battle of the Trebia (218 B.C.), Hannibal engaged the Romans with a frontal attack. After the engagement had started, he set upon the Romans with a cavalry force that had been lying in ambuscade upon their right. Of this method of attack Gilbert [7] says with all the emphasis of italics:

> "*It remained for Hannibal to establish the true principle of a flank attack combined with a frontal attack.*"

He points out that Alexander's flank attack by an oblique march is not free from certain inherent tactical defects and regards Hannibal's flank manoeuvres as a marked advance.

When Hannibal was making his way south from northern Italy in 217 B.C., he learned that his way was blocked at Arretium by the consul Flaminius. Instead of coming to battle, he made a precarious passage across the marshes of the Arno, went around the left flank of the Roman, and cut him off from his communications with Rome. Here again, Dodge[8] informs us, is a clear conception of the enemy's strategic flank.

One of the world's masterpieces of battle tactics is Cannae, which was fought on the Aufidus in Southern Italy in 216 B.C.[9] Hannibal drew up his forces in the shape of a crescent, as Polybius tells us. His centre was rather thin and gave way gradually before the fierce onset of the Roman legionaries. Gradually the line straightened, but not even then did the centre stop. It continued to yield and the enthusias-

6. *Hannibal.*
7. *The Evolution of Tactics.*
8. *Hannibal.*
9. See Polyb., III.; Livy, XXII.

tic legionaries followed into the hollow of the sagging line. Hereupon Hannibal's wings closed in and the Romans were trapped. The disaster was completed by the return of the cavalry which, after putting to flight the Roman horse upon the flanks, assailed the Romans from the rear. Such, in brief, were Hannibal's tactics at Cannae.

No battle in history is a finer example of tactics than Cannae.[10]

This conflict has been the subject of the most intense study by the German military staff. By them it is considered a model battle. Among the most important books of General Count von Schlieffen, whom Ludendorff calls "one of the greatest soldiers who ever lived," is one called *Cannae.* Upon the basis of this ancient battle he worked out his own theories.

> Schlieffen believed in retaining the enemy's centre, or even yielding to him a little there, while outflanking and enclosing him on both wings. A victory of the Cannae type, he held, was the only sort which would ensure the annihilation of an opponent. [11]

By him was conceived a German plan of campaign to be put in operation on the West Front in case of a war with France and Russia. With his elaborate enveloping movement through Belgium in mind,[12] Admiral von Tirpitz, in his *My Memoirs*, says of the Great War prior to the Battle of the Marne:

> Until then the army had been animated by one idea: Cannae.

The best exemplification of Cannae is the Battle of Tannenberg, which was fought in August 1914 by Hindenburg, one of Count von Schlieffen's pupils. [13]

He engaged the invading Russians with retiring bodies of troops to delude them into the belief that they were pushing through weak opposition.

Suddenly (August 26) the Russians, advancing on a wide front,

---

10. Dodge, Hannibal.

11. Wm. L. McPherson, The Strategy of the Great War, New York, 1920.

12. The younger Moltke made changes in Von Schlieffen's plan, notably in greatly strengthening the left wing, but the idea of a great strategic turning movement through Belgium was Von Schlieffen's.

13. A diagram of the German conception of ideal battle tactics, based on Cannae, can be found in *The Times History of the War*, London, I. (1914).

encountered serious resistance. They had come to the prepared trap of Hindenburg. At first the centre seemed to yield, and the Russian general pushed forward. Then there was pressure from the south on his left. Sending troops to overcome this, Samsonoff was surprised by a wide sweep of strong German forces on his right flank. [14] For two days the Russians fought desperately against systematic attacks that closed in around their doomed army. On the third day Samsonoff was practically surrounded, his troops in a bewildering tangle of undergrowth, and his army a demoralized mass struggling in confusion. The fighting was protracted, but only the debris of an army escaped from the deadly circle. It was one of the few cases in history of the complete destruction of an army in battle.[15]

The double turning movement, the object of which was the envelopment of the Russians, had achieved for the Germans the same results that Hannibal gained at Cannae. Tannenberg is already considered a classic by military students. It is a striking fact that the only victory of the World War which resulted in the destruction of the enemy's army was won by tactics over 2100 years old.

When in 211 B.C. Hannibal's last effort to raise the siege of Capua by the Romans had failed and he saw that he could not attack the Romans in their entrenched positions, he decided to try to lure them away by marching on Rome.

> This is the first instance of which we have any record in which a thrust at the enemy's capital has been used as a feint to withdraw him from a compromising position.[16]

This statement would seem to be contradictory to what has been said about Epaminondas and his attempt upon Sparta. Polybius[17] was so struck by the similarity of the moves that he digresses from his story long enough to institute a comparison. There is, however, quite a difference. Epaminondas was capable of taking Sparta and would have succeeded had his plans not been betrayed to the Spartan leader.

---

14. The encircling movement was extended by troops and some cavalry brought down from the North from the army in front of another invading Russian force under Rennenkampf.

15. Thomas G. Frothingham, *A Guide to the Military History of the World War, 1914-1918,* Boston, 1920.

16. Dodge, *Hannibal.*

17. IX.

Rome, unlike Sparta, was amply garrisoned, and, in addition, Hannibal had made no preparation for siege operations and knew he could not take the city. His effort was a pure feint.

After the disaster at Lake Trasimenus in 217 B.C. Quintus Fabius Maximus was put in charge of the Roman arms. It had hitherto been the policy of Roman generals to attack, to take the initiative on every possible occasion. Fabius clearly saw the need of caution. He dogged Hannibal's line of march, but kept to the hilly country to render the Numidian cavalry useless. He cut off foraging parties and interfered with his adversary's movements in every way compatible with safety. He could not be lured or provoked to battle, but wherever Hannibal went, he followed so that he was nicknamed *paedagogus*, in allusion to the Greek slave who accompanied boys to and from school. Another epithet was *Cunctator*, 'Delayer.'

Small war had been resorted to before this by barbarian tribes, but the Romans were the first powerful nation to develop it into a science. We still pay tribute to the innovator when we speak of Fabian tactics.

Marcellus, 'the sword of Rome,' as Fabius was its 'shield,' did a novel thing for a Roman commander when Hannibal made his second attempt upon Nola (215 B.C.). He armed the citizens of the town and held them in reserve between his own ranks and the walls. [18] Hitherto the *triarii*, men in the third rank, had acted as reserves, but for their own legion. The act of Marcellus is a step toward recognition of the error of systematically and rigidly distributing reserves. The Hannibalic War impressed upon the Romans the necessity of a free or mobile reserve.

Before the first lustrum had elapsed after peace with Carthage, reserves were a matter of course in the Roman army. Polybius [19] uses the Battle of Cynocephalae (197 B.C.) as a peg on which to hang the information that in meeting the phalanx the Romans did not extend their front to equal length, but, instead, kept some of their forces in reserve. These reserves were of necessity mobile, since they had to be available to protect either flank from envelopment.

The Roman general of the Second Punic War who learned most from Hannibal was Caius Claudius Nero. This apt pupil used his lessons against his teacher. In 207 B.C, as he was blocking Hannibal at Canusium, he got possession of Hasdrubal's plans to effect a junction with his brother. It was imperative for Rome to frustrate the invader's designs. Nero acted with promptitude. He decided to leave a 'containing' force against Hannibal and to go to the help of Livius in the North. Keeping Hannibal in the dark as to his purpose, he marched north with unprecedented speed, using carts and wagons to hasten his progress, effected a junction with his colleague, exerted upon Hasdrubal the full moral effect of his achievement, was the chief instrument in the destruction of the Carthaginian army at the Metaurus, and returned in safety to his original position. [20]

In two weeks he had covered some five hundred miles and gained for Rome the greatest victory of the war. The masterly execution of the whole operation challenges our admiration. This campaign finds a place here because it is the first instance of the effective use of interior lines. It will always remain a conspicuous illustration of this type of strategy. Napoleon's offensive-defensive on interior lines in his campaigns of 1796 and 1814 has been called a brilliant exposition of the same principle. [21] In spite of the smaller number of men engaged and the crude means of transportation that Nero impressed into service to speed up his line of march, the achievement is a worthy forerunner of the German shifting of forces from one front to another during the Great War.

Of Nero's march Creasy writes as follows:

> Viewed only as a military exploit, it remains unparalleled save by Marlborough's bold march from Flanders to the Danube in the campaign of Blenheim, and perhaps also by the Archduke Charles's lateral march in 1796, by which he overwhelmed the French under Jourdain, and then, driving Moreau through the Black Forest and across the Rhine, for a while freed Germany from her invaders.

In the Battle of the Metaurus Nero executed a brilliant manoeuvre. When the Romans were failing to make headway, he detached a force from the right wing, which he was commanding, made a detour of the Roman left flank, and debouched upon the rear of the Carthaginian right. This movement decided the engagement in favour of the Romans.

A similar manoeuvre makes the Battle of Ramillies Marlborough's masterpiece. Jomini [22] tells us that:

---

18. Livy, XXIII.
19. XVIII.
20. Livy, XXVII.
21. Gilbert, *Op. cit.*
22. *The Art of War.*

> The real cause of Marlborough's success was his seeing that Villeroi had paralysed half his army behind Anderkirch and Gette, and his having the good sense to withdraw thirty-eight squadrons from this wing to reinforce his left, which in this way had twice as many cavalry as the French, and outflanked them.

At the Trebia Hannibal had had a cavalry force in ambush upon a flank of the Romans before battle; Nero combined a front and flank attack by deployment *after* the battle had started;

> But at Türkheim Turenne made a still further advance by illustrating how this principle could be put in practice by manoeuvre whilst on the march and before contact with the enemy.[23]

The battle which Scipio fought in 206 B.C. near Baecula in Spain against Hasdrubal, son of Gisgo, is described by Denison [24] as "the highest development of tactical skill in the history of Roman arms." We shall, however, stop only long enough to note that Dodge [25] finds here another illustration of a threat against the strategic flank, since Scipio's position endangered Hasdrubal's line of retreat to Gades.

At Zama in 202 B.C. Scipio gave another demonstration of tactical ability. Here he met the great Hannibal at bay. [26] Both armies were drawn up with cavalry on the wings. Reversing the situation at Cannae the Roman cavalry, composed chiefly of Numidians, drove Hannibal's horse from the field. Returning from the pursuit while the infantrymen were engaged in a terrible struggle, they fell upon the Carthaginian flanks and rear. Keeping their banners flying, Hannibal's veterans fought fiercely with the courage of despair, but their doom was sealed. The enemies of Carthage had used Carthaginian tactics to her undoing.

The leader of the lion's brood was beaten at last. A life's work was nullified, a life's ambition frustrated, but an ideal of ardent patriotism still remains for the world.

Polybius [27] is unstinted in his praise of Hannibal and even Livy, [28] a calumniator of his personal character, cannot refrain from admiring his great ability. For sixteen years without active support from home,

---

23. Gilbert.
24. *A History of Cavalry.*
25. *Hannibal.*
26. Livy, XXX.
27. XL.
28. XXVIII.

Hannibal maintained his army in a hostile country which had better soldiers than his own. His polyglot army, consisting of Libyans, Iberians, Ligurians, Celts, Phoenicians, Italians, Greeks, differing as widely in temperament and customs as in language, had no bond to hold them together other than the magnetism of their leader.

Intensely human, possessed of a sense of humour, gifted with a fertile imagination, courageous in adversity as in success, an ardent patriot, this great commander calls forth our greatest admiration. I have never heard in a moving-picture theatre applause, as spontaneous and as protracted, as that which greeted the flashing on the screen, in D'Annunzio's *Cabiria*, of Hannibal's army surmounting the heights of the snow-clad Alps.

Carthaginian victory would have been a calamity for the Aryan race, yet one reads with sadness Livy's final chapters of Hannibal's career. Had Hannibal's good-fortune been as great as Alexander's, or even commensurate with his own ability, the world would have been his.

With lessons learned in the Second Punic War and under the inspiration of Metaurus and Zama, Roman generalship should have improved, yet it fell back into the more or less traditional methods. This was the character of the reaction inevitable after an unprecedented effort.

The square, which was so common in Greek tactics, was employed by Crassus in his fear of the Parthian cavalry. We are told by Plutarch[29] that he drew up his men in a deep square with twelve cohorts on each side.

The Battle of Carrhae is, however, more remarkable for other aspects of warfare. In 53 B.C. vain-glorious Publius Crassus endeavoured to lead an army across the Mesopotamian desert to attack the redoubtable Parthians. When the Romans were in a sea of sand, where there were no natural features to make strategic dispositions possible, the Parthians suddenly attacked. Realising the helplessness of their infantry against Romans, they had concentrated on cavalry. With their fleet horses and open order they themselves were unassailable, while the serried ranks of their opponents provided easy targets for their long-range bows.

When they were galling the Romans with their fire and threatening to encircle them, the son of Crassus charged them with thirteen

---

29. Crassus, 23. Antony too used the hollow square to protect himself from the Parthians. See Plut, Ant., 42. 1.

hundred horse, five hundred archers and eight *cohorts* of *legionaries*. The Parthians fled, but when they had lured their pursuers far out of sight of the rest of the Romans, they turned upon them. Equipped with light, but powerful javelins that outranged the *pilum* and other Roman weapons, they rode round and round the Roman army, showering upon them their missiles so thick and fast that one writer compares them to a hail-storm. Of the detachment of Romans but five hundred survived and they were made prisoners. Under cover of the night, the main body of Romans set out for Carrhae, about thirty miles from the first battle-ground, and finally reached it with difficulty.

The Romans had been outwitted strategically and surpassed tactically.

> Here, where the Roman weapons of close combat and the Roman system of concentration yielded for the first time before the weapons of more distant warfare and the system of deploying, was initiated that military revolution which only reached its completion with the introduction of firearms.[30]

The deployed order is seen again in the tactics of Petreius and Afranius, Pompey's lieutenants in Spain. They had been fighting the native tribes of Spain and had adopted in modified form their methods of warfare. They did not keep rank, but fought in loose open order and "did not think it disgraceful to withdraw and yield ground." Caesar's men experienced considerable difficulty on first meeting such tactics. [31] In the American Revolution British regulars at Lexington and Concord, and; in fact throughout the war, seemed helpless against the extended order which took advantage of every natural shelter, a method of warfare that the Colonists had learned in Indian fighting.

When Caesar was thirty-three years old,[32] he lamented that at his age Alexander had conquered the world. The Macedonian had been a student of war from childhood, yet Caesar as a mature man had not even begun his military career. In him were lacking the youthful fire and impetuosity and rashness that characterized Alexander. His late start in war had its influence in making him the purely intellectual type of leader.

That Caesar was not so great a tactician as Alexander and Hannibal and has not left us striking new tactical formations, may be attrib-

---

30. Mommsen, *Op. cit.*, V.
31. *B. C*, I.
32. Suet., *Div. Jul.*, 7, and Dio Cassius, XXXVII. 52; but compare Plut., *Caes.*, 11.

uted in part to the discipline and matter-of-fact temperament of the Romans. Having better fighting material than either of his predecessors, he probably realized that the familiar methodical distribution of legionaries left less to chance and the personal equation of subordinates.

Naturally he made his plan of battle conform to the character of the ground.[33] Perhaps his greatest deviation from customary tactics was in a battle with Ariovistus.[34] He tells us that he opened the battle against the German left wing because he had noticed that that wing was the weakest part of the enemy line. The implication is that his own left flank was 'refused' and weak. In fact it with difficulty held out until Caesar could send it help after beating the enemy in front of him.

The great Condé, who was an enthusiastic student of Caesar's *Commentaries*, admired especially the clever manner in which Caesar outmanoeuvred Petreius and Afranius in Spain and forced them to surrender without a battle.[35]

At the Battle of Pharsalia[36] Caesar stationed himself on the right wing intending to fight in his favourite tenth *legion*. Pompey's cavalry concentrated opposite this wing, planning to attack it from the flank and rear, fully confident that no *legionaries* could stand up against them. To meet this threat, Caesar secretly withdrew six *cohorts* from his third line and hid them in the rear in reserve.

When the infantry joined battle, Pompey's proud cavalry began to extend their companies with the intention of enclosing Caesar's right. Thereupon the reserve *cohorts* sprang forward, and using their spears, not for throwing, but for thrusting at the eyes and face of the horsemen, they drove them shamefully from the field. (These were *Roman* horsemen.) Thereupon the *cohorts* continued their advance and turned the opposing wing of the enemy.

Gilbert thus sums up Caesar's contribution to military science in this battle:

> Caesar here proved the advantage of keeping the third line or reserve concentrated, and not spread out over the whole length of the line of battle, as had hitherto been the Roman practice.[37]

---

33. *E.g., B. G.*, II.
34. *B. G.*, I.
35. *B. C*, I. Cf. J. B. De Bossuet, *Oraison Funèbre de Louis de Bourbon, Prince de Condé, in Oraisons Funèbres*, Paris, 1886.
36. *B. C*, III.; Plut, *Pomp.*
37. Compare previous comments on reserves.

> He moreover retained the reserve under his immediate personal command. It was posted first in rear of his centre, then moved to the threatened flank, and finally employed to confirm the victory. Caesar had solved the difficult problem of how to sustain the shock of a frontal attack, and at the same time repulse a cavalry attack on flanks or rear.

The attack upon the flank, when skilfully executed by a larger force, had been uniformly successful since the days of Hannibal.

Napoleon says in one of his maxims:

> The distances permitted between corps of an army upon the march must be governed by the localities, by circumstances, and by the object in view.

This maxim might well have been framed from Caesar's procedure.[38] The student of the Gallic War recalls how the Nervii were informed that after each of Caesar's *legions* there was a vast amount of baggage, and that it would not be any trouble when the first *legion* had come into camp to attack it while the others were a great distance off. The Nervii, however, met with a surprise, for Caesar changed the order and sent six *legions* in advance "because he was nearing the enemy."

To illustrate Caesar's strategy, we may, as in the case of Alexander, call attention to a ruse of his in effecting the passage of a river in the face of opposition.[39] In 52 B.C. he wished to cross the Elaver (now Allier). Upon the other side was Vercingetorix who had broken down the bridges.

One morning Caesar concealed two *legions* in a forest and ordered the remaining four to march up the river with the formation of six. Upon the other side, Vercingetorix kept parallel with the Romans. When he had gone a considerable distance, Caesar set to work to repair a bridge of which the piles had not been entirely destroyed. He led his two *legions* across without molestation and then summoned the rest of his forces.

> A similar stratagem was successfully employed in 1915. The German and Austrian commanders wished to cross the Vistula in Poland at a point northwest of Ivangorod. They moved their forces upstream in such a way as to lead the Russians to be-

---

38. *B. G.,* II.
39. *B. G.,*VII.

lieve that they intended to force a crossing at some distance northeast of the city. At the point previously determined upon, material for pontoon bridges was brought to the bank of the river loaded on wagons which were covered with straw, so that they were reported by the Russian aviators merely as loads of straw; since the Russian commander had no information to the contrary, slight attention was paid to them. The ruse made it possible for the pontooners to start building the bridges before their presence or purpose was suspected. When the Russians finally brought their artillery to bear at the threatened point, it was too late to check the work; the Teutonic forces completed four bridges over the river and marched across.[40]

Appreciating the importance of speed in military operations, Caesar kept trained engineers in his legions. The expedition with which in one day he threw a bridge across the Arar (Saône), a feat that the Helvetii accomplished with the utmost difficulty in twenty days, so impressed his opponents that they at once sent ambassadors to him.[41] There can hardly be any doubt that this was a pontoon bridge, as was the one constructed over the Sequana (Seine) by Labienus.[42]

In speaking of his indebtedness to Caesar, the Duke of Wellington says of his campaigns in India:

> I passed over the rivers as he did by means of baskets and boats of wicker work; only I think I improved upon him, constructing them into bridges and always fortifying them, and leaving them guarded to return by them if necessary.

The duke here refers to the Roman method of using wicker baskets filled with stones as a means of mooring the boats constituting the pontoon bridge.[43]

On the Column of Trajan, which preserves for us a pictorial record of the emperor's Dacian campaigns, there is to be seen a representation of a very fine pontoon bridge. This obviously served its purpose as well as does its modern counterpart.

The bridge which Caesar threw across the Rhine, to the conster-

40. F. W. Kelsey, *Caesar's Commentaries*, New York, 1918.

41. *B. G.*, I.

42. *Ibid.*, VII.

43. Caesar certainly employed this method on the Guadalquiver in Spain (*Bell. Hisp.*, 5). Arrian, V., digresses from his story long enough to record Roman ways of construction.

nation of modern students of Latin as well as of the ancient Germans, was a remarkable engineering feat. Ten days after he had started to collect material, the army was on the other side. A recent, (1923), United States army pamphlet on fortification says of Caesar's bridge:

> It will be noted that the character of construction used by him is extremely similar to that in use at the present day.[44]

There were three outstanding features of Caesar's campaigns: the capture of decisive points at the outset; the use of the entrenched camp as a movable fortress both to aid in victory and to provide an impregnable rallying place; and the discomfiture of the enemy by breaking up his line of communications.[45] His promptness of decision and rapidity of execution were about on a par with Alexander's. *Veni, vidi, vici* will always be a memorial of his ability to think and act quickly.

He never lost a set battle. Napoleon's enemies finally divined his system of bringing to bear upon some important point a large force against a small one; Caesar's foes never could anticipate his plans.

We have noted Condé's admiration for Caesar's generalship in forcing Afranius and Petreius to surrender without a battle. We have seen that Caesar recognized the real province of a general during a battle. No ancient surpassed him in the art of fortifying. No Roman was his equal in strategy. Of his forces Mommsen says:

> Perhaps there never was an army which was more perfectly what an army ought to be.

With him the military science of a military and militaristic nation had reached flood-tide.

No general ever wrote a better military narrative than did Caesar. His *Commentaries* were intended to be used as notes, but the ancients shrewdly recognized the futility of trying to improve them.

> *With what his valour did enrich his wit,*
> *His wit set down to make his valour live.*

The Romans were the first nation to undertake an elaborate system of road-construction with the idea of securing mobility. With this end in view they made throughout practically their whole empire a network of roads which were so well designed and built that today after the lapse of some 2,000 years portions of them are still service-

---

44. Page 28 of the pamphlet prepared under Major General Black.
45. Dodge, *Caesar.*

able. This system made it possible for Roman armies to swoop down upon their foes with unexpected speed. It has been said that all roads lead to Rome. From a military point of view it was truer that all roads led from Rome.

The Roman word for baggage, *impedimenta*, 'hindrances,' is an indication that the Romans appreciated at its true value the part played by speed and mobility in military operations.[46] Of the ancient generals, certainly, Alexander and Caesar appreciated as fully as do contemporary generals the value of the time factor in warfare. It required modern methods of transportation to exceed the despatch with which they conducted operations.

> The real art of war had ended with Caesar. For its renaissance we are indebted to Gustavus Adolphus.[47]

So highly developed was the Greek and Roman art of war that, once it was lost, it took centuries to restore it to its former position. Without the invention of gunpowder and high explosives, how much farther could modern soldiers have carried the art?

---

46. We are told that Philip of Macedon made his soldiers carry their own provisions, thus getting rid of a large number of wagons. He also limited the number of servants (Frontinus, *Strat.*, IV. 1. 6).
47. Gilbert, *Op. cit.*

12. Roman Cavalry

One cannot speak with enthusiasm about the cavalry achievements of the Romans. They themselves never became wonderful horsemen. Like the Greeks, they first put men upon horses to accelerate their movements. Their first horsemen were called *celeres*, 'quickmen.' The early *equites* were accompanied by squires who likewise dismounted during the fighting, a situation paralleled in the early history of Greek cavalry. A step forward in the evolution of Roman cavalry occurred when mounted footmen were assigned genuine cavalry duties. At a critical time in a fight between Romans and Volscians, for instance,[1] a Roman exclaims to the horsemen:

> Show to Romans and Volscians that no cavalry are equal to you as cavalry and no infantry as infantry.

Even among barbarians the same course of development was followed. The Iberians after conquering horsemen opposed to them would leap to the ground and fight on foot.[2] As late as the Battle of Cannae we find a detachment of Roman cavalry dismounting and fighting on foot, when the consul Paulus no longer had strength to control his horse.[3]

At the beginning of the Second Punic War reconnoitring was already a well recognized duty of Roman cavalry. When in 218 the consul Publius Cornelius was on his way to Spain hoping to obstruct Hannibal's army, he learned that his opponent was planning the passage of the Rhone. To get accurate information, he sent a force of three hundred cavalrymen up the Rhone to make a reconnaissance. They fell in with a body of five hundred Numidian horsemen sent

1. Livy, IV.
2. Diod. *Sic*, V.
3. Livy, XXII.

out for a similar purpose. After a clash, fierce out of all proportion to the number of combatants, they retired victoriously, carrying with them an omen of victory for the entire war. [4]

The Romans had their first object-lesson in the handling of cavalry at the battle of the Trebia late in 218 B.C. [5] In this engagement Carthaginian cavalry forced the retreat of the Roman horsemen upon the wings. This allowed attacks to be made upon the flanks of the Romans, but still they maintained an obstinate and successful resistance until an ambuscade of Numidian horsemen charged the rear of the Roman centre. Hannibal owed his victory here to his numerous and well led cavalry. He was destined to continue to make the most of this branch of the service.

The best demonstration of Hannibal's theory of cavalry tactics was at Cannae. [6] It was the defeat and flight of the Roman cavalry on the right which paved the way for this colossal disaster to Roman arms. In the dispositions for the battle Hannibal placed Numidian cavalry on his right wing facing the cavalry of the Roman allies; on his left he stationed his Gallic and Spanish horse to oppose the Roman horse. Hannibal's horsemen on his left drove the Roman horse from the field and then crossed over in the rear of the Roman lines to aid their own right wing. After overwhelming the Roman squadrons opposed to them, they assailed the Roman *legionaries* from the rear. Gilbert [7] says of this operation:

> The same manoeuvre was successfully carried out in a precisely similar manner by Condé at the Battle of Rocroy, and partially by Cromwell at Naseby.

Of these manoeuvres of Hannibal a cavalry critic writes:

> His extraordinary skill displayed in the distribution of his cavalry, by which he opposed 8,000 to 2,400, and held back his Numidians on the right until they were assisted by the victorious horse from the other wing is beyond all praise, and proves how thoroughly he appreciated one of the best established principles of modern warfare, that of opposing masses of your own army to fractions of the enemy.[8]

---

4. Livy, XXI.
5. Polyb., III.
6. Polyb., III.; Livy, XXII.
7. *Op. cit.*
8. Denison, *Op. cit.*.

After Cannae Hannibal continued to seek to lure the Romans into engagements in the open where he could manoeuvre, but the Romans had learned their lessons and with equal assiduity kept to the hilly country. With great discernment Polybius [9] remarks:

> I think the reason of the strategy adopted by the two sides respectively was that they both had seen that Hannibal's cavalry was the main cause of the Carthaginian victory and Roman defeat.

The Romans gradually mastered Hannibal's lesson in cavalry tactics, and, strange to say, put an end to the war by a victory which was decided by the tactical action of horsemen. When African allied cavalry under Masinissa attacked the Carthaginians in flank and rear, the cavalry arm of the Roman army had reached its highest efficiency and value.

Of Masinissa who, prior to his defection from the Carthaginians, had ravaged the towns and fields of the Romans in Spain and had brought aid to allies, Dodge[10] writes:

> The work of this cavalry-general affords one of the most interesting examples of the proper use of cavalry on a large scale in the history of war.

Of the Battle of Carrhae, which has been referred to previously, Denison[11] writes:

> The history of war does not show a more brilliant illustration of the cavalry service, nor any instance where so great a result was due solely to the unaided efforts of horsemen. It is remarkable how thoroughly the Parthians appreciated the true value and real use of the horse for military purposes, and how skilfully they utilized two great advantages in war, namely, superior speed in movement, and superior range of missile weapons. These two points, well understood, and ably handled, should always secure success.

The Romans did not, then, handle cavalry skilfully or with imagination. At the Battle of Pharsalia, Pompey's cavalry, greatly outnumbering Caesar's as it did, should have carried the day, but it was badly organised and poorly commanded and made a disgraceful showing.

---

9. IX.
10. *Hannibal.*
11. *Op. cit.*

Even Caesar himself never employed horse in a way comparable to the magnificent use of cavalry made by Alexander and Hannibal. This, however, may be more to his credit than otherwise, since he probably recognized the limited possibilities of Roman horsemen.

As a rule, after the Second Punic War the Romans were content to entrust the cavalry branch of the service to allies. In his campaigns in Gaul Caesar relied on Gallic horse with a small admixture of German, Spanish and Numidian auxiliaries. For a long period afterwards the Gauls furnished a great part of the cavalry.

Of these auxiliaries the Numidians were the most efficient. To them we find the adjective "bridleless" applied several times. The adjective is not used figuratively. In describing the cavalry engagement at the Ticinus (219 B.C.), Polybius [12] says that Hannibal put on his front the cavalry "that rode with bridles," while on either flank he placed the Numidians.

The very expression, "that rode with bridles," shows that there were some horsemen, obviously the Numidians, who did not use them.

> It is a curious circumstance in this connection that General Hood, of the army of the late Confederate States of America, has always maintained that if the reins of the cavalry could be cut at the moment of the charge, the horses would break down the opposition of any infantry, and that the charge would always be successful.[13]

He believed that there was a tendency of the riders to pull up at the moment of impact and thus to check the impetuosity of the horses.

Caesar[14] tells us that German cavalry were accompanied into battle by footmen who were so agile and swift that they could support themselves by catching hold of the manes of the horses and so equal their speed. In his war with Rome the Macedonian king, Perseus, had from his allies, the Basternae, ten thousand horsemen with ten thousand men trained to run at their sides. [15] In a charge of the Scots Greys at St. Quentin in 1914, Highlanders accompanied the horsemen and managed to keep up with them. [16]

---

12. III.
13. Denison, *Op. cit.*
14. *B. G.*, I.
15. Plut., *Paul.*, 12. 2.
16. See Kelsey, *Op. cit.*

It is remarkable how the enemies of Rome in different parts of the world recognized at about the same time the irresistible superiority of the *legion* and began to resort to cavalry and long-distance weapons to fight it. The Armenians, when Lucullus was conducting a campaign against them in 68 B.C., would not allow their infantry to be involved in a conflict, but used their cavalry, and especially their mounted archers, to skirmish with the invaders. [17] Cassivellaunus in Britain saw that nothing could avail against Caesar's infantry and so dismissed the greater part of his forces, keeping 4,000 chariots to harass the line of march. [18] After the Gauls had fought Caesar for several years, Vercingetorix advised them to use the cavalry to devastate the surrounding country, to cut off foraging parties, and to hinder the Romans at every turn. [19] Nowhere, however, were cavalry tactics so successful as at Carrhae.

During the latter days of the Empire, as Rome's enemies, especially on the borders, began to resort more and more to the use of cavalry, the Romans were forced to do likewise. Oman, *A History of the Art of War, The Middle Ages*, puts the last days of the Roman *legion* at 235-450 and the commencement of the supremacy of cavalry at 450-552. At the Battle of Daras against the Persians in 530 *A.D.* the dispositions of the Roman force under Belisarius were such as to put the brunt of the fighting upon the cavalry.

---

17. Plut., *Lucullus*.
18. *B. G.*, V.
19. *B. G.*, VII.

13. Ancient and Modern Analogies

The Greeks were a military people, but were never militaristic with the exception of the Macedonian period. The Romans were always militaristic and upon militarism Rome depended as much as did modern Germany for the extension and control of her boundaries. Prior to the Great War we all thought of military Germany as comparable to the Romans, for upon her seemed to have descended the military spirit with many of its attendant qualities.

Neither nation invented the great weapons which it used with greatest effect, but both transformed and transfused those of other nations with their own adaptive and assimilative originality. If we disregard the Zeppelin, which fell far short of expectations, and the long-range gun, used for moral effect, we discover the trend of the inventive skill of the Germans.

They did not have the magic genius to invent the submarine, but carried its development farther than did any other nation; they did not invent the airplane, but constructed new models with great success; they did not invent the machine gun, but the outbreak of the war found them equipped with a greater number of such weapons than any other nation and with a greater realization of their value; they were not the first to make gas, but were the first to employ the poison gas wave; even their most effective weapon, the big siege gun, was but a super-howitzer. In tactics, modifications and improvements were made as experience dictated, but they waged the war without a great deal of imagination.

The same sort of originality is seen among the Romans. Even the *pilum*, 'spear,' which they thought of as being as purely Roman as was satire, was simply a super-javelin with modifications and improvements suggested by the weapons of other nations as well as by their own experience. The sword which conquered the world is said to have been of Iberian type. Even their defensive equipment was patterned after foreign models. From the Greeks they learned the art of constructing and operating siege machines. Their legion was a development of the Doric phalanx which worked its way up from Magna Graecia. Hannibal taught them tactics and strategy. The poet Ovid says:

It is meet to be taught even by an enemy.

We have many acknowledgments, both specific and general, of Roman indebtedness for arms and equipment.

Modern armies have returned to a number of accoutrements and devices employed by the ancients. Military atavism, so to speak, is seen nowhere more clearly than in the return to armour for the body. In the Great War helmets proved serviceable against shrapnel shells breaking overhead. *Cuirasses*, which had apparently been discarded forever, were again resorted to. Even greaves were used by Italian barbed-wire cutters and metal shields were not unknown among French grenadiers. The title of a recent book, *Helmets and Body Armour in Modern Warfare*,[1] shows how persistently we revert to ancient ideas.

A tribute to ancient methods of warfare is seen in the advent of the tank. Ancient counterparts of this contrivance are found in the sheds or *mantlets* and towers mounted on wheels, and even on Assyrian reliefs.[2] As is the case with the tank they were of different sizes and types of construction. Some of them were designed to protect besiegers approaching a wall, especially for the purpose of filling trenches, sapping, or for undermining fortifications. Others were intended to shelter men operating a ram. Against Massilia 'tortoises'[3] or sheds 60 feet long were employed.

A certain Hegetor of Byzantium constructed a 'tortoise' the base of which was 42 feet by 63 feet. It was moved by eight wheels the height of which was six feet, nine inches. In it was suspended a ram 180 feet long which could be elevated to a height sufficient to throw down a wall 100 feet high.[4]

Still other machines were so high that they could command the tops of walls and at the same time attack the base with rams below. The largest moving tower, 'city-taker,' as the Greeks called such a de-

1. By Bashford Dean, New Haven, 1920.
2. In the British Museum visitors are told that the Assyrian reliefs inspired the idea of a protecting device that could be moved against the enemy. Certainly the American caterpillar tractor solved the problem of the means of locomotion.
3. Caes., *B. C*, II. 2. 4; II.
4. Vitruv., X.

vice, which Demetrius brought against the Rhodians in 305 B.C., is described by Plutarch. [5]

> Its base was square, and each of its sides measured at the bottom forty-eight cubits. It rose to a height of sixty-six cubits, and tapered from base to summit. Within, it was divided off into many storeys and chambers, and the side of it which faced the enemy had windows opening out of every storey, and out through these issued missiles of every sort; for it was full of men who fought in every style of fighting. Moreover, it did not totter or lean when it moved, but remained firm and erect on its base, advancing evenly with much noise and great impetus, and this astounded the minds and at the same time greatly charmed the eyes of those who beheld it. [6]

Another writer [7] says that this tower was but little short of being 100 cubits high, that it had eight huge wheels under it, and that it required 3,400 of the strongest men in the army to move it. The 'city-taker' that Demetrius used against Thebes was so big and heavy that in two months it was advanced barely two furlongs. [8]

A Greek whose works were consulted by Vitruvius informs us that the smallest tower should be 60 cubits high with 10 stories, and the largest 120 cubits with 20 stories. [9] For the siege of Jotapata Vespasian ordered three towers 50 feet high to be erected, [10] while at Jerusalem Titus arranged for the construction of three 50 cubits high. [11]

The approach of a moving tower, surmounting the topmost walls, was as terrifying as the attack of an aeroplane and the defence was almost as hopeless. [12] Once it reached fortifications, soldiers in the upper stories could drive off defenders and lower a bridge to the walls. When from the walls of their stronghold the Aduatuci saw Caesar's men constructing such a tower at a distance, they began to jeer at them and to ask how men so small expected to move forward so pon-

---

5. *Demetrius*.
6. Translation, B. Perrin, in *The Loeb Classical Library*, New York, 1920.
7. Diod. *Sic*, XX.
8. Plut., *Demetrius*.
9. Vitruvius, X.
10. Josephus, *The Jewish War*, III.
11. *Op. cit.*, V.
12. The defence consisted in setting fire to the towers, digging mines beneath the course they were to take, or erecting counter-towers, methods which were not very frequently successful.

derous a machine. On seeing it approach they were panic-stricken and sent ambassadors to beg for peace, saying that they did not believe that without the help of the gods the Romans could move such a machine at such a pace. [13]

Vegetius, says:[14]

> What resource is there when those who were putting their entire hope in the height of the wall suddenly see a battlement of the enemy above them?

This was in reality an attack from the air.

There were still other methods of attacking from above. Against Massilia in the Civil War there was erected a rampart 80 feet high. [15] At Uxellodunum upon a mound 60 feet high was built a tower of ten stories. [16]

Even the conquest of the air does not seem to have been beyond the imagination of the ancients. Disregarding the story of Daedalus and Icarus, we hear of a wooden machine, called the 'Dove,' which by a system of springs and balances and other contrivances could be made to fly a limited distance. It was the invention of a Pythagorean philosopher named Archytas.[17]

Even the problem of making ' listening devices ' was tackled by the ancients. A brazen shield placed upon a wall would indicate by audible vibrations where a tunnel was being dug beneath it. [18]

In 189 B.C. the Romans under Marcus Fulvius Nobilior were besieging Ambracia in Epirus. Under shelter of a covered wall or *stoa* about 200 feet long, which they constructed parallel to the town fortifications, the Romans started to mine and tunnel. When the height of the excavated material finally betrayed their operations, the besieged set to work to dig a trench parallel to the Roman protection. In order to locate the approaching tunnels, they placed at intervals in the trench a number of very thin brazen vessels. Since these were "extraordinarily sensitive and vibrated to the sound outside," the besieged were able to dig counter-tunnels so accurately that they hit those of the enemy [19]

---

13. *B. G.*, II.
14. IV.
15. Caes., *B. C,* II. 1; cf. *B. G.*, VII. 24.
16. Caes., *B. G.*, VIII.
17. Aul. Gell., *Noct. Att.*, X.
18. Aeneas Tacticus.
19. Polyb., XXI.

This siege gives us also an interesting prototype of a modern gas attack. When the defenders had located the tunnels of the Romans and made counter-mines, they resorted to the following device: [20]

> Putting in front of them an earthenware jar, made to the width of the mine, they bored a hole in its bottom, and, inserting an iron funnel of the same length as the depth of the vessel, they filled the jar itself with fine feathers, and putting a little fire in it close to the mouth of the jar, they clapped on an iron lid pierced full of holes. They carried this without accident to the mine with its mouth towards the enemy. When they got near the besiegers they stopped up the space all around the rim of the jar, leaving only two holes on each side through which they thrust spears to prevent the enemy coming near the jar. They then took a pair of bellows such as blacksmiths use, and, having attached them to the orifice of the funnel, they vigorously blew up the fire placed on the feathers near the mouth of the jar, continually withdrawing the funnel in proportion as the feathers became ignited lower down. The plan was successfully executed; the volume of smoke created was very great, and, from the peculiar nature of feathers, exceedingly pungent, and was all carried into the faces of the enemy. The Romans, therefore, found themselves in a very distressing and embarrassing position, as they could neither stop nor endure the smoke in the mines. [21]

There is an ancient analogy even to the tear-gas attack, which places the enemy temporarily *hors de combat*. On one occasion Sertorius was defied by a Spanish tribe, the Charactani, who dwelt in caves on an impregnable cliff. Now it happened that the region abounded in a loose clayey soil. Of this the soldiers made a big pile. The next day the wind blew against the mouths of the caves, and the soldiers stirred up the dust and even drove horses to and fro in it. They repeated the process until the cave dwellers were temporarily blinded and surrendered. [22]

The smoke-screen, which played such a prominent part in naval

20. Polyb., XXI.

21. In a note to the passage Shuckburgh says: "Smoking out an enemy was one of the regular manoeuvres. See Aen. Tact., 37. It was perhaps suggested by the illegal means taken by workmen in the silver mines to annoy a rival; for we find an Athenian law directed against it."

22. Plut., Sert., 17. 1-7.

warfare during the Great War, is not without its ancient analogy. When the Bellovaci and Caesar were encamped close together on one occasion, the Gauls wished to deceive Caesar as to their intentions. Accordingly they set fire to brush and other inflammable material. As Caesar was unable to see through the smoke and feared an ambuscade in case he should advance quickly, the main body of the enemy managed to get a good start before he was sure of their purpose. [23]

In the Peloponnesian War the Spartans brought up fire-throwing engines against the Athenians fortified in Lecythus. [24] References to such contrivances are not infrequent. [25] They remind one of the *Flammenwerfer* of the Great War.

In a modest way the ancients had even a meteorological bureau. They did the best their limited means permitted. They studied the moon, the sun, the clouds and air for indications of the weather and we find Vegetius [26] stressing the importance of noting the actions of birds and fishes for weather forecasts.

But in other ways the actions of birds were found to be much more reliable. Scouts detected the presence of the enemy by noting the alarm manifested by birds frightened from their retreat. [27] This method was practised on the western front in the Great War before it developed into a stalemate. In commenting on the Battle of Chancellorsville, Steele[28] writes:

> The lines started through the wilderness. The first warning the Eleventh Corps received was not given by its outposts, for they hardly reached the main position ahead of the Confederates; it was given by the deer and rabbits and wild-turkeys of the forest, put to flight by the advance of the enemy.

The use of homing pigeons for military purposes was not unknown to the ancients. In 43 B.C., Decimus Brutus, who was besieged at Mutina by Antony, sent pigeons with messages to the consuls who had approached to relieve him.[29]

It is easy to see that it was not for lack of imagination that warfare was less complex in antiquity than it is today, but rather for want of

---

23. *B. G.*, VIII.

24. Thuc, IV.

25. *E. g.,* Diod. Sic, XX..; Plut., *Sulla*, 12. 3.

26. IV.

27. Frontinus, *Strat.*, I. 2. 7-8.

28. *American Campaigns*, I.

29. Plin., *N. H.*, X. no; cf. Frontinus, *Strat.*, III.

industries. The imagination of the ancients often inspired on a small scale things that were impossible on a large scale prior to the industrialization of war. [30]

Hitherto we have been concerned chiefly with concrete analogies. Naturally parallels exist with regard to the mental outlook and attitude of the ancients toward war and things military.

In discussing the critical days of the World War during the summer of 1918, Ludendorff, the power behind the German army at that time, thus expresses himself in *The Atlantic Monthly:* [31]

> The German troops were not lacking in bravery, nor in tenacity. But, to be successful, they needed something which the leader had no influence on, but with which he cannot dispense, good luck. More than once fortune smiled upon me; but in the decisive moment of the war it left me alone and favoured the enemy.

This is an old old cry. Polybius [32] indulges in similar reflections:

> It is quite the way of Fortune to confound human calculations by surprises; and when she has helped a man for a time, and caused her balance to incline in his favour, to turn round upon him as though she repented, throw her weight into the opposite scale, and mar all his successes.

Plutarch too comments in the same vein, especially in his *Life of Nicias*, who is a conspicuous example of the mutability of Fortune. Readers who have trudged through Cicero's oration on the Manilian Law will recall that *felicitas*, 'good luck,' is one of the orator's four cardinal requisites for a general. In his *Great Captains*, Dodge notes the part played by Fortune in the careers of the three greatest generals of antiquity. [33]

National emblems were as much objects of reverence as they are today. Augustus was extremely proud of his achievement in forcing the Parthians to restore the standards of three Roman armies which they

---

30. An interesting collection of analogies between ancient and modern methods of warfare has been made by Professor F. W. Kelsey, *Caesar's Commentaries*, New York, 1918, ix-xxvii. A number of parallels may be found in two articles written by myself, "The Ancients and the War," in *The Classical Weekly*, XI. 142-144 (1018), and "The Ancients and the War: Addenda," in *The Classical Weekly*, XII. 129-132 (1919).
31. "The American Effort," in *The Atlantic Monthly*, CXXIX. 683 (1922).
32. XXIX.
33. See *Alexander, Hannibal, Caesar.*

had defeated. The recovery of the standards lost to the Germans under Arminius at the Battle of Teutoberg Forest in 9 A.D. was a subject for national jubilation. In the Treaty of Versailles the French stipulated that the Germans should return the flags captured in 1870.

For extended comparisons between ancient and modern situations, it must suffice at this point merely to quote two titles, namely: *Our Great War and the Great War of the Ancient Greeks,* [34] by Gilbert Murray, and *Pan-Germanism in the Age of Pericles,* [35] by W. J. Battle.

The basic human passions and impulses were the same in antiquity as they are today, (1923). It is the essential oneness of the human race that makes so vital and instructive the experiences of the gifted peoples of antiquity.

---

34. New York, 1920.

35. *The Texas Review*, III. (1918); IV. (1918).

14. Naval Indebtedness

Could some feat of magic recreate an ancient fleet, fully equipped and fully manned, to be sent against a single modern battleship, that ancient fleet would have as much chance as a school of minnows against a whale, yet on the sea too the influence of antiquity still spans the centuries.

> That comparatively small sheet of water, the Mediterranean, served as the cradle for sea-power. Those principles of naval warfare, the adherence to or the disobedience of which has resulted in victory or defeat of nations, and has determined the mastery of the world for certain periods, were first demonstrated upon this inland sea. (So writes a naval critic). [1]

Lessons are still being drawn from dramas enacted in this restricted body of water. The mere title of a work by Sir Reginald Custance, *War at Sea, Modern Theory and Ancient Practice,* which appeared in the year following the Great War, is a glowing tribute to the ancients.

In E. K. Rawson's *Twenty Famous Naval Battles, Salamis to Santiago*, two ancient engagements by sea are described, Salamis, 480 B.C., and Actium, 31 B.C. Not until sixteen centuries later was there another decisive one, namely, Lepanto in 1571 between the Turks and Don Juan of Austria. Salamis and Actium are included among the fourteen engagements described in J. R. Hale's *Famous Sea Fights from Salamis to Tsu-Shima.*, (republished by Leonaur as *Sea Battles* by John Richard Hale).

Many classical parallels to modern manoeuvres likewise attest the alertness and resourcefulness of naval men of antiquity. Even in prehistoric Crete there were prototypes of the island kingdom of Great Britain, *thalassocracies* which owed their security and their independence to control of the sea. With the loss of their naval power they were

1. P. A. B. Silburn, *The Evolution of Sea-Power.*

PLATE IV

Naval Tactics (Perhaps a Gladiatorial Combat)

(From a wall-painting in the Temple of Isis, Pompeii)

Reproduced from Schreiber, *Atlas of Classical Antiquities*

unable to maintain their position and their dominion ended.

In historic Greek times the first ships built especially for use in warfare were constructed at Corinth and Samos about 700 B.C. We have a passing reference in Thucydides [2] to the first recorded naval engagement between Greeks, which was fought by Corinthians and Corcyraeans. Polycrates, a Samian who flourished in the second half of the sixth century B.C., seems to have been the first Greek who was a serious aspirant to sea-power. [3] It was fortunate for the Greeks that they took to the sea before the Persian menace became serious.

War by sea slowly but surely developed into a distinct art. The lengthening of the ships with attendant narrowing of the beam and the introduction of rowers to render the ship independent of the wind are both due to the recognition of the special needs of war by sea.

Data about the dimensions of the trireme, the regular fighting ship of the Greeks, are not available from ancient sources. At Zea, however, a port-town of Athens, there are remains of docks which must have been some one hundred and fifty feet in length and twenty feet in breadth. Presumably the docks are not much larger than the ships they were intended to accommodate. We do not have definite knowledge about the position and arrangement of the rowers and it has even been questioned whether they sat in tiers. Ships have been mentioned with ten, twenty, and even forty banks of oars, in which it is inconceivable that one tier was placed upon another. Fortunately a knowledge of these things is not essential for our problem.

A fight at sea was in some measure a reproduction upon floating platforms of a land engagement. At Salamis there were *epibatai*, 'marines,' who had no nautical duties whatever, but were expected to engage the enemy in a hand-to-hand encounter when the ships clashed. We shall see that boarding tactics as a means of forcing the submission of the foe were practised by the Romans too and in fact continued long after the introduction of cannon on frigates.

As regards battle tactics, the Greeks had two favourite ways of dealing with a hostile ship, by sweeping the banks of oars with a broadside movement and by ramming. The first method was in purpose and effect exactly the same expedient as the modern effort to hit the part of the vessel nearest the engine room. It put the opponent *hors de combat* by destroying his motive power.

Ramming was, however, the device employed to destroy a ship.

2. I. 13.

3. Herod., III.

The thing that made ramming possible as a part of scientific tactics was the emancipation of ships from dependence upon the wind by the introduction of oarsmen. When in more recent times the rough waters of the Atlantic made it imperative to increase the size of ships to such an extent that oars were of no avail, again we see them rendered independent of the wind, this time by the use of steam, and again we find ramming tactics reintroduced in what is virtually a return to the methods of the Greeks and the Romans.

In the Civil War ramming proved effective in the confined spaces of rivers and bays. The Merrimac rammed the Cumberland, but the first fight of steam-driven rams in the history of the world was the battle of Memphis in 1862. Here the Confederates had a fleet of eight rams, while the Union forces had five gunboats and two rams. As late as the Spanish War we had a ram, the Katahdin. It is only the long-range gun that has caused the discarding of the ram. The periscope, however, still makes this method of fighting possible for submarines fighting submarines.

An effective manoeuvre was the *diekplous*, which consisted of sailing through the enemy's line and attacking him from the stern while he was otherwise engaged. In the Battle of Lake Erie, Perry sailed through the British formation in this manner, a manoeuvre which enabled him to deliver broadsides from both port and starboard.

An outstanding figure in the naval history of all time is the Athenian Themistocles. Though we are inclined to regard Marathon as a decisive battle, he saw that the struggle with the Persian could be terminated successfully only by victory upon the water. Accordingly during the years between Marathon and Salamis he was instrumental in having built and equipped a fleet that not merely saved, but exalted his country. He it was who persuaded the Greeks that ships were meant when the oracle advised them to put their dependence in a "wooden wall." It is not impossible that it was he who inspired the oracle. He was the first European to have a thorough comprehension of the importance of the command of the sea. It is said in fact that in the history of sea-power the name of Themistocles stands without a peer.

The strategy employed by Themistocles may be briefly noted. In the face of strong objections he had the Greek fleet take a position in the strait between Salamis and Attica as the Persians were proceeding southward along the coast of Greece in 480 B.C. This strategic flanking position constituted a menace that the Persians could not disregard. Themistocles precipitated an engagement by giving the Persians the impression that the Greeks were on the point of trying to escape. The *mêlée* took place in the narrow waters where the superior numbers of the Persians availed not and where the superior seamanship and fighting ability of the Greeks were exerted to the best advantage. Darkness finally ended the struggle. The next morning when the Greeks embarked with hearts fortified and encouraged to renew the struggle, they found that the enemy had fled. The Persian threat by sea was past.

In spite of their many ships the Persians had no traditions of success upon the water. [4] Athens had saved herself and Greece through her realization that it takes a sea-power to defeat a nation with a navy, a lesson the truth of which Napoleon was reluctant to admit.

> The Battle of Salamis is one of the most instructive battles in the history of the world, in that it proves the overwhelming possibilities of the genius of the strategist; for by nothing else than the genius of Themistocles was the expedition of the Persians brought to naught and Greece saved from ruin.[5]

Admiral Custance [6] says:

> The flanking position used by Themistocles . . . to limit the movements of a hostile fleet remains the chief foundation, on which rests all strategy at sea. For more than three centuries the defence of this country [England] from invasion has been based upon it, the detachments of small ships holding the channel and the narrow seas being covered from an enemy advancing in force out of the Atlantic by the main fleet based on a western port—*e.g.*, Plymouth or Torbay. The same principle might have been applied in the North Sea during the war with Germany, since a fleet in the Forth would have covered the detachments holding the Straits of Dover and the northern exits.

According to the same authority,[7] similar strategy to that of Salamis was employed in the Armada Campaign, 1588, and by Togo off Port Arthur, 1904, and in the straits of Tsu-Shima, 1905.

After Salamis the fear of a return of the Persians gave Athens a handle for the formation of the Delian Confederacy. With the tribute

4. Mardonius himself referred to the Persians as "landsmen" (Plut., *Aristides*, 10. 2).

5. Fiske, *The Art of Fighting*.

6. *War at Sea*.

7. *Ibid*.

from the confederated states Athens started the practice of paying her crews, which at Salamis had consisted of freemen serving without pay. Higher speed and skill were developed and the seaman began to feel a professional pride in handling his ship and to regard himself as a seaman rather than as a soldier. He began to manoeuvre and to realize to the full the possibilities of the prow as a ram. Here we see the beginning in Europe of a professional navy.

A half century of development drew very clearly the line of demarcation between war by sea and by land. At the very inception of the Peloponnesian War (431 B.C-404 B.C.), Pericles says with emphasis:

> Maritime skill is like skill of other kinds, not a thing to be cultivated by the way or at chance times; it is jealous of any other pursuit which distracts the mind for an instant from itself.[8]

In this great conflict with Sparta the Athenian ships had better prows and greater mobility than formerly, but the narrower beam entailed a reduction in the number of marines. This was the beginning of the age-long conflict between fighting power and speed.

An advance in tactics was attained in the same war by the skilful disposition of ships in groups or squadrons and methods by which they were thrown into battle. Naturally flanking movements were carried out on a large scale, but the greatest improvement was seen in the endeavour to bring overpowering forces to bear upon parts of the enemy formation while weaker detachments of the attacking force ' contained ' or checked the rest of the enemy.

In the Battle of Arginusae, which was fought in 406 B.C. in the northern Aegean, the Spartans and their friends had the longer line and intended to overlap the Athenians. Admiral Custance says:[9]

> The Athenian dispositions seem designed to hold the centre with a force equal to that of the enemy, while two masses, each of sixty ships, were launched against the thirty ships on either side of the centre; in other words, their aim was to throw the whole fleet of one hundred and fifty ships on to eighty or ninety of the enemy with the view of getting a decision before the ships in the overlap could come into action. The result was a complete defeat of the allies, who lost seventy-seven *triremes* as against twenty-five lost by the Athenians. If the above view is

8. Thuc, I.

9. Custance.

correct, the tactical skill of the Athenians in the battle was of a high order.

The same writer says that "Arginusae was the prototype of Trafalgar," a statement that should not be construed to mean that Nelson had Arginusae in mind, but that, like the Greeks, he was employing the principle of concentrating the bulk of his fleet upon a fraction of the enemy.

At the Battle of Cynossema, 411 B.C., in the Hellespont, new tactics were tried against the Athenians by the commander of the allied fleet under the Lacedaemonians:

> The battle illustrates a step in the development of tactics, in that the centre and one wing were held by a frontal attack while an attempt was made to outflank the other wing.[10]

Still other Greek naval battles exemplify this principle of concentration of force.

During the long course of the Peloponnesian War the Syracusans had a fine chance to use to advantage the principles of strategy employed by Themistocles at Salamis. In June 415 B.C. an Athenian fleet gathered at Corcyra for an attack on Sicily. The Syracusans were urged by Hermocrates, whom Captain Mahan styles an "untaught genius," to send all their available ships to take up a strategic flanking position at Tarentum, so that they might set upon the Athenians as they rounded the promontory of Iapygia at the heel of Italy. The Syracusans could not, however, be convinced that the Athenian concentration at Corcyra was aimed at them and so lost a golden opportunity.

How permanent the basic principles of naval strategy are and how thoroughly the Greeks had mastered them cannot be better shown than by quoting Captain Mahan,[11] who thus sums up the naval side of the Athenian expedition against Sicily:

> This episode in the Peloponnesian War . . . gives us all the conditions of a distant maritime expedition in any age. We have the home base, Athens; the advanced intermediate bases at Corcyra and other points, which played for Athens the part that Gibraltar, Malta, and foreign coaling stations have done and still do for Great Britain; the objective, Syracuse; the neutral, doubtful, or hostile country to be passed, across the Ionian Sea or along the

10. Custance.
11. *Naval Strategy.*

coasts of Italy; the enemy's advanced post in Tarentum and sister cities; the greater naval power in Athens; the smaller but still respectable fleet of Syracuse; the difficulty of communications; the tactical embarrassment of a train of supply ships; the tactical difficulty of ships deeply laden for a long voyage, which exists in a degree today; the tactical difficulty of the fatigue of rowers, which has disappeared; the wisdom of meeting the enemy half way and harassing his progress; the danger of awaiting him at home on the defensive; the perception of the navy's true sphere, the offensive. All these broad outlines, with many lesser details, are to be found in this Athenian expedition, *and most of them involve principles of present application.* In fact, put this early galley expedition under a microscope and there is (*sic*) seen realized the essential leading features of any maritime invasion.

In Thucydides [12] a significant comment is put into the mouth of Pericles as he advocates the vigorous prosecution of the Peloponnesian War. As he contrasts the position of the Spartans and Athenians he says:

> If they attack our country by land, we shall attack theirs by sea; and the devastation, even of part of Peloponnesus, will be a very different thing from that of all Attica. For they, if they want fresh territory, must take it by arms, whereas we have abundance of land both in the islands and on the continent; such is the power which the empire of the sea (τὸ τῆς θαλάσσης κράτος) gives.

The Greek words really mean 'sea-power' in all the fullness of meaning with which that term is employed by Captain Mahan and other technical writers. Thucydides would surely include under this term "all that tends to make a people great upon the sea or by the sea."[13]

The writer of the article on *Sea-Power* in the Encyclopaedia Britannica (1902) thus pays his respects to Thucydides:

> Before Mahan no historian—not even one of those who specially devoted themselves to the narration of naval occurrences—had evinced a more correct appreciation of the general principles of naval warfare than Thucydides. He alludes several times to the importance of getting command of the sea. Great

12. I. 143 (Jowett's translation).
13. Cf. Mahan, *Influence of Sea Power upon History.*

> Britain would have been saved some disasters and been less often in peril had British writers . . . possessed the same grasp of the true principles of defence as Thucydides did."

The span from the Greek historian to Mahan is a long, long one. As we shall see later, however, Thucydides's fellow-countryman, Polybius, was not much inferior in his appreciation of the value of sea-power.

Napoleon quotes an adage to the effect that he who is master of the sea is master of the land. The ancients realized as clearly as the nations engaged in the Great War the difficulty of conducting successful operations on land without control of the sea. Alexander did not feel free to advance into the heart of Persia until he had neutralized the power of the Persian fleet by subduing the coast towns in Asia Minor and Phoenicia. He has been accused of wasting seven months in the siege of Tyre, but Napoleon said that he would have stayed there seven years if necessary. Just before undertaking the siege, Alexander said:

> I see that the expedition against Egypt is not safe while the Persians are in command of the sea, nor is it safe to pursue Darius if we leave behind us the city of the Tyrians wavering in her loyalty.[14]

Alexander understood how to combine the actions of land and naval forces. After describing the cooperation of the Japanese fleet and army as they pushed their base northward from Korea in their war against China, Baron Von der Goltz continues:

> In the ages of antiquity we see the same thing carried out on a large scale by Alexander, who caused his land forces to be accompanied by the fleet of Nearchus, on the march to and from India.[15]

As for the Romans, their sea-power was artificially stimulated, since, like that of the Germans, it was not built upon the maritime character or tradition of the people, but founded upon a clear realisation of the relation of sea-power to conquest and world-dominion.

When Antony decided to fight Octavius upon the sea off Actium, a *centurion* who had suffered many wounds in service thus addressed his commander with tears:

> *Imperator*, why do you distrust these wounds or this sword, and

---

14. Arrian, II.

15. *The Conduct of War*, translated by J. T. Dickman, Kansas City, Mo., 1896.

> rest your hopes in miserable logs of wood? Let Egyptians and Phoenicians fight on sea, but give us land, on which we are accustomed to stand and to die or to vanquish our enemies.[16]

The attitude of the centurion may be regarded as fairly representative. It was cool reasoning that put the Roman navy upon the sea. When emergencies passed, Rome was apt to be indifferent to its navy.

As soon as the Roman octopus began to reach out its tentacles beyond the confines of Italy, the Romans grasped the significance of sea-power. We find that in 261 B.C., three years after the inception of the First Punic War, the Romans were eager to meet the Carthaginians upon the water, because "so long as the Carthaginians were in undisturbed command of the sea, the balance of success could not incline decisively in their favour." [17]

After this same war had dragged out its weary length for twenty-two years, the Romans in 242 B.C. despatched a fleet to Sicily under the command of Gaius Lutatius Catulus. Of him Polybius says: [18]

> He kept in mind the original idea of this expedition, that it was by a victory at sea alone that the result of the whole war could be decided.

Again in the Second Punic War the Romans showed a clear vision as to the value of seapower. Its advantage was fully manifested when, after Hannibal had eluded Scipio at the Rhone, they were enabled to transport their army to Italy and to face the invader at the Po. The command of the sea finally made it possible for the Romans to carry the war into Africa. By the terms of the ensuing peace Carthage was forced to give up all but ten *triremes*, a surrender that showed that her conqueror appreciated the meaning of supremacy upon the water as fully as did the vanquishers of Germany in the World War.

In May 49 B.C., during the conflict between Caesar and Pompey, Cicero in a letter to his friend Atticus [19] states that even if Pompey loses the Spains, the contest will not be decided, for Pompey has a fleet and is going to resort to the plan of Themistocles:

> For he thinks the man who holds the sea must come off master.

---

16. Plut., *Anton.*
17. Polyb., I.
18. I.
19. *Epistulae*, X.

Of the battle off Actium fought in 31 B.C. between Antony and Octavius a naval authority writes:

> Actium affords us the spectacle of two experienced generals commanding large armies facing each other, acknowledging the all-importance of sea-power by leaving those armies inactive and taking to the sea and deciding the sovereignty of the then known world with maritime forces far inferior in number to the available land forces impotently standing by as spectators. Actium witnessed the full development of sea-power; its firm establishment as the first and governing principle of warfare occurred in the centuries that followed.[20]

As regards battle formations, perhaps the most conspicuous example of Roman originality is at the Battle of Ecnomus, where they met the Carthaginians in 256 B.C. Two files of ships were arranged in the form of a wedge while a third squadron took position in a single line at the base so that the completed formation resembled a triangle, at the apex of which were the ships of the two consuls. In this formation they bore down upon the enemy. Unwilling to face the impact, the Carthaginian centre made a 'strategic retreat.' Silburn says:

> This action is celebrated, and marks a distinct advance in sea-power, as the first example of 'breaking the line.'[21]

In the naval battle of the Saints, fought between Rodney and De Grasse off San Domingo in 1782, Rodney cut the line of his opponent and "unconsciously repeated the Roman admiral's tactics at Ecnomus."[22]

The Romans, realizing their inferior seamanship, went much farther than the Greeks in reproducing the conditions of war by land. At the battle of Actium the ships of Antony were too heavy to acquire sufficient speed to ram and Caesar's ships were too light to stand an impact upon them.

Plutarch says:[23]

---

20. Silburn, *Op. cit.*

21. *Ibid.*

22. Since the Carthaginians retreated under orders, with the intention of permitting the Roman dispositions to be scattered by the confusion of pursuit, it is more accurate to speak of the Roman formation *as designed to break the line.* In the *diekplous*, 'sailing through,' ships penetrated the enemy's line, but did not necessarily break it

23. *Anton.*

> The battle, there fore, was like land fights, or, to speak more exactly, like the assailing of a fortress; for three and four of Caesar's ships at the same time were engaged about one of the ships of Antony and the men fought with light shields and spears and poles and fiery missiles; the soldiers of Antony assailed them also with catapults from wooden towers.

Besides Plutarch, we find that Polybius, Livy, Vegetius and other writers were struck by the resemblance of Roman naval engagements to fights on land. While the Romans did employ naval tactics and even made some additions to what they learned from the Greeks, they realised the limitations of their ships and of their seamanship. In general the tendency of their tactics was to reproduce the conditions obtaining on land. In order to neutralize their hopeless inferiority in seamanship at the Battles of Mylae, 260 B.C., and Ecnomus, 256 B.C., in the First Punic War, they equipped their vessels with a 'crow,' a sort of gangway that could be raised and lowered at will. This was fitted with a heavy spike at the elevated end so that when it fell, it not only grappled the two ships, but provided a bridge. Thus we see the ramming tactics of the Greeks superseded by boarding tactics. Such tactics persisted and even in the days of frigates many engagements were terminated only when the ships had been lashed together and victory decided by hand to hand engagements of boarding parties. John Paul Jones said of the fight with the Serapis:

> The enemy's bowsprit, however, came over the *Bon Homme Richard's* poop by the mizzenmast, and I made both ships fast together in that situation.

Plutarch's second comparison of the seafight at Actium to a siege operation is by far the more accurate one. The similarity struck Vegetius, too, for he says that men fought from ramparts and towers on ships just as if from walls. Artillery, which was not always employed in field operations, was freely used. Hooks, such as besiegers used to loosen stones in the walls, were employed to catch and cut rigging. The chemical warfare of the defenders of cities was likewise imitated by the use of oil, pitch, bitumen, resin and other highly combustible material. Even with these tactics bridges were still used. [24] Occasionally even the Greeks used clumsy tactics. Thucydides [25] tells us that an engagement between Corinth and Corcyra in 432 B.C. had "almost

---

24. Veg., IV.
25. I.

the appearance of a battle by land," and he remarks that "brute force and rage made up for the want of tactics."

The towers that were placed in the prows to provide a means of raking the enemy's decks, are lineal ancestors of the forecastles of modern ships which were used originally for the same purpose.

Military-tops were not used on Greek and Roman war-ships, although merchantmen employed them as part of their defence against pirates. Long before the days of the classical nations, Egyptian war-ships had used them and they were to appear again in the Byzantine period.[26]

We have seen that tactics of the ancients have been repeated in succeeding ages and that the principles of strategy which they inaugurated are as fundamental and as far reaching as those on land. Their achievements on the water are a fitting complement to those on land and will still reward the student of naval history and progress. That the lessons of sea-power have passed unheeded has been ascribed to their being buried under the volume of detail concerning engagements by land. The writings of Captain Mahan have again focused attention upon them.

Every war possesses features of its own by land and sea which differentiate it from all its predecessors, yet in broad outlines warfare even today retains characteristics which have long since been worked out as fundamental.

---

26. Torr, *Ancient Ships.*

15. Conclusion

The principles of warfare through the correct application or disregard of which battles are won or lost on both land and sea were first demonstrated in Europe by the Greeks and Romans. From dramas that were enacted in so small a theatre of operations lessons may still be drawn. Writing in 1890 Colonel Dodge [1] says:

> War is scarcely more perfect today, according to our resources in arts and mechanics, than it was twenty odd centuries ago among the Greeks according to theirs.

The thoughtful reader, having the Great War in mind, may, perhaps, regret that the Greeks and Romans have made lasting contributions to a science that carries death and destruction in its path. Arts and culture and the sciences in general thrive, however, only in an atmosphere of freedom. Without their martial skill the Greeks would not have had a chance in their day to cultivate their special gifts; without recourse to arms Rome would not, anciently, have been able to spread law and order and civilization in Western Europe.

The classical nations, it must be noted, are not the sole peoples that have, unhappily, used military power to protect their independence and their growth, and then, with the attainment of these objects, diverted that same power to reduce other nations to a condition they themselves found intolerable.

Alexander aspired to "sow Greece" [2] throughout the world. The Germans seized upon this statement to justify their own method of spreading *kultur*. That the Greeks sowed their civilization more successfully by the arts of peace than by those of war is one of the lessons of history that the world is slow to learn.

---

1. *Alexander*.
2. Plut., *Moralia*.

Our own nation too might have profited by lessons that antiquity has to teach. Pericles said to the Athenians: [3]

> To remain at peace when you should be going to war may often be very dangerous.

If there are degrees of truth, such a statement was never more true than during the first two years and a half of the Great War.

Vegetius [4] is thoroughly Rooseveltian:

> No one has the courage to provoke or to do injury to that realm or people which he knows to be prepared and disposed to resist and requite.

Ex-President Wilson says:

> We should have scant capital to trade on were we to throw away the wisdom we have inherited and seek our fortunes with the slender stock we ourselves have accumulated.

In this connection I cannot forbear quoting Gilbert [5] once more:

> With perhaps the sole exception of such men as Parmenio, Craterus, Ptolemy, Hephaestion, Meleager, Coenus, and others of the Alexandrian galaxy of subordinate commanders, history does not show us a body of officers that had gone through the amount of hard fighting experienced by Ney, Soult, Davout, Victor, Junot, Masséna, and others of Napoleon's marshals. This experience was spread over a period of twenty years, and was gained under the most varied conditions. Yet it is a remarkable fact that without exception they one and all failed to justify the trust imposed in them when in independent command and left in a great measure to their own resources and initiative, and that one of them, by no means the least famous [Ney], we find charged with stupidity. Their chief, on the other hand, is a standing example of the result of the fruits of study applied in this field.

Advances in civilization are effected by building upon the heritage of the past. The ancient treasures of experience and wisdom will always be a source of enrichment for those sufficiently enlightened to use them. The art of war is only one of the many arts and fundamental

3. Thuc, I.
4. IV.
5. *Op. cit.*

branches of human endeavour whose recorded history begins with a resume of the contributions of the ancients. It too illustrates the continuity of human progress.

It has been well said that the roots of the present lie deep in the past and that he who would know the present must study the past. We think what we think and do what we do and are what we are largely because of what the Greeks and Romans thought and did and were. The military and naval history of these ancient nations, which lies at the foundation of European experience, must be part of our knowledge if we are to apprehend our own instincts truly, if we are to avert inherent evils and above all create a more enlightened future.

Five Decisive Battles of the World

(Extract from Fifteen Decisive Battles of the World From Marathon to Waterloo)

Contents

Chapter 1

The Battle of Marathon

Two thousand three hundred and forty years ago, a council of Athenian officers was summoned on the slope of one of the mountains that look over the plain of Marathon, on the eastern coast of Attica. The immediate subject of their meeting was to consider whether they should give battle to an enemy that lay encamped on the shore beneath them; but on the result of their deliberations depended not merely the fate of two armies, but the whole future progress of human civilization.

There were eleven members of that council of war. Ten were the generals, who were then annually elected at Athens, one for each of the local tribes into which the Athenians were divided. Each general led the men of his own tribe, and each was invested with equal military authority. One also of the Archons was associated with them in the joint command of the collective force. This magistrate was termed the Polemarch or War-Ruler: he had the privilege of leading the right wing of the army in battle, and of taking part in all councils of war. A noble Athenian, named Callimachus, was the War-Ruler of this year; and as such, stood listening to the earnest discussion of the ten generals. They had, indeed, deep matter for anxiety, though little aware how momentous to mankind were the votes they were about to give, or how the generations to come would read with interest that record of their debate.

They saw before them the invading forces of a mighty empire, which had in the last fifty years shattered and enslaved nearly all the kingdoms and principalities of the then known world. They knew that all the resources of their own country were comprised in the little army entrusted to their guidance. They saw before them a chosen host of the Great King sent to wreak his special wrath on that country, and on the other insolent little Greek community, which had dared to aid his rebels and burn the capital of one of his provinces. That victorious host had already fulfilled half its mission of vengeance. Eretria, the confederate of Athens in the bold march against Sardis nine years before, had fallen in the last few days; and the Athenian generals could discern from the heights the island of Ægilia, in which the Persians had deposited their Eretrian prisoners, whom they had reserved to be led away captives into Upper Asia, there to hear their doom from the lips of King Darius himself. Moreover, the men of Athens knew that in the camp before them was their own banished tyrant, Hippias, who was seeking to be reinstated by foreign scimitars in despotic sway over any remnant of his countrymen that might survive the sack of their town, and might be left behind as too worthless for leading away into Median bondage.

The numerical disparity between the force which the Athenian commanders had under them, and that which they were called on to encounter, was fearfully apparent to some of the council. The historians who wrote nearest to the time of the battle do not pretend to give any detailed statements of the numbers engaged, but there are sufficient data for our making a general estimate. Every free Greek was trained to military duty: and, from the incessant border wars between the different states, few Greeks reached the age of manhood without having seen some service. But the muster-roll of free Athenian citizens of an age fit for military duty never exceeded thirty thousand, and at this epoch probably did not amount to two-thirds of that number. Moreover, the poorer portion of these were unprovided with the equipments, and untrained to the operations of the regular infantry. Some detachments of the best armed troops would be required to garrison the city itself, and man the various fortified posts in the territory; so that it is impossible to reckon the fully equipped force that marched from Athens to Marathon, when the news of the Persian landing arrived, at higher than ten thousand men.[1]

With one exception, the other Greeks held back from aiding them. Sparta had promised assistance; but the Persians had landed on the

1. The historians who lived long after the time of the battle, such as Justin, Plutarch and others, give ten thousand as the number of the Athenian army. Not much reliance could be placed on their authority, if unsupported by other evidence; but a calculation made from the number of the Athenian free population remarkably confirms it. For the data of this, see Boeck's *Public Economy of Athens*, the number of resident aliens at Athens cannot have been large at this period.

sixth day of the moon, and a religious scruple delayed the march of Spartan troops till the moon should have reached its full. From one quarter only, and that a most unexpected one, did Athens receive aid at the moment of her great peril.

For some years before this time, the little state of Plataea in Boeotia, being hard pressed by her powerful neighbour, Thebes, had asked the protection of Athens, and had owed to an Athenian army the rescue of her independence. Now when it was noised over Greece that the Mede had come from the uttermost parts of the earth to destroy Athens, the brave Plataeans, unsolicited, marched with their whole force to assist in the defence, and to share the fortunes of their benefactors. The general levy of the Plataeans only amounted to a thousand men: and this little column, marching from their city along the southern ridge of Mount Cithaeron, and thence across the Attic territory, joined the Athenian forces above Marathon almost immediately before the battle. The reinforcement was numerically small; but the gallant spirit of the men who composed it must have made it of tenfold value to the Athenians: and its presence must have gone far to dispel the cheerless feeling of being deserted and friendless, which the delay of the Spartan succours was calculated to create among the Athenian ranks.

This generous daring of their weak but true-hearted ally was never forgotten at Athens. The Plataeans were made the fellow-countrymen of the Athenians, except the right of exercising certain political functions; and from that time forth in the solemn sacrifices at Athens, the public prayers were offered up for a joint blessing from Heaven upon the Athenians, and the Plataeans also.[2]

After the junction of the column from Plataea, the Athenians commanders must have had under them about eleven thousand fully-armed and disciplined infantry, and probably a larger number of irregular light-armed troops; as, besides the poorer citizens who went to the field armed with javelins, cutlasses, and targets, each regular heavy-

---

2. Mr. Grote observes that "this volunteer march of the whole Plataean force to Marathon is one of the most affecting incidents of all Grecian history." In truth, the whole career of Plataea, and the friendship, strong even unto death, between her and Athens, form one of the most affecting episodes in the history of antiquity. In the Peloponnesian War the Plataeans again were true to the Athenians against all risks and all calculation of self-interest; and the destruction of Plataea was the consequence. There are few nobler passages in the classics than the speech in which the Plataean prisoners of war, after the memorable siege of their city, justify before their Spartan executioners their loyal adherence to Athens. (See Thucydides, *lib.* iii.)

armed soldier was attended in the camp by one or more slaves, who were armed like the inferior freemen.[3] Cavalry or archers the Athenians (on this occasion) had none: and the use in the field of military engines was not at that period introduced into ancient warfare.

Contrasted with their own scanty forces, the Greek commanders saw stretched before them, along the shores of the winding bay, the tents and shipping of the varied nations that marched to do the bidding of the King of the Eastern world. The difficulty of finding transports and of securing provisions would form the only limit to the numbers of a Persian army. Nor is there any reason to suppose the estimate of Justin exaggerated, who rates at a hundred thousand the force which on this occasion had sailed, under the satraps Datis and Artaphernes, from the Cilician shores, against the devoted coasts of Euboea and Attica. And after largely deducting from this total, so as to allow for mere mariners and camp followers, there must still have remained fearful odds against the national levies of the Athenians.

Nor could Greek generals then feel that confidence in the superior quality of their troops which ever since the battle of Marathon has animated Europeans in conflicts with Asiatics; as, for instance, in the after struggles between Greece and Persia, or when the Roman legions encountered the myriads of Mithridates and Tigranes, or as is the case in the Indian campaigns of our own regiments. On the contrary, up to the day of Marathon the Medes and Persians were reputed invincible. They had more than once met Greek troops in Asia Minor, in Cyprus, in Egypt, and had invariably beaten them. Nothing can be stronger than the expressions used by the early Greek writers respecting the terror which the name of the Medes inspired, and the prostration of men's spirits before the apparently resistless career of the Persian arms.

It is therefore, little to be wondered at, that five of the ten Athenian generals shrank from the prospect of fighting a pitched battle against an enemy so superior in numbers, and so formidable in military renown. Their own position on the heights was strong, and offered great advantages to a small defending force against assailing masses. They deemed it mere foolhardiness to descend into the plain to be trampled down by the Asiatic horse, overwhelmed with the archery, or cut to pieces by the invincible veterans of Cambyses and Cyrus. Moreover,

---

3. At the Battle of Plataea, eleven years after Marathon, each of the eight thousand Athenian regular infantry who served there, was attended by a light-armed slave. (Herod. lib. viii.).

Sparta, the great war-state of Greece, had been applied to, and had promised succour to Athens, though the religious observance which the Dorians paid to certain times and seasons had for the present delayed their march. Was it not wise, at any rate, to wait till the Spartans came up, and to have the help of the best troops in Greece, before they exposed themselves to the shock of the dreaded Medes?

Specious as these reasons might appear, the other five generals were for speedier and bolder operations. And, fortunately for Athens and for the world, one of them was a man, not only of the highest military genius, but also of that energetic character which impresses its own type and ideas upon spirits feebler in conception.

Miltiades was the head of one of the noblest houses at Athens: he ranked the Æacidae among his ancestry, and the blood of Achilles flowed in the veins of the hero of Marathon. One of his immediate ancestors had acquired the dominion of the Thracian Chersonese, and thus the family became at the same time Athenian citizens and Thracian princes. This occurred at the time when Pisistratus was tyrant of Athens. Two of the relatives of Miltiades—an uncle of the same name, and a brother named Stesagoras—had ruled the Chersonese before Miltiades became its prince. He had been brought up at Athens in the house of his father Cimon, who was renowned throughout Greece for his victories in the Olympic chariot-races, and who must have been possessed of great wealth.

The sons of Pisistratus, who succeeded their father in the tyranny at Athens, caused Cimon to be assassinated, but they treated the young Miltiades with favour and kindness; and when his brother Stesagoras died in the Chersonese, they sent him out there as lord of the principality. This was about twenty-eight years before the battle of Marathon, and it is with his arrival in the Chersonese that our first knowledge of the career and character of Miltiades commences. We find, in the first act recorded of him, proof of the same resolute and unscrupulous spirit that marked his mature age. His brother's authority in the principality had been shaken by war and revolt: Miltiades determined to rule more securely. On his arrival he kept close within his house, as if he was mourning for his brother. The principal men of the Chersonese, hearing of this, assembled from all the towns and districts, and went together to the house of Miltiades on a visit of condolence. As soon as he had thus got them in his power, he made them all prisoners. He then asserted and maintained his own absolute authority in the peninsula, taking into his pay a body of five hundred regular troops, and strengthening his interest by marrying the daughter of the king of the neighbouring Thracians.

When the Persian power was extended to the Hellespont and its neighbourhood, Miltiades, as prince of the Chersonese, submitted to King Darius; and he was one of the numerous tributary rulers who led their contingents of men to serve in the Persian army in the expedition against Scythia. Miltiades and the vassal Greeks of Asia Minor were left by the Persian king in charge of the bridge across the Danube, when the invading army crossed that river, and plunged into the wilds of the country that now is Russia, in vain pursuit of the ancestors of the modern Cossacks. On learning the reverses that Darius met with in the Scythian wilderness, Miltiades proposed to his companions that they should break the bridge down, and leave the Persian king and his army to perish by famine and the Scythian arrows.

The rulers of the Asiatic Greek cities whom Miltiades addressed, shrank from this bold and ruthless stroke against the Persian power, and Darius returned in safety. But it was known what advice Miltiades had given; and the vengeance of Darius was thenceforth specially directed against the man who had counselled such a deadly blow against his empire and his person. The occupation of the Persian arms in other quarters left Miltiades for some years after this in possession of the Chersonese; but it was precarious and interrupted. He, however, availed himself of the opportunity which his position gave him of conciliating the goodwill of his fellow-countrymen at Athens, by conquering and placing under Athenian authority the islands of Lemnos and Imbros, to which Athens had ancient claims, but which she had never previously been able to bring into complete subjection.

At length, in 494 B.C., the complete suppression of the Ionian revolt by the Persians left their armies and fleets at liberty to act against the enemies of the Great King to the west of the Hellespont. A strong squadron of Phoenician galleys was sent against the Chersonese. Miltiades knew that resistance was hopeless; and while the Phoenicians were at Tenedos, he loaded five galleys with all the treasure that he could collect, and sailed away for Athens. The Phoenicians fell in with him, and chased him hard along the north of the Ægean. One of his galleys, on board of which was his eldest son, Metiochus, was actually captured; but Miltiades, with the other four, succeeded in reaching the friendly coast of Imbros in safety. Thence he afterwards proceeded to Athens, and resumed his station as a free citizen of the Athenian commonwealth.

The Athenians at this time had recently expelled Hippias, the son of Pisistratus, the last of their tyrants. They were in the full glow of their newly-recovered liberty and equality; and the constitutional changes of Cleisthenes had inflamed their republican zeal to the utmost. Miltiades had enemies at Athens; and these, availing themselves of the state of popular feeling, brought him to trial for his life for having been tyrant of the Chersonese. The charge did not necessarily import any acts of cruelty or wrong to individuals: it was founded on so specific law; but it was based on the horror with which the Greeks of that age regarded every man who made himself compulsory master of his fellow-men, and exercised irresponsible dominion over them. The fact of Miltiades having so ruled in the Chersonese was undeniable; but the question which the Athenians, assembled in judgment, must have tried, was, whether Miltiades, by becoming tyrant of the Chersonese, deserved punishment as an Athenian citizen. The eminent service that he had done the state in conquering Lemnos and Imbros for it, pleaded strongly in his favour. The people refused to convict him. He stood high in public opinion; and when the coming invasion of the Persians was known, the people wisely elected him one of their generals for the year.

Two other men of signal eminence in history, though their renown was achieved at a later period than that of Miltiades, were also among the ten Athenian generals at Marathon. One was Themistocles, the future founder of the Athenian Navy and the destined victor of Salamis: the other was Aristides, who afterwards led the Athenian troops at Plataea, and whose integrity and just popularity acquired for his country, when the Persians had finally been repulsed, the advantageous pre-eminence of being acknowledged by half of the Greeks as their impartial leader and protector. It is not recorded what part either Themistocles or Aristides took in the debate of the council of war at Marathon. But from the character of Themistocles, his boldness, and his intuitive genius for extemporizing the best measures in every emergency (a quality which the greatest of historians ascribes to him beyond all his contemporaries), we may well believe that the vote of Themistocles was for prompt and decisive action.

On the vote of Aristides it may be more difficult to speculate. His predilection for the Spartans may have made him wish to wait till they came up; but, though circumspect, he was neither timid as a soldier nor as a politician; and the bold advice of Miltiades may probably have found in Aristides a willing, most assuredly it found in him a candid, hearer.

Miltiades felt no hesitation as to the course which the Athenian army ought to pursue: and earnestly did he press his opinion on his brother-generals. Practically acquainted with the organization of the Persian armies, Miltiades was convinced of the superiority of the Greek troops, if properly handled: he saw with the military eye of a great general the advantage which the position of the forces gave him for a sudden attack, and as a profound politician he felt the perils of remaining inactive, and of giving treachery time to ruin the Athenian cause.

One officer in the council of war had not yet voted. This was Callimachus, the War-Ruler. The votes of the generals were five and five, so that the voice of Callimachus would be decisive.

On that vote, in all human probability, the destiny of all the nations of the world depended. Miltiades turned to him, and in simple soldierly eloquence, the substance of which we may read faithfully reported in Herodotus, who had conversed with the veterans of Marathon, the great Athenian thus adjured his countryman to vote for giving battle:—

> It now rests with you, Callimachus, either to enslave Athens, or, by assuring her freedom, to win yourself an immortality of fame, such as not even Harmodius and Aristogeiton have acquired. For never, since the Athenians were a people, were they in such danger as they are in at this moment. If they bow the knee to these Medes, they are to be given up to Hippias, and you know what they then will have to suffer. But if Athens comes victorious out of this contest, she has it in her to become the first city of Greece. Your vote is to decide whether we are to join battle or not. If we do not bring on a battle presently, some factious intrigue will disunite the Athenians, and the city will be betrayed to the Medes. But if we fight, before there is anything rotten in the state of Athens, I believe that, provided the Gods will give fair play and no favour, we are able to get the best of it in the engagement.[4]

The vote of the brave War-Ruler was gained; the council deter-

4. Herodotus, lib. vi. sec. 209. The 116th section is to my mind clear proof that Herodotus had personally conversed with Epizelus, one of the veterans of Marathon. The substance of the speech of Miltiades would naturally become known by the report of some of his colleagues.

mined to give battle; and such was the ascendancy and military eminence of Miltiades, that his brother-generals, one and all, gave up their days of command to him, and cheerfully acted under his orders. Fearful, however, of creating any jealousy, and of so failing to obtain the co-operation of all parts of his small army, Miltiades waited till the day when the chief command would have come round to him in regular rotation, before he led the troops against the enemy.

The inaction of the Asiatic commanders, during this interval, appears strange at first sight; but Hippias was with them, and they and he were aware of their chance of a bloodless conquest through the machinations of his partisans among the Athenians. The nature of the ground also explains, in many points, the tactics of the opposite generals before the battle, as well as the operations of the troops during the engagement.

The plain of Marathon, which is about twenty-two miles distant from Athens, lies along the bay of the same name on the north-eastern coast of Attica. The plain is nearly in the form of a crescent, and about six miles in length. It is about two miles broad in the centre, where the space between the mountains and the sea is greatest, but it narrows towards either extremity, the mountains coming close down to the water at the horns of the bay. There is a valley trending inwards from the middle of the plain, and a ravine comes down to it to the southward. Elsewhere it is closely girt round on the land side by rugged limestone mountains, which are thickly studded with pines, olive-trees, and cedars, and overgrown with the myrtle, arbutus, and the other low odoriferous shrubs that everywhere perfume the Attic air. The level of the ground is now varied by the mound raised over those who fell in the battle, but it was an unbroken plain when the Persians encamped on it. There are marshes at each end, which are dry in spring and summer, and then offer no obstruction to the horseman, but are commonly flooded with rain, and so rendered impracticable for cavalry, in the autumn, the time of year at which the action took place. (See plan on the following page).

The Greeks, lying encamped on the mountains, could watch every movement of the Persians on the plain below, while they were enabled completely to mask their own. Miltiades also had, from his position, the power of giving battle whenever he pleased, or of delaying it at his discretion, unless Datis were to attempt the perilous operation of storming the heights.

If we turn to the map of the old world, to test the comparative

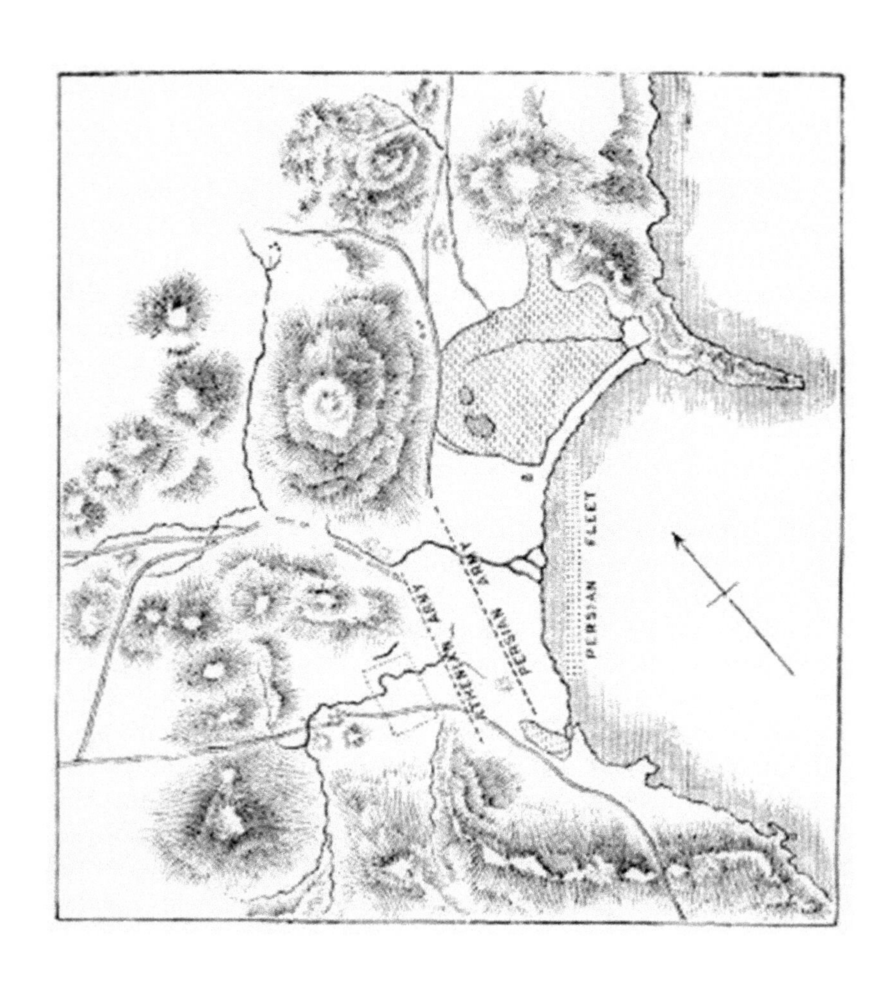

Plan of the Battle of Marathon

territorial resources of the two states whose armies were now about to come into conflict, the immense preponderance of the material power of the Persian king over that of the Athenian republic is more striking than any similar contrast which history can supply. It has been truly remarked, that, in estimating mere areas, Attica, containing on its whole surface only seven hundred square miles, shrinks into insignificance if compared with many a baronial fief of the Middle Ages, or many a colonial allotment of modern times. Its antagonist, the Persian empire, comprised the whole of modern Asiatic and much of modern European Turkey, the modern kingdom of Persia, and the countries of modern Georgia, Armenia, Balkh, the Punjaub, Affghanistan, Beloochistan, Egypt, and Tripoli.

Nor could a European, in the beginning of the fifth century before our era, look upon this huge accumulation of power beneath the sceptre of a single Asiatic ruler, with the indifference with which we now observe on the map the extensive dominions of modern Oriental sovereigns. For, as has been already remarked, before Marathon was fought, the prestige of success and of supposed superiority of race was on the side of the Asiatic against the European. Asia was the original seat of human societies and long before any trace can be found of the inhabitants of the rest of the world having emerged from the rudest barbarism, we can perceive that mighty and brilliant empires flourished in the Asiatic continent. They appear before us through the twilight of primeval history, dim and indistinct, but massive and majestic, like mountains in the early dawn.

Instead, however, of the infinite variety and restless change which have characterised the institutions and fortunes of European states ever since the commencement of the civilization of our continent, a monotonous uniformity pervades the histories of nearly all Oriental empires, from the most ancient down to the most recent times. They are characterised by the rapidity of their early conquests; by the immense extent of the dominions comprised in them; by the establishment of a *satrap* or *pacha* system of governing the provinces; by an invariable and speedy degeneracy in the princes of the royal house, the effeminate nurslings of the seraglio succeeding to the warrior-sovereigns reared in the camp; and by the internal anarchy and insurrections, which indicate and accelerate the decline and fall of those unwieldy and ill-organised fabrics of power. It is also a striking fact that the governments of all the great Asiatic empires have in all ages been absolute despotisms. And Heeren is right in connecting this with another great fact, which is important from its influence both on the political and the social life of Asiatics.

> Among all the considerable nations of Inner Asia, the paternal government of every household was corrupted by polygamy; where that custom exists, a good political constitution is impossible. Fathers being converted into domestic despots, are ready to pay the same abject obedience to their sovereign which they exact from their family and dependants in their domestic economy.

We should bear in mind also the inseparable connexion between the state religion and all legislation, which has always prevailed in the East, and the constant existence of a powerful sacerdotal body, exercising some check, though precarious and irregular, over the throne itself, grasping at all civil administration, claiming the supreme control of education, stereotyping the lines in which literature and science must move, and limiting the extent to which it shall be lawful for the human mind to prosecute its inquiries.

With these general characteristics rightly felt and understood, it becomes a comparatively easy task to investigate and appreciate the origin, progress, and principles of Oriental empires in general, as well as of the Persian monarchy in particular. And we are thus better enabled to appreciate the repulse which Greece gave to the arms of the East, and to judge of the probable consequences to human civilization, if the Persians had succeeded in bringing Europe under their yoke, as they had already subjugated the fairest portions of the rest of the then known world.

The Greeks, from their geographical position, formed the natural vanguard of European liberty against Persian ambition; and they pre-eminently displayed the salient points of distinctive national character, which have rendered European civilization so far superior to Asiatic. The nations that dwelt in ancient times around and near the northern shores of the Mediterranean Sea, were the first in our continent to receive from the East the rudiments of art and literature, and the germs of social and political organization. Of these nations, the Greeks, through their vicinity to Asia Minor, Phoenicia, and Egypt, were among the very foremost in acquiring the principles and habits of civilized life; and they also at once imparted a new and wholly original stamp on all which they received.

Thus, in their religion they received from foreign settlers the names of all their deities and many of their rites, but they discarded the loathsome monstrosities of the Nile, the Orontes, and the Ganges;—they nationalized their creed; and their own poets created their beautiful mythology. No sacerdotal caste ever existed in Greece. So, in their governments they lived long under hereditary kings, but never endured the permanent establishment of absolute monarchy. Their early kings were constitutional rulers, governing with defined prerogatives. And long before the Persian invasion the kingly form of government had given way in almost all the Greek states to republican institutions, presenting infinite varieties of the balancing or the alternate predominance of the oligarchical and democratical principles.

In literature and science the Greek intellect followed no beaten track, and acknowledged no limitary rules. The Greeks thought their subjects boldly out; and the novelty of a speculation invested it in their minds with interest, and not with criminality. Versatile, restless, enterprising and self-confident, the Greeks presented the most striking contrast to the habitual quietude and submissiveness of the Orientals. And, of all the Greeks, the Athenians exhibited these national characteristics in the strongest degree. This spirit of activity and daring, joined to a generous sympathy for the fate of their fellow-Greeks in Asia, had led them to join in the last Ionian war; and now, mingling with their abhorrence of the usurping family of their own citizens, which for a period had forcibly seized on and exercised despotic power at Athens, it nerved them to defy the wrath of King Darius, and to refuse to receive back at his bidding the tyrant whom they had some years before driven from their land.

The enterprise and genius of an Englishman have lately confirmed by fresh evidence, and invested with fresh interest, the might of the Persian monarch, who sent his troops to combat at Marathon. Inscriptions in a character termed the Arrow-headed, or Cuneiform, had long been known to exist on the marble monuments at Persepolis, near the site of the ancient Susa, and on the faces of rocks in other places formerly ruled over by the early Persian kings. But for thousands of years they had been mere unintelligible enigmas to the curious but baffled beholder: and they were often referred to as instances of the folly of human pride, which could indeed write its own praises in the solid rock, but only for the rock to outlive the language as well as the memory of the vain-glorious inscribers.

The elder Niebuhr, Grotefend, and Lassen had made some guesses at the meaning of the Cuneiform letters; but Major Rawlinson, of the East India Company's service, after years of labour, has at last accomplished the glorious achievement of fully revealing the alphabet and the grammar of this long unknown tongue. He has, in particular, fully deciphered and expounded the inscriptions on the sacred rock of Behistun, on the western frontiers of Media. These records of the Achaemenidae have at length found their interpreter; and Darius himself speaks to us from the consecrated mountain, and tells us the names of the nations that obeyed him, the revolts that he suppressed, his victories, his piety, and his glory.

Kings who thus seek the admiration of posterity are little likely to dim the record of their successes by the mention of their occasional defeats; and it throws no suspicion on the narrative of the Greek historians, that we find these inscriptions silent respecting the overthrow of Datis and Artaphernes, as well as respecting the reverses which Darius sustained in person during his Scythian campaigns. But these indisputable monuments of Persian fame confirm, and even increase, the opinion with which Herodotus inspires us, of the vast power which Cyrus founded and Cambyses increased; which Darius augmented by Indian and Arabian conquests, and seemed likely, when he directed his arms against Europe, to make the predominant monarchy of the world.

With the exception of the Chinese empire, in which, throughout all ages down to the last few years, one-third of the human race has dwelt almost unconnected with the other portions, all the great kingdoms which we know to have existed in Ancient Asia, were, in Darius's time, blended with the Persian. The northern Indians, the Assyrians, the Syrians, the Babylonians, the Chaldees, the Phoenicians, the nations of Palestine, the Armenians, the Bactrians, the Lydians, the Phrygians, the Parthians, and the Medes,—all obeyed the sceptre of the Great King: the Medes standing next to the native Persians in honour, and the empire being frequently spoken of as that of the Medes, or as that of the Medes and Persians. Egypt and Cyrene were Persian provinces; the Greek colonists in Asia Minor and the islands of the Ægean were Darius's subjects; and their gallant but unsuccessful attempts to throw off the Persian yoke had only served to rivet it more strongly, and to increase the general belief: that the Greeks could not stand before the Persians in a field of battle. Darius's Scythian war, though unsuccessful in its immediate object, had brought about the subjugation of Thrace and the submission of Macedonia. From the Indus to the Peneus, all was his.

We may imagine the wrath with which the lord of so many nations must have heard, nine years before the battle of Marathon, that a strange nation towards the setting sun, called the Athenians, had dared to help his rebels in Ionia against him, and that they had plundered and burnt the capital of one of his provinces. Before the burning of Sardis, Darius seems never to have heard of the existence of Athens; but his satraps in Asia Minor had for some time seen Athenian refugees at their provincial courts imploring assistance against their fellow-countrymen. When Hippias was driven away from Athens, and the tyrannic dynasty of the Pisistratidae finally overthrown in 510 B.C., the banished tyrant and his adherents, after vainly seeking to be restored by Spartan intervention, had betaken themselves to Sardis, the capital city of the satrapy of Artaphernes.

There Hippias (in the expressive words of Herodotus) began every kind of agitation, slandering the Athenians before Artaphernes, and doing all he could to induce the satrap to place Athens in subjection to him, as the tributary vassal of King Darius. When the Athenians heard of his practices, they sent envoys to Sardis to remonstrate with the Persians against taking up the quarrel of the Athenian refugees. But Artaphernes gave them in reply a menacing command to receive Hippias back again if they looked for safety. The Athenians were resolved not to purchase safety at such a price; and after rejecting the satrap's terms, they considered that they and the Persians were declared enemies.

At this very crisis the Ionian Greeks implored the assistance of their European brethren, to enable them to recover their independence from Persia. Athens, and the city of Eretria in Euboea, alone consented. Twenty Athenian galleys, and five Eretrian, crossed the Ægean Sea; and by a bold and sudden march upon Sardis the Athenians and their allies succeeded in capturing the capital city of the haughty satrap, who had recently menaced them with servitude or destruction. The Persian forces were soon rallied, and the Greeks were compelled to retire. They were pursued, and defeated on their return to the coast, and Athens took no further part in the Ionian war. But the insult that she had put upon the Persian power was speedily made known throughout that empire, and was never to be forgiven or forgotten. In the emphatic simplicity of the narrative of Herodotus, the wrath of the Great King is thus described:—

Now when it was told to King Darius that Sardis had been

taken and burnt by the Athenians and Ionians, he took small heed of the Ionians, well knowing who they were, and that their revolt would soon be put down: but he asked who, and what manner of men, the Athenians were. And when he had been told, he called for his bow; and, having taken it, and placed an arrow on the string, he let the arrow fly towards heaven; and as he shot it into the air, he said, 'O Supreme God! grant me that I may avenge myself on the Athenians.' And when he had said this, he appointed one of his servants to say to him every day as he sat at meat, 'Sire, remember the Athenians.'

Some years were occupied in the complete reduction of Ionia. But when this was effected, Darius ordered his victorious forces to proceed to punish Athens and Eretria, and to conquer European Greece. The first armament sent for this purpose was shattered by shipwreck, and nearly destroyed off Mount Athos, But the purpose of King Darius was not easily shaken. A larger army was ordered to be collected in Cilicia; and requisitions were sent to all the maritime cities of the Persian empire for ships of war, and for transports of sufficient size for carrying cavalry as well as infantry across the Ægean. While these preparations were being made, Darius sent heralds round to the Grecian cities demanding their submission to Persia. It was proclaimed in the market-place of each little Hellenic state (some with territories not larger than the Isle of Wight), that King Darius, the lord of all men, from the rising to the setting sun, required earth and water to be delivered to his heralds, as a symbolical acknowledgment that he was head and master of the country.[5]

Terror-stricken at the power of Persia and at the severe punishment that had recently been inflicted on the refractory Ionians, many of the continental Greeks and nearly all the islanders submitted, and gave the required tokens of vassalage. At Sparta and Athens an indignant refusal was returned: a refusal which was disgraced by outrage and violence against the persons of the Asiatic heralds.

Fresh fuel was thus added to the anger of Darius against Athens, and the Persian preparations went on with renewed vigour. In the

5. Aeschines in *Ctes.* is speaking of Xerxes, but Mitford is probably right in considering it as the style of the Persian kings in their proclamations. In one of the inscriptions at Persepolis, Darius terms himself "Darius the great king, king of kings, the king of the many peopled countries, the supporter also of this great world." In another, he styles himself "the king of all inhabited countries." See Asiatic Journal, and Major Rawlinson's Comments.

summer of 490 B.C., the army destined for the invasion was assembled in the Aleian plain of Cilicia, near the sea. A fleet of six hundred galleys and numerous transports was collected on the coast for the embarkation of troops, horse as well as foot. A Median general named Datis, and Artaphernes, the son of the satrap of Sardis, and who was also nephew of Darius, were placed in titular joint command of the expedition. That the real supreme authority was given to Datis alone is probable, from the way in which the Greek writers speak of him.

We know no details of the previous career of this officer; but there is every reason to believe that his abilities and bravery had been proved by experience, or his Median birth would have prevented his being placed in high command by Darius. He appears to have been the first Mede who was thus trusted by the Persian kings after the overthrow of the conspiracy of the Median Magi against the Persians immediately before Darius obtained the throne. Datis received instructions to complete the subjugation of Greece, and especial orders were given him with regard to Eretria and Athens. He was to take these two cities; and he was to lead the inhabitants away captive, and bring them as slaves into the presence of the Great King.

Datis embarked his forces in the fleet that awaited them; and coasting along the shores of Asia Minor till he was off Samos, he thence sailed due westward through the Ægean Sea for Greece, taking the islands in his way. The Naxians had, ten years before, successfully stood a siege against a Persian armament, but they now were too terrified to offer any resistance, and fled to the mountain-tops, while the enemy burnt their town and laid waste their lands. Thence Datis, compelling the Greek islanders to join him with their ships and men, sailed onward to the coast of Euboea. The little town of Carystus essayed resistance, but was quickly overpowered. He next attacked Eretria. The Athenians sent four thousand men to its aid.

But treachery was at work among the Eretrians; and the Athenian force received timely warning from one of the leading men of the city to retire to aid in saving their own country, instead of remaining to share in the inevitable destruction of Eretria. Left to themselves, the Eretrians repulsed the assaults of the Persians against their walls for six days; on the seventh day they were betrayed by two of their chiefs and the Persians occupied the city. The temples were burnt in revenge for the burning of Sardis, and the inhabitants were bound and placed as prisoners in the neighbouring islet of Ægylia, to wait there till Datis should bring the Athenians to join them in captivity, when both populations were to be led into Upper Asia, there to learn their doom from the lips of King Darius himself.

Flushed with success, and with half his mission thus accomplished, Datis reimbarked his troops, and crossing the little channel that separates Euboea from the mainland, he encamped his troops on the Attic coast at Marathon, drawing up his galleys on the shelving beach, as was the custom with the navies of antiquity. The conquered islands behind him served as places of deposit for his provisions and military stores. His position at Marathon seemed to him in every respect advantageous; and the level nature of the ground on which he camped was favourable for the employment of his cavalry, if the Athenians should venture to engage him. Hippias, who accompanied him, and acted as the guide of the invaders, had pointed out Marathon as the best place for a landing, for this very reason. Probably Hippias was also influenced by the recollection, that forty-seven years previously he, with his father Pisistratus, had crossed with an army from Eretria to Marathon, and had won an easy victory over their Athenian enemies on that very plain, which had restored them to tyrannic power. The omen seemed cheering. The place was the same; but Hippias soon learned to his cost how great a change had come over the spirit of the Athenians.

But though "the fierce democracy" of Athens was zealous and true against foreign invader and domestic tyrant, a faction existed in Athens, as at Eretria, of men willing to purchase a party triumph over their fellow-citizens at the price of their country's ruin. Communications were opened between these men and the Persian camp, which would have led to a catastrophe like that of Eretria, if Miltiades had not resolved, and had not persuaded his colleagues to resolve, on fighting at all hazards.

When Miltiades arrayed his men for action, he staked on the arbitrement of one battle not only the fate of Athens, but that of all Greece; for if Athens had fallen, no other Greek state, except Lacedaemon, would have had the courage to resist; and the Lacedaemonians, though they would probably have died in their ranks to the last man, never could have successfully resisted the victorious Persians, and the numerous Greek troops, which would have soon marched under the Persian satraps, had they prevailed over Athens.

Nor was there any power to the westward of Greece that could have offered an effectual opposition to Persia, had she once conquered Greece, and made that country a basis for future military operations.

Rome was at this time in her season of utmost weakness. Her dynasty of powerful Etruscan kings had been driven out, and her infant commonwealth was reeling under the attacks of the Etruscans and Volscians from without, and the fierce dissensions between the patricians and plebeians within. Etruria, with her Lucumos and serfs, was no match for Persia. Samnium had not grown into the might which she afterwards put forth: nor could the Greek colonies in South Italy and Sicily hope to survive when their parent states had perished.

Carthage had escaped the Persian yoke in the time of Cambyses, through the reluctance of the Phoenician mariners to serve against their kinsmen. But such forbearance could not long have been relied on, and the future rival of Rome would have become as submissive a minister of the Persian power as were the Phoenician cities themselves. If we turn to Spain, or if we pass the great mountain chain which, prolonged through the Pyrenees, the Cevennes, the Alps, and the Balkan, divides Northern from Southern Europe, we shall find nothing at that period but mere savage Finns, Celts, Slaves, and Teutons. Had Persia beaten Athens at Marathon, she could have found no obstacle to prevent Darius, the chosen servant of Ormuzd, from advancing his sway over all the known Western races of mankind.

The infant energies of Europe would have been trodden out beneath universal conquest; and the history of the world, like the history of Asia, would have become a mere record of the rise and fall of despotic dynasties, of the incursions of barbarous hordes, and of the mental and political prostration of millions beneath the diadem, the tiara, and the sword.

Great as the preponderance of the Persian over the Athenian power at that crisis seems to have been, it would be unjust to impute wild rashness to the policy of Miltiades, and those who voted with him in the Athenian council of war, or to look on the after-current of events as the mere result of successful indiscretion, as before has been remarked, Miltiades, whilst prince of the Chersonese, had seen service in the Persian armies; and he knew by personal observation how many elements of weakness lurked beneath their imposing aspect of strength. He knew that the bulk of their troops no longer consisted of the hardy shepherds and mountaineers from Persia Proper and Kurdistan, who won Cyrus's battles: but that unwilling contingents from conquered nations now largely filled up the Persian muster rolls, fighting more from compulsion than from any zeal in the cause of their masters. He had also the sagacity and the spirit to appreciate the superiority of the Greek armour and organization over the Asiatic, notwithstanding former reverses. Above all, he felt and worthily trusted the enthusiasm of the men under his command.

The Athenians, whom he led, had proved by their new-born valour in recent wars against the neighbouring states, that "Liberty and Equality of civic rights are brave spirit-stirring things: and they who, while under the yoke of a despot, had been no better men of war than any of their neighbours, as soon as they were free, became the foremost men of all; for each felt that in fighting for a free commonwealth, he fought for himself, and, whatever he took in hand, he was zealous to do the work thoroughly." So the nearly contemporaneous historian describes the change of spirit that was seen in the Athenians after their tyrants were expelled; and Miltiades knew that in leading them against the invading army, where they had Hippias, the foe they most hated, before them, he was bringing into battle no ordinary men, and could calculate on no ordinary heroism.

As for traitors, he was sure, that whatever treachery might lurk among some of the higher-born and wealthier Athenians, the rank and file whom he commanded were ready to do their utmost in his and their own cause. With regard to future attacks from Asia, he might reasonably hope that one victory would inspirit all Greece to combine against common foe; and that the latent seeds of revolt and disunion in the Persian empire would soon burst forth and paralyse its energies, so as to leave Greek independence secure.

With these hopes and risks, Miltiades, on the afternoon of a September day, 490 B.C., gave the word for the Athenian army to prepare for battle. There were many local associations connected with those mountain heights, which were calculated powerfully to excite the spirits of the men, and of which the commanders well knew how to avail themselves in their exhortations to their troops before the encounter. Marathon itself was a region sacred to; Hercules. Close to them was the fountain of Macaria, who had in days of yore devoted herself to death for the liberty of her people.

The very plain on which they were to fight was the scene of the exploits of their national hero, Theseus; and there, too, as old legends told, the Athenians and the Heraclidae had routed the invader, Eurystheus. These traditions were not mere cloudy myths, or idle fictions, but matters of implicit earnest faith to the men of that day: and many a fervent prayer arose from the Athenian ranks to the heroic spirits who while on earth had striven and suffered on that very spot, and who were believed to be now heavenly powers, looking down with interest on their still beloved country, and capable of interposing with superhuman aid in its behalf.

According to old national custom, the warriors of each tribe were arrayed together; neighbour thus fighting by the side of neighbour, friend by friend, and the spirit of emulation and the consciousness of responsibility excited to the very utmost. The War-Ruler, Callimachus, had the leading of the right wing; the Plataeans formed the extreme left; and Themistocles and Aristides commanded the centre. The line consisted of the heavy-armed spearmen only. For the Greeks (until the time of Iphicrates) took little or no account of light-armed soldiers in a pitched battle, using them only in skirmishes or for the pursuit of a defeated enemy. The panoply of the regular infantry consisted of a long spear, of a shield, helmet, breast-plate, greaves, and short sword.

Thus equipped, they usually advanced slowly and steadily into action in an uniform phalanx of about eight spears deep. But the military genius of Miltiades led him to deviate on this occasion from the commonplace tactics of his countrymen. It was essential for him to extend his line so as to cover all the practicable ground, and to secure himself from being outflanked and charged in the rear by the Persian horse. This extension involved the weakening of his line. Instead of an uniform reduction of its strength, he determined on detaching principally from his centre, which, from the nature of the ground, would have the best opportunities for rallying if broken; and on strengthening his wings, so as to insure advantage at those points; and he trusted to his own skill, and to his soldiers' discipline, for the improvement of that advantage into decisive victory. [6]

In this order, and availing himself probably of the inequalities of the ground, so as to conceal his preparations from the enemy till the last possible moment, Miltiades drew up the eleven thousand infantry whose spears were to decide this crisis in the struggle between the European and the Asiatic worlds. The sacrifices, by which the favour of Heaven was sought, and its will consulted, were announced to show

6. It is remarkable that there is no other instance of a Greek general deviating from the ordinary mode of bringing a *phalanx* of spearmen into action, until the Battles of Leuctra and Mantineia, more than a century after Marathon, when Epaminondas introduced the tactics (which Alexander the Great in ancient times, and Frederic the Great in modern times, made so famous) of concentrating an overpowering force on some decisive point of the enemy's line, while he kept back, or, in military phrase, refused the weaker part of his own.

propitious omens. The trumpet sounded for action, and, chanting the hymn of battle, the little army bore down upon the host of the foe. Then, too, along the mountain slopes of Marathon must have resounded the mutual exhortation which Æschylus, who fought in both battles, tells us was afterwards heard over the waves of Salamis,—

> On, sons of the Greeks! Strike for the freedom of your country! strike for the freedom of your children and of your wives—for the shrines of your fathers' gods, and for the sepulchres of your sires. All—all are now staked upon the strife!

Instead of advancing at the usual slow pace of the *phalanx*, Miltiades brought his men on at a run. They were all trained in the exercises of the *palaestra*, so that there was no fear of their ending the charge in breathless exhaustion: and it was of the deepest importance for him to traverse as rapidly as possible the space of about a mile of level ground, that lay between the mountain foot and the Persian outposts, and so to get his troops into close action before the Asiatic cavalry could mount, form, and manoeuvre against him, or their archers keep him long under bow-shot, and before the enemy's generals could fairly deploy their masses. Herodotus says:

> When the Persians saw the Athenians running down on them, without horse or bowmen, and scanty in numbers, they thought them a set of madmen rushing upon certain destruction.

They began, however, to prepare to receive them and the Eastern chiefs arrayed, as quickly as time and place allowed, the varied races who served in their motley ranks. Mountaineers from Hyrcania and Affghanistan, wild horsemen from the steppes of Khorassan, the black archers of Ethiopia, swordsmen from the banks of the Indus, the Oxus, the Euphrates, and the Nile, made ready against the enemies of the Great King. But no national cause inspired them, except the division of native Persians; and in the large host there was no uniformity of language, creed, race, or military system. Still, among them there were many gallant men, under a veteran general; they were familiarized with victory; and in contemptuous confidence their infantry, which alone had time to form, awaited the Athenian charge.

On came the Greeks, with one unwavering line of levelled spears, against which the light targets, the short lances and scimitars of the Orientals offered weak defence. The front rank of the Asiatics must have gone down to a man at the first shock. Still they recoiled not, but strove by individual gallantry, and by the weight of numbers, to make up for the disadvantages of weapons and tactics, and to bear back the shallow line of the Europeans. In the centre, where the native Persians and the Sacae fought, they succeeded in breaking through the weaker part of the Athenian phalanx; and the tribes led by Aristides and Themistocles were, after a brave resistance, driven back over the plain, and chased by the Persians up the valley towards the inner country.

There the nature of the ground gave the opportunity of rallying and renewing the struggle: and meanwhile, the Greek wings, where Miltiades had concentrated his chief strength, had routed the Asiatics opposed to them; and the Athenian and Plataean officers, instead of pursuing the fugitives, kept their troops well in hand, and wheeling round they formed the two wings together.

Miltiades instantly led them against the Persian centre, which had hitherto been triumphant, but which now fell back, and prepared to encounter these new and unexpected assailants. Aristides and Themistocles renewed the fight with their re-organised troops, and the full force of the Greeks was brought into close action with the Persian and Sacian divisions of the enemy. Datis's veterans strove hard to keep their ground, and evening was approaching before the stern encounter was decided.

But the Persians, with their slight wicker shields, destitute of body-armour, and never taught by training to keep the even front and act with the regular movement of the Greek infantry, fought at grievous disadvantage with their shorter and feebler weapons against the compact array of well-armed Athenian and Plataean spearmen, all perfectly drilled to perform each necessary evolution in concert, and to preserve an uniform and unwavering line in battle. In personal courage and in bodily activity the Persians were not inferior to their adversaries. Their spirits were not yet cowed by the recollection of former defeats; and they lavished their lives freely, rather than forfeit the fame which they had won by so many victories.

While their rear ranks poured an incessant shower of arrows over the heads of their comrades, the foremost Persians kept rushing forward, sometimes singly, sometimes in desperate groups of twelve or ten upon the projecting spears of the Greeks, striving to force a lane into the *phalanx*, and to bring their scimitars and daggers into play. But the Greeks felt their superiority, and though the fatigue of the long-continued action told heavily on their inferior numbers, the sight of the carnage that they dealt amongst their assailants nerved them to fight still more fiercely on.[7]

At last the previously unvanquished lords of Asia turned their backs and fled, and the Greeks followed, striking them down, to the water's edge, where the invaders were now hastily launching their galleys, and seeking to embark and fly. Flushed with success, the Athenians dashed at the fleet.

"Bring fire, bring fire," was their cry; and they began to lay hold of the ships. But here the Asiatics resisted desperately, and the principal loss sustained by the Greeks was in the assault on the fleet. Here fell the brave War-Ruler Callimachus, the general Stesilaus, and other Athenians of note. Conspicuous among them was Cynaegeirus, the brother of the tragic poet Æschylus. He had grasped the ornamental work on the stern of one of the galleys, and had his hand struck off by an axe. Seven galleys were captured; but the Persians succeeded in saving the rest. They pushed off from the fatal shore: but even here the skill of Datis did not desert him, and he sailed round to the western coast of Attica, in hopes to find the city unprotected, and to gain possession of it from some of the partisans of Hippias. Miltiades, however, saw and counteracted his manoeuvre.

Leaving Aristides, and the troops of his tribe, to guard the spoil and the slain, the Athenian commander led his conquering army by a rapid night-march back across the country to Athens. And when the Persian fleet had doubled the Cape of Sunium and sailed up to the Athenian harbour in the morning, Datis saw arrayed on the heights above the city the troops before whom his men had fled on the preceding evening. All hope of further conquest in Europe for the time was abandoned, and the baffled armada returned to the Asiatic coasts.

After the battle had been fought, but while the dead bodies were yet on the ground, the promised reinforcement from Sparta arrived. Two thousand Lacedaemonian spearmen, starting immediately after the full moon, had marched the hundred and fifty miles between Athens and Sparta in the wonderfully short time of three days. Though too late to share in the glory of the action, they requested to be allowed to march to the battlefield to behold the Medes. They proceeded thither, gazed

7. See the description in Herodotus, 9, 62, of the gallantry shown by the Persian infantry against the Lacedaemonians at Plataea. We have no similar detail of the fight at Marathon, but we know that it was long and obstinately contested, and the spirit of the Persians must have been even higher at Marathon than at Plataea. In both battles it was only the true Persians and the Sacae who showed this valour; the other Asiatics fled like sheep.

on the dead bodies of the invaders, and then, praising the Athenians and what they had done, they returned to Lacedaemon.

The number of the Persian dead was six thousand four hundred; of the Athenians, a hundred and ninety-two. The number of Plataeans who fell is not mentioned, but as they fought in the part of the army which was not broken, it cannot have been large.

The apparent disproportion between the losses of the two armies is not surprising, when we remember the armour of the Greek spearmen, and the impossibility of heavy slaughter being inflicted by sword or lance on troops so armed, as long as they kept firm in their ranks.

The Athenian slain were buried on the field of battle. This was contrary to the usual custom, according to which the bones of all who fell fighting for their country in each year were deposited in a public sepulchre in the suburb of Athens called the Cerameicus. But it was felt that a distinction ought to be made in the funeral honours paid to the men of Marathon, even as their merit had been distinguished over that of all other Athenians. A lofty mound was raised on the plain of Marathon, beneath which the remains of the men of Athens who fell in the battle were deposited. Ten columns were erected on the spot, one for each of the Athenian tribes; and on the monumental column of each tribe were graven the names of those of its members whose glory it was to have fallen in the great battle of liberation. The antiquary Pausanias read those names there six hundred years after the time when they were first graven.[8] The columns have long perished, but the mound still marks the spot where the noblest heroes of antiquity, the *Marathonomakhoi* repose.

A separate *tumulus* was raised over the bodies of the slain Plataeans, and another over the light-armed slaves who had taken part and had fallen in the battle.[9] There was also a distinct sepulchral monument to the general to whose genius the victory was mainly due. Miltiades did not live long after his achievement at Marathon, but he lived long enough to experience a lamentable reverse of his popularity and good fortune. As soon as the Persians had quitted the western coasts of the

8. Pausanias states, with implicit belief, that the battlefield was haunted at night by supernatural beings, and that the noise of combatants and the snorting of horses were heard to resound on it. The superstition has survived the change of creeds, and the shepherds of the neighbourhood still believe that spectral warriors contend on the plain at midnight, and they say that they have heard the shouts of the combatants and the neighing of the steeds. See Grote and Thirlwall.

9. It is probable that the Greek light-armed irregulars were active in the attack on the Persian ships and it was in this attack that the Greeks suffered their principal loss.

Ægean, he proposed to an assembly of the Athenian people that they should fit out seventy galleys, with a proportionate force of soldiers and military stores, and place them at his disposal; not telling them whither he meant to proceed, but promising them that if they would equip the force he asked for, and give him discretionary powers, he would lead it to a land where there was gold in abundance to be won with ease.

The Greeks of that time believed in the existence of Eastern realms teeming with gold, as firmly as the Europeans of the sixteenth century believed in Eldorado of the West. The Athenians probably thought that the recent victor of Marathon, and former officer of Darius, was about to guide them on a secret expedition against some wealthy and unprotected cities of treasure in the Persian dominions. The armament was voted and equipped, and sailed eastward from Attica, no one but Miltiades knowing its destination, until the Greek isle of Paros was reached, when his true object appeared. In former years, while connected with the Persians as prince of the Chersonese, Miltiades had been involved in a quarrel with one of the leading men among the Parians, who had injured his credit and caused some slights to be put upon him at the court of the Persian satrap, Hydarnes. The feud had ever since rankled in the heart of the Athenian chief, and he now attacked Paros for the sake of avenging himself on his ancient enemy.

His pretext, as general of the Athenians, was, that the Parians had aided the armament of Datis with a war-galley. The Parians pretended to treat about terms of surrender, but used the time which they thus gained in repairing the defective parts of the fortifications of their city; and they then set the Athenians at defiance. So far, says Herodotus, the accounts of all the Greeks agree. But the Parians, in after years, told also a wild legend, how a captive priestess of a Parian temple of the Deities of the Earth promised Miltiades to give him the means of capturing Paros: how, at her bidding, the Athenian general went alone at night and forced his way into a holy shrine, near the city gate, but with what purpose it was not known: how a supernatural awe came over him, and in his flight he fell and fractured his leg: how an oracle afterwards forbad the Parians to punish the sacrilegious and traitorous priestess, "because it was fated that Miltiades should come to an ill end, and she was only the instrument to lead him to evil."

Such was the tale that Herodotus heard at Paros. Certain it was that Miltiades either dislocated or broke his leg during an unsuccessful siege of that city, and returned home in evil plight with his baffled and defeated forces.

The indignation of the Athenians was proportionate to the hope and excitement which his promises had raised. Xanthippus, the head of one of the first families in Athens, indicted him before the supreme popular tribunal for the capital offence of having deceived the people. His guilt was undeniable, and the Athenians passed their verdict accordingly. But the recollections of Lemnos and Marathon, and the sight of the fallen general who lay stretched on a couch before them, pleaded successfully in mitigation of punishment, and the sentence was commuted from death to a fine of fifty *talents*. This was paid by his son, the afterwards illustrious Cimon, Miltiades dying, soon after the trial, of the injury which he had received at Paros. [10]

The melancholy end of Miltiades, after his elevation to such a height of power and glory, must often have been recalled to the mind of the ancient Greeks by the sight of one, in particular, of the memorials of the great battle which he won. This was the remarkable statue (minutely described by Pausanias) which the Athenians, in the time of Pericles, caused to be hewn out of a huge block of marble, which, it was believed, had been provided by Datis to form a trophy of the anticipated victory of the Persians. Phidias fashioned out of this a colossal image of the goddess Nemesis, the deity whose peculiar function was to visit the exuberant prosperity both of nations and individuals with sudden and awful reverses. This statue was placed in a temple of the goddess at Rhamnus, about eight miles from Marathon, Athens herself contained numerous memorials of her primary great victory. Panenus, the cousin of Phidias, represented it in fresco on the walls of the painted porch; and, centuries afterwards, the figures of Miltiades and Callimachus at the head of the Athenians were conspicuous in

10. "Looking to the practice of the Athenian dicastery in criminal cases, fifty talents was the minor penalty actually proposed by the defenders of Miltiades themselves as a substitute for the punishment of death. In those penal cases at Athens, where the punishment was not fixed beforehand by the terms of the law, if the person accused was found guilty, it was customary to submit to the jurors subsequently and separately, the question as to the amount of punishment. First, the accuser named the penalty which he thought suitable; next, the accused person was called upon to name an amount of penalty for himself, and the jurors were constrained to take their choice between these two; no third gradation of penalty being admissible for consideration. Of course, under such circumstances, it was the interest of the accused party to name, even in his own case, some real and serious penalty, something which the jurors might be likely to deem not wholly inadequate to his crime just proved; for if he proposed some penalty only trifling, he drove them to far the heavier sentence recommended by his opponent." Mr. Grote *History*, 4.

the fresco.

The tutelary deities were exhibited taking part in the fray. In the background were seen the Phoenician galleys; and nearer to the spectator, the Athenians and the Plataeans (distinguished by their leathern helmets) were chasing routed Asiatics into the marshes and the sea. The battle was sculptured also on the Temple of Victory in the Acropolis; and even now there may be traced on the frieze the figures of the Persian combatants with their lunar shields, their bows and quivers, their curved scimitars, their loose trowsers, and Phrygian tiaras.

These and other memorials of Marathon were the produce of the meridian age of Athenian intellectual splendour—of the age of Phidias and Pericles. For it was not merely by the generation of men whom the battle liberated from Hippias and the Medes, that the transcendent importance of their victory was gratefully recognised. Through the whole epoch of her prosperity, through the long Olympiads of her decay, through centuries after her fall, Athens looked back on the day of Marathon as the brightest of her national existence.

By a natural blending of patriotic pride with grateful piety, the very spirits of the Athenians who fell at Marathon were deified by their countrymen. The inhabitants of the districts of Marathon paid religious rites to them; and orators solemnly invoked them in their most impassioned adjurations before the assembled men of Athens.

> Nothing was omitted that could keep alive the remembrance of a deed which had first taught the Athenian people to know its own strength, by measuring it with the power which had subdued the greater part of the known world. The consciousness thus awakened fixed its character, its station, and its destiny; it was the spring of its later great actions and ambitious enterprises.—Thirlwall.

It was not indeed by one defeat, however signal, that the pride of Persia could be broken, and her dreams of universal empire be dispelled. Ten years afterwards she renewed her attempts upon Europe on a grander scale of enterprise, and was repulsed by Greece with greater and reiterated loss. Larger forces and heavier slaughter than had been seen at Marathon signalised the conflicts of Greeks and Persians at Artemisium, Salamis, Plataea, and the Eurymedon. But mighty and momentous as these battles were, they rank not with Marathon in importance. They originated no new impulse. They turned back no current of fate. They were merely confirmatory of the already existing bias which Marathon had created. The day of Marathon is the critical epoch in the history of the two nations.

It broke for ever the spell of Persian invincibility, which had paralysed men's minds. It generated among the Greeks the spirit which beat back Xerxes, and afterwards led on Xenophon, Agesilaus, and Alexander, in terrible retaliation, through their Asiatic campaigns. It secured for mankind the intellectual treasures of Athens, the growth of free institutions the liberal enlightenment of the Western world, and the gradual ascendency for many ages of the great principles of European civilisation.

Explanatory Remarks on Some of the Circumstances of the Battle of Marathon

Nothing is said by Herodotus of the Persian cavalry taking any part in the battle, although he mentions that Hippias recommended the Persians to land at Marathon, because the plain was favourable for cavalry evolutions. In the life of Miltiades, which is usually cited as the production of Cornelius Nepos, but which I believe to be of no authority whatever, it is said that Miltiades protected his flanks from the enemy's horse by an abattis of felled trees. While he was on the high ground he would not have required this defence; and it is not likely that the Persians would have allowed him to erect it on the plain.

Bishop Thirlwall calls our attention to a passage in Suidas, where the proverb *khoris hippeis* is said to have originated from some Ionian Greeks, who were serving compulsorily in the army of Datis, contriving to inform Miltiades that the Persian cavalry had gone away, whereupon Miltiades immediately joined battle and gained the victory. There may probably be a gleam of truth in this legend. If Datis's cavalry was numerous, as the abundant pastures of Euboea were close at hand, the Persian general, when he thought, from the inaction of his enemy, that they did not mean to come down from the heights and give battle, might naturally send the larger part of his horse back across the channel to the neighbourhood of Eretria, where he had already left a detachment, and where his military stores must have been deposited. The knowledge of such a movement would of course confirm Miltiades in his resolution to bring on a speedy engagement.

But, in truth, whatever amount of cavalry we suppose Datis to have had with him on the day of Marathon, their inaction in the battle is intelligible, if we believe the attack of the Athenian spearmen to have been as sudden as it was rapid. The Persian horse-soldier, on an alarm being given, had to take the shackles off his horse, to strap the saddle on, and bridle him, besides equipping himself; and when each individual horseman was ready, the line had to be formed; and the time that it takes to form the Oriental cavalry in line for a charge, has, in all ages, been observed by Europeans.

The wet state of the marshes at each end of the plain, in the time of year when the battle was fought, has been adverted to by Mr Wordsworth; and this would hinder the Persian general from arranging and employing his horsemen on his extreme wings, while it also enabled the Greeks, as they came forward, to occupy the whole breadth of the practicable ground with an unbroken line of levelled spears, against which, if any Persian horse advanced they would be driven back in confusion upon their own foot.

Even numerous and fully-arrayed bodies of cavalry have been repeatedly broken, both in ancient and modern warfare, by resolute charges of infantry. For instance, it was by an attack of some picked cohorts that Caesar routed the Pompeian cavalry, which had previously defeated his own at Pharsalia.

I have represented the Battle of Marathon as beginning in the afternoon, and ending towards evening. If it had lasted all day, Herodotus would have probably mentioned that fact. That it ended towards evening is, I think, proved by the line from the *Vespae*, and to which my attention was called by Sir Edward Bulwer Lytton's account of the battle. I think that the lines in Aristophanes, justify the description which I have given of the rear-ranks of the Persians keeping up a flight of arrows over the heads of their comrades against the Greeks.

Chapter 2

Defeat of the Athenians at Syracuse, B.C.413

Few cities have undergone more memorable sieges during ancient and mediaeval times, than has the city of Syracuse. Athenian, Carthaginian, Roman, Vandal, Byzantine, Saracen, and Norman, have in turns beleaguered her walls; and the resistance which she successfully opposed to some of her early assailants was of the deepest importance, not only to the fortunes of the generations then in being, but to all the subsequent current of human events. To adopt the eloquent expressions of Arnold respecting the check which she gave to the Carthaginian arms,

> Syracuse was a breakwater, which God's providence raised up to protect the yet immature strength of Rome.

And her triumphant repulse of the great Athenian expedition against her was of even more wide-spread and enduring importance. It forms a decisive epoch in the strife for universal empire, in which all the great states of antiquity successively engaged and failed.

The present city of Syracuse is a place of little or no military strength, as the fire of artillery from the neighbouring heights would almost completely command it. But in ancient warfare its position, and the care bestowed on its walls, rendered it formidably strong against the means of offence which then were employed by besieging armies.

The ancient city, in the time of the Peloponnesian war, was chiefly built on the knob of land which projects into the sea on the eastern coast of Sicily, between two bays; one of which, to the north, was called the bay of Thapsus, while the southern one formed the great harbour of the city of Syracuse itself. A small island, or peninsula (for such it soon was rendered), lies at the south-eastern extremity of this knob of land, stretching almost entirely across the mouth of the great harbour, and rendering it nearly land-locked. This island comprised the original settlement of the first Greek colonists from Corinth, who founded Syracuse two thousand five hundred years ago; and the modern city has shrunk again into these primary limits. But, in the fifth century before our era, the growing wealth and population of the Syracusans had led them to occupy and include within their city walls portion after portion of the mainland lying next to the little isle; so that at the time of the Athenian expedition the seaward part of the land between the two bays already spoken of was built over, and fortified from bay to bay; constituting the larger part of Syracuse.

The landward wall, therefore, of the city traversed this knob of land, which continues to slope upwards from the sea, and which to the west of the old fortifications (that is, towards the interior of Sicily) rises rapidly for a mile or two, but diminishes in width, and finally terminates in a long narrow ridge, between which and Mount Hybla a succession of chasms and uneven low ground extend. On each flank of this ridge the descent is steep and precipitous from its summits to the strips of level land that lie immediately below it, both to the south-west and north-west.

The usual mode of assailing fortified towns in the time of the Peloponnesian war, was to build a double wall round them, sufficiently strong to check any sally of the garrison from within, or any attack of a relieving force from without. The interval within the two walls of the circumvallation was roofed over, and formed barracks, in which the besiegers posted themselves, and awaited the effects of want or treachery among the besieged in producing a surrender. And, in every Greek city of those days, as in every Italian republic of the middle ages, the rage of domestic sedition between aristocrats and democrats ran high. Rancorous refugees swarmed in the camp of every invading enemy; and every blockaded city was sure to contain within its walls a body of intriguing malcontents, who were eager to purchase a party-triumph at the expense of a national disaster.

Famine and faction were the allies on whom besiegers relied. The generals of that time trusted to the operation of these sure confederates as soon as they could establish a complete blockade. They rarely ventured on the attempt to storm any fortified post. For the military engines of antiquity were feeble in breaching masonry, before the improvements which the first Dionysius effected in the mechanics of destruction; and the lives of spearmen the boldest and most highly-trained would, of course, have been idly spent in charges against unshattered walls.

A city built, close to the sea, like Syracuse, was impregnable, save by the combined operations of a superior hostile fleet and a superior hostile army. And Syracuse, from her size, her population, and her military and naval resources, not unnaturally thought herself secure from finding in another Greek city a foe capable of sending a sufficient armament to menace her with capture and subjection. But in the spring of 414 B.C. the Athenian navy was mistress of her harbour and the adjacent seas; an Athenian army had defeated her troops, and cooped them within the town; and from bay to bay a blockading wall was being rapidly carried across the strips of level ground and the high ridge outside the city (then termed Epipolae), which, if completed, would have cut the Syracusans off from all succour from the interior of Sicily, and have left them at the mercy of the Athenian generals. The besiegers' works were, indeed, unfinished; but every day the unfortified interval in their lines grew narrower, and with it diminished all apparent hope of safety for the beleaguered town.

Athens was now staking the flower of her forces, and the accumulated fruits of seventy years of glory, on one bold throw for the dominion of the Western world. As Napoleon from Mount Coeur de Lion pointed to St. Jean d'Acre, and told his staff that the capture of that town would decide his destiny, and would change the face of the world; so the Athenian officers, from the heights of Epipolae, must have looked on Syracuse, and felt that with its fall all the known powers of the earth would fall beneath them. They must have felt also that Athens, if repulsed there, must pause for ever in her career of conquest, and sink from an imperial republic into a ruined and subservient community.

At Marathon, the first in date of the Great Battles of the World, we beheld Athens struggling for self-preservation against the invading armies of the East. At Syracuse she appears as the ambitious and oppressive invader of others. In her, as in other republics of old and of modern times, the same energy that had inspired the most heroic efforts in defence of the national independence, soon learned to employ itself in daring and unscrupulous schemes of self-aggrandizement at the expense of neighbouring nations. In the interval between the Persian and Peloponnesian wars she had rapidly grown into a conquering and dominant state, the chief of a thousand tributary cities, and the mistress of the largest and best-manned navy that the Mediterranean had yet beheld. The occupations of her territory by Xerxes and Mardonius, in the second Persian war, had forced her whole population to become mariners; and the glorious results of that struggle confirmed them in their zeal for their country's service at sea. The voluntary suffrage of the Greek cities of the coasts and islands of the Ægean first placed Athens at the head of the confederation formed for the further prosecution of the war against Persia.

But this titular ascendancy was soon converted by her into practical and arbitrary dominion. She protected them from piracy and the Persian power, which soon fell into decrepitude and decay; but she exacted in return implicit obedience to herself. She claimed and enforced a prerogative of taxing them at her discretion; and proudly refused to be accountable for her mode of expending their supplies. Remonstrance against her assessments was treated as factious disloyalty; and refusal to pay was promptly punished as revolt. Permitting and encouraging her subject allies to furnish all their contingents in money, instead of part consisting of ships and men, the sovereign republic gained the double object of training her own citizens by constant and well-paid service in her fleets, and of seeing her confederates lose their skill and discipline by inaction, and become more and more passive and powerless under her yoke.

Their towns were generally dismantled; while the imperial city herself was fortified with the greatest care and sumptuousness: the accumulated revenues from her tributaries serving to strengthen and adorn to the utmost her havens, her docks, her arsenals, her theatres, and her shrines; and to array her in that plenitude of architectural magnificence, the ruins of which still attest the intellectual grandeur of the age and people, which produced a Pericles to plan and a Phidias to execute.

All republics that acquire supremacy over other nations, rule them selfishly and oppressively. There is no exception to this in either ancient or modern times. Carthage, Rome, Venice, Genoa, Florence, Pisa, Holland, and Republican France, all tyrannized over every province and subject state where they gained authority. But none of them openly avowed their system of doing so upon principle, with the candour which the Athenian republicans displayed, when any remonstrance was made against the severe exactions which they imposed upon their vassal allies. They avowed that their empire was a tyranny, and frankly stated that they solely trusted to force and terror to uphold it. They appealed to what they called "the eternal law of nature, that the weak should be coerced by the strong." (Thuc. i.) Sometimes they stated, and not without some truth, that the unjust hatred of Sparta against themselves forced them to be unjust to others in self-defence. To be safe they must be powerful; and to be powerful they must plunder and coerce their neighbours.

They never dreamed of communicating any franchise, or share in office, to their dependents; but jealously monopolized every post of command, and all political and judicial power; exposing themselves to every risk with unflinching gallantry; enduring cheerfully the laborious training and severe discipline which their sea-service required; venturing readily on every ambitious scheme; and never suffering difficulty or disaster to shake their tenacity of purpose. Their hope was to acquire unbounded empire for their country, and the means of maintaining each of the thirty thousand citizens who made up the sovereign republic, in exclusive devotion to military occupations, and to those brilliant sciences and arts in which Athens already had reached the meridian of intellectual splendour.

Her great political, dramatist speaks of the Athenian empire as comprehending a thousand states. The language of the stage must not be taken too literally; but the number of the dependencies of Athens, at the time when the Peloponnesian confederacy attacked her, was undoubtedly very great. With a few trifling exceptions, all the islands of the Ægean, and all the Greek cities, which in that age fringed the coasts of Asia Minor, the Hellespont, and Thrace paid tribute to Athens, and implicitly obeyed her orders. The Ægean Sea was an Attic lake. Westward of Greece, her influence though strong, was not equally predominant. She had colonies and allies among the wealthy and populous Greek settlements in Sicily and South Italy, but she had no organised system of confederates in those regions; and her galleys brought her no tribute from the western seas.

The extension of her empire over Sicily was the favourite project of her ambitious orators and generals. While her great statesman Pericles lived, his commanding genius kept his countrymen under control and forbade them to risk the fortunes of Athens in distant enterprises, while they had unsubdued and powerful enemies at their own doors. He taught Athens this maxim; but he also taught her to know and to use her own strength, and when Pericles had departed the bold spirit which he had fostered overleaped the salutary limits which he had prescribed. When her bitter enemies, the Corinthians, succeeded, in 431 B.C., in inducing Sparta to attack her, and a confederacy was formed of five-sixths of the continental Greeks, all animated by anxious jealousy and bitter hatred of Athens; when armies far superior in numbers and equipment to those which had marched against the Persians were poured into the Athenian territory, and laid it waste to the city walls; the general opinion was that Athens would, in two or three years at the farthest, be reduced to submit to the requisitions of her invaders. But her strong fortifications, by which she was girt and linked to her principal haven, gave her, in those ages, almost all the advantages of an insular position. Pericles had made her trust to her empire of the seas.

Every Athenian in those days was a practised seaman. A state indeed whose members, of an age fit for service, at no time exceeded thirty thousand, and whose territorial extent did not equal half Sussex, could only have acquired such a naval dominion as Athens once held, by devoting, and zealously training, all its sons to service in its fleets. In order to man the numerous galleys which she sent out, she necessarily employed also large numbers of hired mariners and slaves at the oar; but the staple of her crews was Athenian, and all posts of command were held by native citizens. It was by reminding them of this, of their long practice in seamanship, and the certain superiority which their discipline gave them over the enemy's marine, that their great minister mainly encouraged them to resist the combined power of Lacedaemon and her allies. He taught them that Athens might thus reap the fruit of her zealous devotion to maritime affairs ever since the invasion of the Medes:

> She had not, indeed, perfected herself; but the reward of her superior training was the rule of the sea—a mighty dominion, for it gave her the rule of much fair land beyond its waves, safe from the idle ravages with which the Lacedaemonians might harass Attica, but never could subdue Athens.—Thuc. *lib.* i.

Athens accepted the war with which her enemies threatened her, rather than descend from her pride of place. And though the awful visitation of the Plague came upon her, and swept away more of her citizens than the Dorian spear laid low, she held her own gallantly against her foes. If the Peloponnesian armies in irresistible strength wasted every spring her corn lands, her vineyards, and her olive groves with fire and sword, she retaliated on their coasts with her fleets;

which, if resisted, were only resisted to display the pre-eminent skill and bravery of her seamen. Some of her subject-allies revolted, but the revolts were in general sternly and promptly quelled. The genius of one enemy had, indeed, inflicted blows on her power in Thrace which she was unable to remedy; but he fell in battle in the tenth year of the war; and with the loss of Brasidas the Lacedaemonians seemed to have lost all energy and judgment.

Both sides at length grew weary of the war; and in 421 B.C. a truce of fifty years was concluded, which, though ill kept, and though many of the confederates of Sparta refused to recognise it, and hostilities still continued in many parts of Greece, protected the Athenian territory from the ravages of enemies, and enabled Athens to accumulate large sums out of the proceeds of her annual revenues. So also, as a few years passed by, the havoc which the pestilence and the sword had made in her population was repaired; and in 415 B.C. Athens was full of bold and restless spirits, who longed for some field of distant enterprise, wherein they might signalize themselves, and aggrandize the state; and who looked on the alarm of Spartan hostility as a mere old woman's tale. When Sparta had wasted their territory she had done her worst; and the fact of its always being in her power to do so, seemed a strong reason for seeking to increase the transmarine dominion of Athens.

The West was now the quarter towards which the thoughts of every aspiring Athenian were directed. From the very beginning of the war Athens had kept up an interest in Sicily; and her squadrons had from time to time appeared on its coasts and taken part in the dissensions in which the Sicilian Greeks were universally engaged one against the other. There were plausible grounds for a direct quarrel, and an open attack by the Athenians upon Syracuse.

With the capture of Syracuse all Sicily, it was hoped, would be secured. Carthage and Italy were next to be assailed. With large levies of Iberian mercenaries she then meant to overwhelm her Peloponnesian enemies. The Persian monarchy lay in hopeless imbecility, inviting Greek invasion; nor did the known world contain the power that seemed capable of checking the growing might of Athens, if Syracuse once could be hers.

The national historian of Rome has left us, as an episode of his great work, a disquisition on the probable effects that would have followed, if Alexander the Great had invaded Italy. Posterity has generally regarded that disquisition as proving Livy's patriotism more strongly than his impartiality or acuteness. Yet, right or wrong, the speculations of the Roman writer were directed to the consideration of a very remote possibility. To whatever age Alexander's life might have been prolonged, the East would have furnished full occupation for his martial ambition, as well as for those schemes of commercial grandeur and imperial amalgamation of nations, in which the truly great qualities of his mind loved to display themselves.

With his death the dismemberment of his empire among his generals was certain, even as the dismemberment of Napoleon's empire among his marshals would certainly have ensued, if he had been cut off in the zenith of his power. Rome, also, was far weaker when the Athenians were in Sicily, than she was a century afterwards, in Alexander's time. There can be little doubt but that Rome would have been blotted out from the independent powers of the West, had she been attacked at the end of the fifth century B.C., by an Athenian army, largely aided by Spanish mercenaries, and flushed with triumphs over Sicily and Africa; instead of the collision between her and Greece having been deferred until the latter had sunk into decrepitude, and the Roman Mars had grown into full vigour.

The armament which the Athenians equipped against Syracuse was in every way worthy of the state which formed such projects of universal empire; and it has been truly termed "the noblest that ever yet had been sent forth by a free and civilized commonwealth." (Arnold's *History of Rome.*) The fleet consisted of one hundred and thirty-four war galleys, with a multitude of store ships. A powerful force of the best heavy-armed infantry that Athens and her allies could furnish was sent on board, together with a smaller number of slingers and bowmen. The quality of the forces was even more remarkable than the number. The zeal of individuals vied with that of the republic in giving every galley the best possible crew, and every troop the most perfect accoutrements. And with private as well as public wealth eagerly lavished on all that could give splendour as well as efficiency to the expedition, the fated fleet began its voyage for the Sicilian shores in the summer of 415 B.C.

The Syracusans themselves, at the time of the Peloponnesian war, were a bold and turbulent democracy, tyrannizing over the weaker Greek cities in Sicily, and trying to gain in that island the same arbitrary supremacy which Athens maintained along the eastern coast of the Mediterranean. In numbers and in spirit they were fully equal to the Athenians, but far inferior to them in military and naval discipline. When the probability of an Athenian invasion was first publicly discussed at Syracuse, and efforts were made by some of the wiser citizens to improve the state of the national defences, and prepare for the impending danger, the rumours of coming war and the proposals for preparation were received by the mass of the Syracusans with scornful incredulity.

The speech of one of their popular orators is preserved to us in Thucydides, and many of its topics might, by a slight alteration of names and details, serve admirably for the party among ourselves at present which opposes the augmentation of our forces, and derides the idea of our being in any peril from the sudden attack of a French expedition. The Syracusan orator told his countrymen to dismiss with scorn the visionary terrors which a set of designing men among themselves strove to excite, in order to get power and influence thrown into their own hands. He told them that Athens knew her own interest too well to think of wantonly provoking their hostility:—

> Even if the enemies were to come, so distant from their resources, and opposed to such a power as ours, their destruction would be easy and inevitable. Their ships will have enough to do to get to our island at all, and to carry such stores of all sorts as will be needed. They cannot therefore carry, besides, an army large enough to cope with such a population as ours. They will have no fortified place from which to commence their operations; but must rest them on no better base than a set of wretched tents, and such means as the necessities of the moment will allow them. But in truth I do not believe that they would even be able to effect a disembarkation. Let us, therefore, set at nought these reports as altogether of home manufacture; and be sure that if any enemy does come, the state will know how to defend itself in a manner worthy of the national honour.

Such assertions pleased the Syracusan assembly; and their counterparts find favour now among some portion of the English public. But the invaders of Syracuse came; made good their landing in Sicily; and, if they had promptly attacked the city itself, instead of wasting nearly a year in desultory operations in other parts of the island, the Syracusans must have paid the penalty of their self-sufficient carelessness in submission to the Athenian yoke. But, of the three generals who led the Athenian expedition, two only were men of ability, and one was most weak and incompetent. Fortunately for Syracuse, Alcibiades, the most skilful of the three, was soon deposed from his command by a factious and fanatic vote of his fellow-countrymen, and the other competent one, Lamachus, fell early in a skirmish: while, more fortunately still for her, the feeble and vacillating Nicias remained unrecalled and unhurt, to assume the undivided leadership of the Athenian army and fleet, and to mar, by alternate over-caution and over-carelessness, every chance of success which the early part of the operations offered.

Still, even under him, the Athenians nearly won the town. They defeated the raw levies of the Syracusans, cooped them within the walls, and, as before mentioned, almost effected a continuous fortification from bay to bay over Epipolae, the completion of which would certainly have been followed by capitulation.

Alcibiades, the most complete example of genius without principle that history produces, the Bolingbroke of antiquity, but with high military talents superadded to diplomatic and oratorical powers, on being summoned home from his command in Sicily to take his trial before the Athenian tribunal had escaped to Sparta; and he exerted himself there with all the selfish rancour of a renegade to renew the war with Athens, and to send instant assistance to Syracuse.

When we read his words in the pages of Thucydides (who was himself an exile from Athens at this period, and may probably have been at Sparta, and heard Alcibiades speak), we are at loss whether most to admire or abhor his subtile and traitorous counsels. After an artful exordium, in which he tried to disarm the suspicions which he felt must be entertained of him, and to point out to the Spartans how completely his interests and theirs were identified, through hatred of the Athenian democracy, he thus proceeded:—

> Hear me, at any rate, on the matters which require your grave attention, and which I, from the personal knowledge that I have of them, can and ought to bring before you. We Athenians sailed to Sicily with the design of subduing, first the Greek cities there, and next those in Italy. Then we intended to make an attempt on the dominions of Carthage, and on Carthage itself.[1] If all these projects succeeded (nor did we limit ourselves to them in these quarters), we intended to increase our fleet with the inexhaustible supplies of ship timber which Italy affords, to

1. Arnold, in his notes on this passage, well reminds the reader that Agathocles, with a Greek force far inferior to that of the Athenians at this period, did, a century afterwards, very nearly conquer Carthage.

put in requisition the whole military force of the conquered Greek states, and also to hire large armies of the barbarians; of the Iberians, and others in those regions, who are allowed to make the best possible soldiers. [2]

Then, when we had done all this, we intended to assail Peloponnesus with our collected force. Our fleets would blockade you by sea, and desolate your coasts; our armies would be landed at different points, and assail your cities. Some of these we expected to storm and others we meant to take by surrounding them with fortified lines.[3] We thought that it would thus be an easy matter thoroughly to war you down; and then we should become the masters of the whole Greek race. As for expense, we reckoned that each conquered state would give us supplies of money and provisions sufficient to pay for its own conquest, and furnish the means for the conquest of its neighbours.

Such are the designs of the present Athenian expedition to Sicily, and you have heard them from the lips of the man who, of all men living, is most accurately acquainted with them. The other Athenian generals, who remain with the expedition, will endeavour to carry out these plans.

And be sure that without your speedy interference they will all be accomplished. The Sicilian Greeks are deficient in military training; but still if they could be at once brought to combine in an organised resistance to Athens, they might even now be saved. But as for the Syracusans resisting Athens by themselves, they have already with the whole strength of their population fought a battle and been beaten; they cannot face the Athenians at sea; and it is quite impossible for them to hold out against the force of their invaders. And if this city falls into the hands of the Athenians, all Sicily is theirs, and presently Italy also: and the danger which I warned you of from that quarter will soon fall upon yourselves. You must, therefore, in Sicily fight for the safety of Peloponnesus. Send some galleys thither instantly. Put

---

2. It will be remembered that Spanish infantry were the staple of the Carthaginian armies. Doubtless Alcibiades and other leading Athenians had made themselves acquainted with the Carthaginian system of carrying on war, and meant to adopt it. With the marvellous powers which Alcibiades possessed of ingratiating himself with men of every class and every nation, and his high military genius, he would have been as formidable a chief of an army of *condottieri* as Hannibal afterwards was.

3. Alcibiades here alluded to Sparta itself, which was unfortified. His Spartan hearers must have glanced round them at these words, with mixed alarm and indignation.

men on board who can work their own way over, and who, as soon as they land, can do duty as regular troops.

But above all, let one of yourselves, let a man of Sparta, go over to take the chief command, to bring into order and effective discipline the forces that are in Syracuse, and urge those, who at present hang back to come forward and aid the Syracusans. The presence of a Spartan general at this crisis will do more to save the city than a whole army.

The renegade then proceeded to urge on them the necessity of encouraging their friends in Sicily, by showing that they themselves were earnest in hostility to Athens. He exhorted them not only to march their armies into Attica again, but to take up a permanent fortified position in the country: and he gave them in detail information of all that the Athenians most dreaded, and how his country might receive the most distressing and enduring injury at their hands.

The Spartans resolved to act on his advice, and appointed Gylippus to the Sicilian command. Gylippus was a man who, to the national bravery and military skill of a Spartan, united political sagacity that was worthy of his great fellow-countryman Brasidas; but his merits were debased by mean and sordid vice; and his is one of the cases in which history has been austerely just, and where little or no fame has been accorded to the successful but venal soldier. But for the purpose for which he was required in Sicily, an abler man could not have been found in Lacedaemon. His country gave him neither men nor money, but she gave him her authority; and the influence of her name and of his own talents was speedily seen in the zeal with which the Corinthians and other Peloponnesian Greeks began to equip a squadron to act under him for the rescue of Sicily.

As soon as four galleys were ready, he hurried over with them to the southern coast of Italy; and there, though he received such evil tidings of the state of Syracuse that he abandoned all hope of saving that city, he determined to remain on the coast, and do what he could in preserving the Italian cities from the Athenians.

So nearly, indeed, had Nicias completed his beleaguering lines, and so utterly desperate had the state of Syracuse seemingly become, that an assembly of the Syracusans was actually convened, and they were discussing the terms on which they should offer to capitulate, when a galley was seen dashing into the great harbour, and making her way towards the town with all the speed that her rowers could supply.

From her shunning the part of the harbour where the Athenian fleet lay, and making straight for the Syracusan side, it was clear that she was a friend; the enemy's cruisers, careless through confidence of success, made no attempt to cut her off; she touched the beach, and a Corinthian captain springing on shore from her, was eagerly conducted to the assembly of the Syracusan people, just in time to prevent the fatal vote being put for a surrender.

Providentially for Syracuse, Gongylus, the commander of the galley, had been prevented by an Athenian squadron from following Gylippus to South Italy, and he had been obliged to push direct for Syracuse from Greece.

The sight of actual succour, and the promise of more, revived the drooping spirits of the Syracusans. They felt that they were not left desolate to perish; and the tidings that a Spartan was coming to command them confirmed their resolution to continue their resistance. Gylippus was already near the city. He had learned at Locri that the first report which had reached him of the state of Syracuse was exaggerated; and that there was an unfinished space in the besiegers' lines through which it was barely possible to introduce reinforcements into the town. Crossing the straits of Messina, which the culpable negligence of Nicias had left unguarded, Gylippus landed on the northern coast of Sicily, and there began to collect from the Greek cities an army, of which the regular troops that he brought from Peloponnesus formed the nucleus.

Such was the influence of the name of Sparta, [4] and such were his own abilities and activity, that he succeeded in raising a force of about two thousand fully armed infantry, with a larger number of irregular troops. Nicias, as if infatuated, made no attempt to counteract his operations; nor, when Gylippus marched his little army towards Syracuse, did the Athenian commander endeavour to check him. The Syracusans marched out to meet him: and while the Athenians were solely intent on completing their fortifications on the southern side towards the harbour, Gylippus turned their position by occupying the high ground in the extreme rear of Epipolae. He then marched through the unfortified interval of Nicias's lines into the besieged town; and, joining his troops with the Syracusan forces, after some engagements with varying success, gained the mastery over Nicias, drove the Athenians

4. The effect of the presence of a Spartan officer on the troops of the other Greeks, seems to have been like the effect of the presence of an English officer upon native Indian troops.

from Epipolae, and hemmed them into a disadvantageous position in the low grounds near the great harbour.

The attention of all Greece was now fixed on Syracuse; and every enemy of Athens felt the importance of the opportunity now offered of checking her ambition, and, perhaps, of striking a deadly blow at her power. Large reinforcements from Corinth, Thebes, and other cities, now reached the Syracusans; while the baffled and dispirited Athenian general earnestly besought his countrymen to recall him, and represented the further prosecution of the siege as hopeless.

But Athens had made it a maxim never to let difficulty or disaster drive her back from any enterprise once undertaken, so long as she possessed the means of making any effort, however desperate, for its accomplishment. With indomitable pertinacity she now decreed, instead of recalling her first armament from before Syracuse, to send out a second, though her enemies near home had now renewed open warfare against her, and by occupying a permanent fortification in her territory, had severely distressed her population, and were pressing her with almost all the hardships of an actual siege. She still was mistress of the sea, and she sent forth another fleet of seventy galleys, and another army, which seemed to drain the very last reserves of her military population, to try if Syracuse could not yet be won, and the honour of the Athenian arms be preserved from the stigma of a retreat.

Hers was, indeed, a spirit that might be broken, but never would bend. At the head of this second expedition she wisely placed her best general Demosthenes, one of the most distinguished officers whom the long Peloponnesian war had produced, and who, if he had originally held the Sicilian command, would soon have brought Syracuse to submission.

The fame of Demosthenes the general, has been dimmed by the superior lustre of his great countryman, Demosthenes the orator. When the name of Demosthenes is mentioned, it is the latter alone that is thought of. The soldier has found no biographer. Yet out of the long list of the great men of the Athenian republic, there are few that deserve to stand higher than this brave, though finally unsuccessful, leader of her fleets and armies in the first half of the Peloponnesian war. In his first campaign in Ætolia he had shown some of the rashness of youth, and had received a lesson of caution, by which he profited throughout the rest of his career, but without losing any of his natural energy in enterprise or in execution. He had performed the eminent service of rescuing Naupactus from a powerful hostile armament in the seventh year of the war; he had then, at the request of the Acarnanian republics, taken on himself the office of commander-in-chief of all their forces, and at their head he had gained some important advantages over the enemies of Athens in Western Greece.

His most celebrated exploits had been the occupation of Pylos on the Messenian coast, the successful defence of that place against the fleet and armies of Lacedaemon, and the subsequent capture of the Spartan forces on the isle of Sphacteria; which was the severest blow dealt to Sparta throughout the war, and which had mainly caused her to humble herself to make the truce with Athens. Demosthenes was as honourably unknown in the war of party politics at Athens, as he was eminent in the war against the foreign enemy. We read of no intrigues of his on either the aristocratic or democratic side. He was neither in the interest of Nicias, nor of Cleon. His private character was free from any of the stains which polluted that of Alcibiades. On all these points the silence of the comic dramatist is decisive evidence in his favour. He had also the moral courage, not always combined with physical of seeking to do his duty to his country, irrespectively of any odium that he himself might incur, and unhampered by any petty jealousy of those who were associated with him in command. There are few men named in ancient history, of whom posterity would gladly know more, or whom we sympathise with more deeply in the calamities that befell them, than Demosthenes, the son of Alcisthenes, who, in the spring of the year 413 B.C., left Piraeus at the head of the second Athenian expedition against Sicily.

His arrival was critically timed; for Gylippus had encouraged the Syracusans to attack the Athenians under Nicias by sea as well as by land, and by an able stratagem of Ariston, one of the admirals of the Corinthian auxiliary squadron, the Syracusans and their confederates had inflicted on the fleet of Nicias the first defeat that the Athenian navy had ever sustained from a numerically inferior foe. Gylippus was preparing to follow up his advantage by fresh attacks on the Athenians on both elements, when the arrival of Demosthenes completely changed the aspect of affairs, and restored the superiority to the invaders. With seventy-three war-galleys in the highest state of efficiency, and brilliantly equipped, with a force of five thousand picked men of the regular infantry of Athens and her allies, and a still larger number of bowmen, javelin-men, and slingers on board, Demosthenes rowed round the great harbour with loud cheers and martial music, as if in defiance of the Syracusans and their confederates.

His arrival had indeed changed their newly-born hopes into the deepest consternation. The resources of Athens seemed inexhaustible, and resistance to her hopeless. They had been told that she was reduced to the last extremities, and that her territory was occupied by an enemy; and yet, here they saw her, as if in prodigality of power, sending forth, to make foreign conquests, a second armament, not inferior to that with which Nicias had first landed on the Sicilian shores.

With the intuitive decision of a great commander, Demosthenes at once saw that the possession of Epipolae was the key to the possession of Syracuse, and he resolved to make a prompt and vigorous attempt to recover that position, while his force was unimpaired, and the consternation which its arrival had produced among the besieged remained unabated. The Syracusans and their allies had run out an outwork along Epipolae from the city walls, intersecting the fortified lines of circumvallation which Nicias had commenced, but from which they had been driven by Gylippus.[5] Could Demosthenes succeed in storming this outwork, and in re-establishing the Athenian troops on the high ground, he might fairly hope to be able to resume the circumvallation of the city, and become the conqueror of Syracuse: for, when once the besiegers' lines were completed, the number of the troops with which Gylippus had garrisoned the place would only tend to exhaust the stores of provisions, and accelerate its downfall.

An easily-repelled attack was first made on the outwork in the daytime, probably more with the view of blinding the besieged to the nature of the main operations than with any expectation of succeeding in an open assault, with every disadvantage of the ground to contend against. But, when the darkness had set in, Demosthenes formed his men in columns, each soldier taking with him five days' provisions, and the engineers and workmen of the camp following the troops with their tools, and all portable implements of fortification, so as at once to secure any advantage of ground that the army might gain.

Thus equipped and prepared, he led his men along by the foot of the southern flank of Epipolae, in a direction towards the interior of the island, till he came immediately below the narrow ridge that forms the extremity of the high ground looking westward. He then wheeled his vanguard to the right, sent them rapidly up the paths that wind along the face of the cliff, and succeeded in completely surprising the Syracusan outposts, and in placing his troops fairly on the extreme summit of the all-important Epipolae. Thence the Athenians marched

5. See plan of the city of Syracuse.

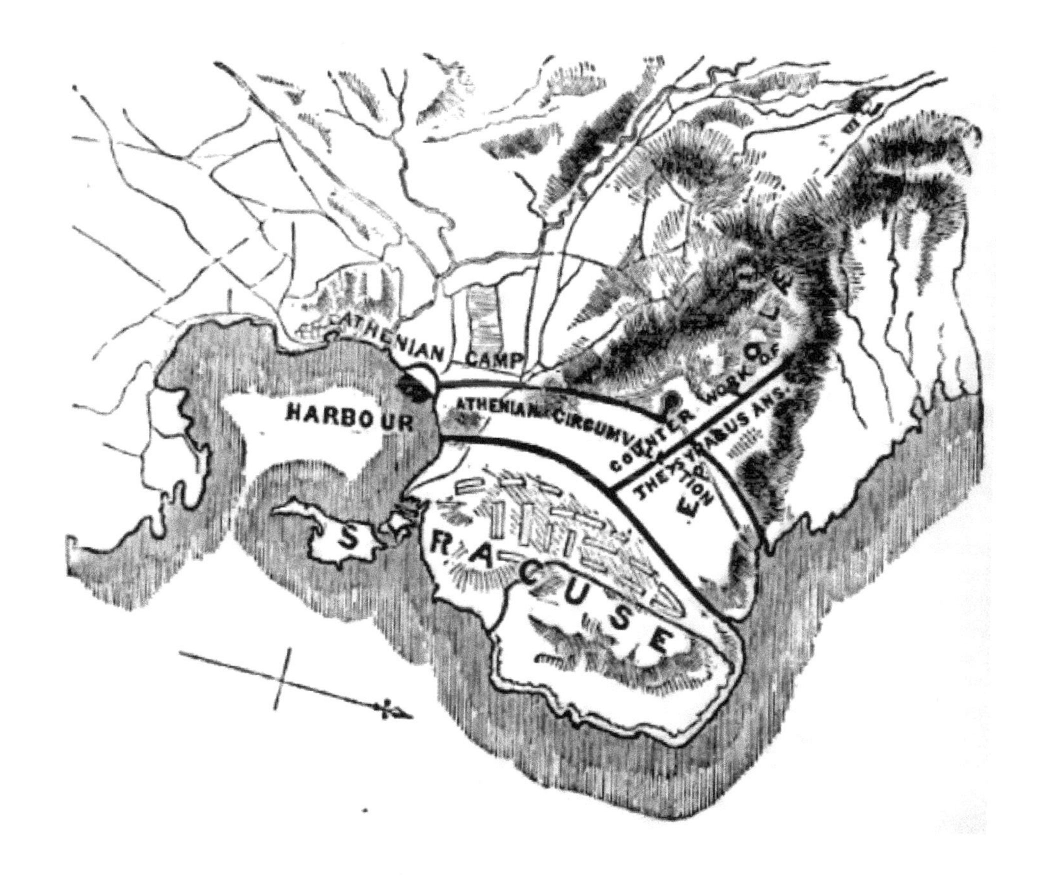

Plan of the City
of Syracuse

eagerly down the slope towards the town, routing some Syracusan detachments that were quartered in their way, and vigorously assailing the unprotected part of the outwork. All at first favoured them. The outwork was abandoned by its garrison, and the Athenian engineers began to dismantle it. In vain Gylippus brought up fresh troops to check the assault: the Athenians broke and drove them back, and continued to press hotly forward, in the full confidence of victory.

But, amid the general consternation of the Syracusans and their confederates, one body of infantry stood firm. This was a brigade of their Boeotian allies, which was posted low down the slope of Epipolae, outside the city walls. Coolly and steadily the Boeotian infantry formed their line, and, undismayed by the current of flight around them, advanced against the advancing Athenians. This was the crisis of the battle. But the Athenian van was disorganised by its own previous successes; and, yielding to the unexpected charge thus made on it by troops in perfect order, and of the most obstinate courage, it was driven back in confusion upon the other divisions of the army that still continued to press forward. When once the tide was thus turned, the Syracusans passed rapidly from the extreme of panic to the extreme of vengeful daring, and with all their forces they now fiercely assailed the embarrassed and receding Athenians.

In vain did the officers of the latter strive to re-form their line. Amid the din and the shouting of the fight, and the confusion inseparable upon a night engagement, especially one where many thousand combatants were pent and whirled together in a narrow and uneven area, the necessary manoeuvres were impracticable; and though many companies still fought on desperately, wherever the moonlight showed them the semblance of a foe, they fought without concert or subordination; and not unfrequently, amid the deadly chaos, Athenian troops assailed each other. Keeping their ranks close, the Syracusans and their allies pressed on against the disorganised masses of the besiegers; and at length drove them, with heavy slaughter, over the cliffs, which, scarce an hour before, they had scaled full of hope, and apparently certain of success.

This defeat was decisive of the event of the siege. The Athenians afterwards struggled only to protect themselves from the vengeance which the Syracusans sought to wreak in the complete destruction of their invaders. Never, however, was vengeance more complete and terrible. A series of sea-fights followed, in which the Athenian galleys were utterly destroyed or captured. The mariners and soldiers who escaped death in disastrous engagements, and in a vain attempt to force a retreat into the interior of the island, became prisoners of war. Nicias and Demosthenes were put to death in cold blood; and their men either perished miserably in the Syracusan dungeons, or were sold into slavery to the very persons whom, in their pride of power, they had crossed the seas to enslave.

All danger from Athens to the independent nations of the West was now for ever at an end. She, indeed, continued to struggle against her combined enemies and revolted allies with unparalleled gallantry; and many more years of varying warfare passed away before she surrendered to their arms. But no success in subsequent conquests could ever have restored her to the pre-eminence in enterprise, resources, and maritime skill which she had acquired before her fatal reverses in Sicily. Nor among the rival Greek republics, whom her own rashness aided to crush her, was there any capable of reorganizing her empire, or resuming her schemes of conquest. The dominion of Western Europe was left for Rome and Carthage to dispute two centuries later, in conflicts still more terrible, and with even higher displays of military daring and genius, than Athens had witnessed either in her rise, her meridian, or her fall.

Chapter 3

The Battle of Arbela, B.C. 331

A long and not uninstructive list might be made out of illustrious men, whose characters have been vindicated during recent times from aspersions which for centuries had been thrown on them. The spirit of modern inquiry, and the tendency of modern scholarship, both of which are often said to be solely negative and destructive, have, in truth, restored to splendour, and almost created anew, far more than they have assailed with censure, or dismissed from consideration as unreal. The truth of many a brilliant narrative of brilliant exploits has of late years been triumphantly demonstrated; and the shallowness of the sceptical scoffs with which little minds have carped at the great minds of antiquity, has been in many instances decisively exposed. The laws, the politics, and the lines of action adopted or recommended by eminent men and powerful nations have been examined with keener investigation, and considered with more comprehensive judgment, than formerly were brought to bear on these subjects. The result has been at least as often favourable as unfavourable to the persons and the states so scrutinized; and many an oft-repeated slander against both measures and men has thus been silenced, we may hope, for ever.

The veracity of Herodotus, the pure patriotism of Pericles, of Demosthenes, and of the Gracchi, the wisdom of Cleisthenes and of Licinius as constitutional reformers, may be mentioned as facts which recent writers have cleared from unjust suspicion and censure. And it might be easily shown that the defensive tendency which distinguishes the present and recent best historians of Germany, France, and England, has been equally manifested in the spirit in which they have treated the heroes of thought and the heroes of action who lived during what we term the Middle Ages and whom it was so long the fashion to sneer at or neglect.

The name of the victor of Arbela has led to these reflections; for, although the rapidity and extent of Alexander's conquests have through all ages challenged admiration and amazement, the grandeur of genius which he displayed in his schemes of commerce, civilization, and of comprehensive union and unity amongst nations, has, until lately, been comparatively unhonoured. This long-continued depreciation was of early date. The ancient rhetoricians—a class of babblers, a school for lies and scandal, as Niebuhr justly termed them—chose among the stock themes for their commonplaces, the character and exploits of Alexander. They had their followers in every age; and until a very recent period, all who wished to "point a moral or adorn a tale" about unreasoning ambition, extravagant pride, and the formidable frenzies of free will when leagued with free power, have never failed to blazon forth the so-called madman of Macedonia as one of the most glaring examples.

Without doubt, many of these writers adopted with implicit credence traditional ideas and supposed, with uninquiring philanthropy, that in blackening Alexander they were doing humanity good service. But also, without doubt, many of his assailants, like those of other great men, have been mainly instigated by "that strongest of all antipathies, the antipathy of a second-rate mind to a first-rate one," (De Stael.) and by the envy which talent too often bears to genius.

Arrian, who wrote his history of Alexander when Hadrian was emperor of the Roman world, and when the spirit of declamation and dogmatism was at its full height, but who was himself, unlike the dreaming pedants of the schools, a statesman and a soldier of practical and proved ability, well rebuked the malevolent aspersions which he heard continually thrown upon the memory of the great conqueror of the East. He truly says:

> Let the man who speaks evil of Alexander not merely bring forward those passages of Alexander's life which were really evil, but let him collect and review *all* the actions of Alexander, and then let him thoroughly consider first who and what manner of man he himself is, and what has been his own career; and then let him consider who and what manner of man Alexander was, and to what an eminence of human grandeur *he* arrived. Let him consider that Alexander was a king, and the undisputed lord of the two continents; and that his name is renowned throughout the whole earth. Let the evil-speaker against Al-

exander bear all this in mind, and then let him reflect on his own insignificance, the pettiness of his own circumstances and affairs, and the blunders that he makes about these, paltry and trifling as they are. Let him then ask himself whether he is a fit person to censure and revile such a man as Alexander. I believe that there was in his time no nation of men, no city, nay, no single individual, with whom Alexander's name had not become a familiar word. I therefore hold that such a man, who was like no ordinary mortal was not born into the world without some special providence.

And one of the most distinguished soldiers and writers of our own nation, Sir Walter Raleigh, though he failed to estimate justly the full merits of Alexander, has expressed his sense of the grandeur of the part played in the world by "The Great Emathian Conqueror" in language that well deserves quotation:—

> So much hath the spirit of some one man excelled as it hath undertaken and effected the alteration of the greatest states and commonwealths, the erection of monarchies, the conquest of kingdoms and empires, guided handfuls of men against multitudes of equal bodily strength, contrived victories beyond all hope and discourse of reason, converted the fearful passions of his own followers into magnanimity, and the valour of his enemies into cowardice; such spirits have been stirred up in sundry ages of the world, and in divers parts thereof, to erect and cast down again, to establish and to destroy, and to bring all things, persons, and states to the same certain ends, which the infinite spirit of the *Universal*, piercing, moving, and governing all things, hath ordained. Certainly, the things that this king did were marvellous, and would hardly have been undertaken by any one else: and though his father had determined to have invaded the Lesser Asia, it is like that he would have contented himself with some part thereof, and not have discovered the river of Indus, as this man did.—*The Historie of the World,* by Sir Walter Raleigh.

A higher authority than either Arrian or Raleigh may now be referred to by those who wish to know the real merit of Alexander as a general, and how far the commonplace assertions are true, that his successes were the mere results of fortunate rashness and unreasoning pugnacity, Napoleon selected Alexander as one of the seven greatest generals whose noble deeds history has handed down to us, and from the study of whose campaigns the principles of war are to be learned. The critique of the greatest conqueror of modern times on the military career of the great conqueror of the old world, is no less graphic than true.

> Alexander crossed the Dardanelles 334 B.C. with an army of about forty thousand men, of which one-eighth was cavalry; he forced the passage of the Granicus in opposition to an army under Memnon, the Greek, who commanded for Darius on the coast of Asia, and he spent the whole of the year 333 in establishing his power in Asia Minor. He was seconded by the Greek colonists, who dwelt on the borders of the Black Sea, and on the Mediterranean, and in Smyrna, Ephesus, Tarsus, Miletus, &c. The kings of Persia left their provinces and towns to be governed according to their own particular laws. Their empire was a union of confederated states, and did not form one nation; this facilitated its conquest. As Alexander only wished for the throne of the monarch, he easily effected the change, by respecting the customs, manners, and laws of the people, who experienced no change in their condition.
>
> In the year 332, he met with Darius at the head of sixty thousand men, who had taken up a position near Tarsus, on the banks of the Issus, in the province of Cilicia. He defeated him, entered Syria, took Damascus, which contained all the riches of the Great King, and laid siege to Tyre. This superb metropolis of the commerce of the world detained him nine months. He took Gaza after a siege of two months; crossed the Desert in seven days; entered Pelusium and Memphis, and founded Alexandria. In less than two years, after two battles and four or five sieges, the coasts of the Black Sea from Phasis to Byzantium, those of the Mediterranean as far as Alexandria, all Asia Minor, Syria, and Egypt, had submitted to his arms.
>
> In 331, he repassed the Desert, encamped in Tyre, recrossed Syria, entered Damascus, passed the Euphrates and Tigris, and defeated Darius on the field of Arbela, when he was at the head of a still stronger army than that which he commanded on the Issus, and Babylon opened her gates to him. In 330, he overran Susa, and took that city, Persepolis, and Pasargada, which contained the tomb of Cyrus. In 329, he directed his course

northward, entered Ecbatana, and extended his conquests to the coasts of the Caspian, punished Bessus, the cowardly assassin of Darius, penetrated into Scythia, and subdued the Scythians. In 328, he forced the passage of the Oxus, received sixteen thousand recruits from Macedonia, and reduced the neighbouring people to subjection.

In 327, he crossed the Indus, vanquished Poros in a pitched battle, took him prisoner, and treated him as a king. He contemplated passing the Ganges, but his army refused. He sailed down the Indus, in the year 326, with eight hundred vessels; having arrived at the ocean, he sent Nearchus with a fleet to run along the coasts of the Indian Ocean and the Persian Gulf, as far as the mouth of the Euphrates. In 325, he took sixty days in crossing from Gedrosia, entered Keramania, returned to Pasargada, Persepolis, and Susa, and married Statira, the daughter of Darius. In 324, he marched once more to the north, passed Ecbatana, and terminated his career at Babylon.—Count Montolon's *Memoirs of Napoleon.*

The enduring importance of Alexander's conquests is to be estimated not by the duration of his own life and empire, or even by the duration of the kingdoms which his generals after his death formed out of the fragments of that mighty dominion. In every region of the world that he traversed, Alexander planted Greek settlements, and founded cities, in the populations of which the Greek element at once asserted its predominance. Among his successors, the Seleucids and the Ptolemies imitated their great captain in blending schemes of civilization, of commercial intercourse, and of literary and scientific research with all their enterprises of military aggrandizement, and with all their systems of civil administration. Such was the ascendancy of the Greek genius, so wonderfully comprehensive and assimilating was the cultivation which it introduced, that, within thirty years after Alexander crossed the Hellespont, the language, the literature, and the arts of Hellas, enforced and promoted by the arms of semi-Hellenic Macedon, predominated in every country from the shores of that sea to the Indian waters.

Even sullen Egypt acknowledged the intellectual supremacy of Greece; and the language of Pericles and Plato became the language of the statesmen and the sages who dwelt in the mysterious land of the Pyramids and the Sphinx. It is not to be supposed that this victory of the Greek tongue was so complete as to exterminate the Coptic, the Syrian, the Armenian, the Persian, or the other native languages of the numerous nations and tribes between the Ægean, the Iaxertes, the Indus, and the Nile; they survived as provincial dialects. Each probably was in use as the vulgar tongue of its own district. But every person with the slightest pretence to education spoke Greek. Greek was universally the State language, and the exclusive language of all literature and science, It formed also for the merchant, the trader, and the traveller, as well as for the courtier, the government official, and the soldier, the organ of intercommunication among the myriads of mankind inhabiting these large portions of the Old World.[1]

Throughout Asia Minor, Syria, and Egypt, the Hellenic character that was thus imparted, remained in full vigour down to the time of the Mahometan conquests. The infinite value of this to humanity in the highest and holiest point of view has often been pointed out; and the workings of the finger of Providence have been gratefully recognised by those who have observed how the early growth and progress of Christianity were aided by that diffusion of the Greek language and civilization throughout Asia Minor, Syria, and Egypt which had been caused by the Macedonian conquest of the East.

In Upper Asia, beyond the Euphrates, the direct and material influence of Greek ascendancy was more short-lived. Yet, during the existence of the Hellenic kingdoms in these regions, especially of the Greek kingdom of Bactria, the modern Bokhara, very important effects were produced on the intellectual tendencies and tastes of the inhabitants of those countries and of the adjacent ones, by the animating contact of the Grecian spirit. Much of Hindoo science and philosophy, much of the literature of the later Persian kingdom of the Arsacidae, either originated from, or was largely modified by, Grecian influences. So, also, the learning and science of the Arabians were in a far less degree the result of original invention and genius, than the reproduction, in an altered form, of the Greek philosophy and the Greek lore, acquired by the Saracenic conquerors together with their acquisition of the provinces which Alexander had subjugated nearly a thousand years before the armed disciples of Mahomet commenced their career in the East.

It is well known that Western Europe in the Middle ages drew its philosophy, its arts, and its science, principally from Arabian teachers. And thus we see how the intellectual influence of ancient Greece,

1. See Arnold, *Hist. Rome*, ii.

poured on the Eastern world by Alexander's victories, and then brought back to bear on Mediaeval Europe by the spread of the Saracenic powers, has exerted its action on the elements of modern civilization by this powerful though indirect channel as well as by the more obvious effects of the remnants of classic civilization which survived in Italy, Gaul, Britain, and Spain, after the irruption of the Germanic nations.[2]

These considerations invest the Macedonian triumphs in the East with never-dying interest, such as the most showy and sanguinary successes of mere "low ambition and the pride of kings," however they may dazzle for a moment, can never retain with posterity. Whether the old Persian empire, which Cyrus founded, could have survived much longer than it did, even if Darius had been victorious at Arbela, may safely be disputed. That ancient dominion, like the Turkish at the present time, laboured under every cause of decay and dissolution. The *satraps*, like the modern *pachas*, continually rebelled against the central power, and Egypt, in particular, was almost always in a state of insurrection against its nominal sovereign.

There was no longer any effective central control, or any internal principle of unity fused through the huge mass of the empire, and binding it together. Persia was evidently about to fall; but, had it not been for Alexander's invasion of Asia, she would most probably have fallen beneath some other Oriental power, as Media and Babylon had formerly fallen before herself, and as, in after times, the Parthian supremacy gave way to the revived ascendancy of Persia in the East, under the sceptres of the Arsacidae. A revolution that merely substituted one Eastern power for another would have been utterly barren and unprofitable to mankind.

Alexander's victory at Arbela not only overthrew an Oriental dynasty, but established European rulers in its stead. It broke the monotony, of the Eastern world by the impression of Western energy and superior civilization; even as England's present mission is to break up the mental and moral stagnation of India and Cathay, by pouring upon and through them the impulsive current of Anglo-Saxon commerce and conquest.

Arbela, the city which has furnished its name to the decisive battle that gave Asia to Alexander, lies more than twenty miles from the actual scene of conflict. The little village then named Gaugamela is close to the spot where the armies met, but has ceded the honour of naming

2. See Humboldt's *Cosmos*.

the battle to its more euphonious neighbour. Gaugamela is situate in one of the wide plains that lie between the Tigris and the mountains of Kurdistan. A few undulating hillocks diversify the surface of this sandy track; but the ground is generally level, and admirably qualified for the evolutions of cavalry, and also calculated to give the larger of two armies the full advantage of numerical superiority. The Persian King (who before he came to the throne, had proved his personal valour as a soldier, and his skill as a general) had wisely selected this region for the third and decisive encounter between his forces and the invaders. The previous defeats of his troops, however severe they had been, were not looked on as irreparable.

The Granicus had been fought by his generals rashly and without mutual concert. And, though Darius himself had commanded and been beaten at Issus, that defeat might be attributed to the disadvantageous nature of the ground; where, cooped up between the mountains, the river, and the sea, the numbers of the Persians confused and clogged alike the general's skill and the soldiers' prowess, so that their very strength became their weakness. Here, on the broad plains of Kurdistan, there was scope for Asia's largest host to array its lines, to wheel, to skirmish, to condense or expand its squadrons, to manoeuvre, and to charge at will. Should Alexander and his scanty band dare to plunge into that living sea of war, their destruction seemed inevitable.

Darius felt, however, the critical nature to himself as well as to his adversary of the coming encounter. He could not hope to retrieve the consequences of a third overthrow. The great cities of Mesopotamia and Upper Asia, the central provinces of the Persian empire, were certain to be at the mercy of the victor. Darius knew also the Asiatic character well enough to be aware how it yields to the prestige of success, and the apparent career of destiny. He felt that the diadem was now either to be firmly replaced on his own brow, or to be irrevocably transferred to the head of his European conqueror. He, therefore, during the long interval left him after the battle of Issus, while Alexander was subjugating Syria and Egypt, assiduously busied himself in selecting the best troops which his vast empire supplied, and in training his varied forces to act together with some uniformity of discipline and system.

The hardy mountaineers of Affghanistan, Bokhara, Khiva, and Thibet, were then, as at present, far different from the generality of Asiatics in warlike spirit and endurance. From these districts Darius collected large bodies of admirable infantry; and the countries of the modern

Kurds and Turkomans supplied, as they do now, squadrons of horsemen, strong, skilful, bold, and trained to a life of constant activity and warfare. It is not uninteresting to notice that the ancestors of our own late enemies, the Sikhs, served as allies of Darius against the Macedonians. They are spoken of in Arrian as Indians who dwelt near Bactria. They were attached to the troops of that satrapy, and their cavalry was one of the most formidable forces in the whole Persian army.

Besides these picked troops, contingents also came in from the numerous other provinces that yet obeyed the Great King. Altogether, the horse are said to have been forty thousand, the scythe-bearing chariots two hundred, and the armed elephants fifteen in number. The amount of the infantry is uncertain; but the knowledge which both ancient and modern times supply of the usual character of Oriental armies, and of their populations of camp-followers, may warrant us in believing that many myriads were prepared to fight, or to encumber those who fought, for the last Darius.

The position of the Persian king near Mesopotamia was chosen with great military skill. It was certain that Alexander on his return from Egypt must march northward along the Syrian coast, before he attacked the central provinces of the Persian empire. A direct eastward march from the lower part of Palestine across the great Syrian Desert was then, as now, utterly impracticable. Marching eastward from Syria, Alexander would, on crossing the Euphrates, arrive at the vast Mesopotamian plains. The wealthy capitals of the empire, Babylon, Susa, and Persepolis, would then lie to his south; and if he marched down through Mesopotamia to attack them, Darius might reasonably hope to follow the Macedonians with his immense force of cavalry, and, without even risking a pitched battle, to harass and finally overwhelm them.

We may remember that three centuries afterwards a Roman army under Crassus was thus actually destroyed by the Oriental archers and horsemen in these very plains; and that the ancestors of the Parthians who thus vanquished the Roman legions, served by thousands under King Darius. If, on the contrary, Alexander should defer his march against Babylon, and first seek an encounter with the Persian army, the country on each side of the Tigris in this latitude was highly advantageous for such an army as Darius commanded; and he had close in his rear the mountainous districts of Northern Media, where he himself had in early life been *satrap*, where he had acquired reputation as a soldier and a general, and where he justly expected to find loyalty to his person, and a safe refuge in case of defeat.

His great antagonist came on across the Euphrates against him, at the head of an army which Arrian, copying from the journals of Macedonian officers, states to have consisted of forty thousand foot, and seven thousand horse. In studying the campaigns of Alexander, we possess the peculiar advantage of deriving our information from two of Alexander's generals of division, who bore an important part in all his enterprises. Aristobulus and Ptolemy (who afterwards became king of Egypt) kept regular journals of the military events which they witnessed; and these journals were in the possession of Arrian, when he drew up his history of Alexander's expedition.

The high character of Arrian for integrity makes us confident that he used them fairly, and his comments on the occasional discrepancies between the two Macedonian narratives prove that he used them sensibly. He frequently quotes the very words of his authorities: and his history thus acquires a charm such as very few ancient or modern military narratives possess. The anecdotes and expressions which he records we fairly believe to be genuine, and not to be the coinage of a rhetorician, like those in Curtius. In fact, in reading Arrian, we read General Aristobulus and General Ptolemy on the campaigns of the Macedonians; and it is like reading General Jomini or General Foy on the campaigns of the French.

The estimate which we find in Arrian of the strength of Alexander's army, seems reasonable when we take into account both the losses which he had sustained, and the reinforcements which he had received since he left Europe. Indeed, to Englishmen, who know with what mere handfuls of men our own generals have, at Plassy, at Assaye, at Meeanee, and other Indian battles, routed large hosts of Asiatics, the disparity of numbers that we read of in the victories won by the Macedonians over the Persians presents nothing incredible. The army which Alexander now led was wholly composed of veteran troops in the highest possible state of equipment and discipline, enthusiastically devoted to their leader, and full of confidence in his military genius and his victorious destiny.

The celebrated Macedonian *phalanx* formed the main strength of his infantry. This force had been raised and organised by his father Philip, who on his accession to the Macedonian throne needed a numerous and quickly-formed army, and who, by lengthening the spear of the ordinary Greek *phalanx*, and increasing the depth of the files, brought the tactic of armed masses to the greatest efficiency of which it was capable with such materials as he possessed.[3] He formed his men sixteen deep, and placed in their grasp the *sarissa*, as the Macedonian pike was called, which was four-and-twenty feet in length, and when couched for action, reached eighteen feet in front of the soldier: so that, as a space of about two feet was allowed between the ranks, the spears of the five files behind him projected in advance of each front-rank man. The *phalangite* soldier was fully equipped in the defensive armour of the regular Greek infantry. And thus the *phalanx* presented a ponderous and bristling mass, which as long as its order was kept compact, was sure to bear down all opposition. The defects of such an organization are obvious, and were proved in after years, when the Macedonians were opposed to the Roman *legions*.

But it is clear that, under Alexander, the *phalanx* was not the cumbrous unwieldy body which it was at Cynoscephalae and Pydna. His men were veterans; and he could obtain from them an accuracy of movement and steadiness of evolution, such as probably the recruits of his father would only have floundered in attempting, and such as certainly were impracticable in the phalanx when handled by his successors: especially as under them it ceased to be a standing force, and became only a militia. Under Alexander the *phalanx* consisted of an aggregate of eighteen thousand men, who were divided into six brigades of three thousand each.

These were again subdivided into regiments and companies; and the men were carefully trained to wheel, to face about, to take more ground, or to close up, as the emergencies of the battle required. Alexander also arrayed in the intervals of the regiments of his *phalangites*, troops armed in a different manner, which could prevent their line from being pierced, and their companies taken in flank, when the nature of the ground prevented a close formation; and which could be withdrawn, when a favourable opportunity arrived for closing up the phalanx or any of its brigades for a charge, or when it was necessary to prepare to receive cavalry.

Besides the *phalanx*, Alexander had a considerable force of infantry who were called shield-bearers: they were not so heavily armed as the *phalangites*, or as was the case with the Greek regular infantry in general; but they were equipped for close fight, as well as for skirmishing, and were far superior to the ordinary irregular troops of Greek warfare. They were about six thousand strong. Besides these, he had several bodies of Greek regular infantry; and he had archers, slingers, and

3. See Niebuhr's *Hist. of Rome*, iii.

javelin-men, who fought also with broadsword and target. These were principally supplied to him by the highlanders of Illyria and Thracia. The main strength of his cavalry consisted in two chosen corps of cuirassiers, one Macedonian, and one Thessalian each of which was about fifteen hundred strong. They were provided with long lances and heavy swords, and horse as well as man was fully equipped with defensive armour. Other regiments of regular cavalry were less heavily armed, and there were several bodies of light horsemen, whom Alexander's conquests in Egypt and Syria had enabled him to mount superbly.

A little before the end of August, Alexander crossed the Euphrates at Thapsacus, a small corps of Persian cavalry under Mazaeus retiring before him. Alexander was too prudent to march down through the Mesopotamian deserts, and continued to advance eastward with the intention of passing the Tigris, and then, if he was unable to find Darius and bring him to action, of marching southward on the left side of that river along the skirts of a mountainous district where his men would suffer less from heat and thirst, and where provisions would be more abundant.

Darius, finding that his adversary was not to be enticed into the march through Mesopotamia against his capital, determined to remain on the battle-ground which he had chosen on the left of the Tigris; where, if his enemy met a defeat or a check, the destruction of the invaders would be certain with two such rivers as the Euphrates and the Tigris in their rear. The Persian king availed himself to the utmost of every advantage in his power. He caused a large space of ground to be carefully levelled for the operation of his scythe-armed chariots; and he deposited his military stores in the strong town of Arbela, about twenty miles in his rear. The rhetoricians of after ages have loved to describe Darius Codomannus as a second Xerxes in ostentation and imbecility; but a fair examination of his generalship in this his last campaign, shows that he was worthy of bearing the same name as his great predecessor, the royal son of Hystaspes.

On learning that Darius was with a large army on the left of the Tigris, Alexander hurried forward and crossed that river without opposition. He was at first unable to procure any certain intelligence of the precise position of the enemy, and after giving his army a short interval of rest, he marched for four days down the left bank of the river. A moralist may pause upon the fact, that Alexander must in this march have passed within a few miles of the remains of Nineveh, the great, city of the primaeval conquerors of the human race. Neither the Macedonian king nor any of his followers knew what those vast mounds had once been. They had already become nameless masses of grass-grown ruins; and it is only within the last few years that the intellectual energy of one of our own countrymen has rescued Nineveh from its long centuries of oblivion.[4]

On the fourth day of Alexander's southward march, his advanced guard reported that a body of the enemy's cavalry was in sight. He instantly formed his army in order for battle, and directing them to advance steadily, he rode forward at the head of some squadrons of cavalry, and charged the Persian horse whom he found before him. This was a mere reconnoitring party, and they broke and fled immediately; but the Macedonians made some prisoners, and from them Alexander found that Darius was posted only a few miles off and learned the strength of the army that he had with him. On receiving this news, Alexander halted, and gave his men repose for four days, so that they should go into action fresh and vigorous. He also fortified his camp, and deposited in it all his military stores, and all his sick and disabled soldiers; intending to advance upon the enemy with the serviceable part of his army perfectly unencumbered.

After this halt, he moved forward, while it was yet dark, with the intention of reaching the enemy, and attacking them at break of day. About half-way between the camps there were some undulations of the ground, which concealed the two armies from each other's view. But, on Alexander arriving at their summit, he saw by the early light the Persian host arrayed before him; and he probably also observed traces of some engineering operation having been carried on along part of the ground in front of them. Not knowing that these marks had been caused by the Persians having levelled the ground for the free use of their war-chariots, Alexander suspected that hidden pitfalls had been prepared with a view of disordering the approach of his cavalry. He summoned a council of war forthwith, some of the officers were for attacking instantly at all hazards, but the more prudent opinion of Parmenio prevailed, and it was determined not to advance farther till the battle-ground had been carefully surveyed.

Alexander halted his army on the heights; and taking with him some light-armed infantry and some cavalry, he passed part of the day in reconnoitring the enemy, and observing the nature of the ground which he had to fight on. Darius wisely refrained from moving from

4. See Layard's *Nineveh*, and also Vaux's *Nineveh and Persepolis*.

his position to attack the Macedonians on eminences which they occupied, and the two armies remained until night without molesting each other. On Alexander's return to his headquarters, he summoned his generals and superior officers together, and telling them that he well knew that *their* zeal wanted no exhortation, he besought them to do their utmost in encouraging and instructing those whom each commanded, to do their best in the next day's battle. They were to remind them that they were now not going to fight for a province, as they had hitherto fought, but they were about to decide by their swords the dominion of all Asia.

Each officer ought to impress this upon his subalterns and they should urge it on their men. Their natural courage required no long words to excite its ardour: but they should be reminded of the paramount importance of steadiness in action. The silence in the ranks must be unbroken as long as silence was proper; but when the time came for the charge, the shout and the cheer must be full of terror for the foe. The officers were to be alert in receiving and communicating orders; and every one was to act as if he felt that the whole result of the battle depended on his own single good conduct.

Having thus briefly instructed his generals, Alexander ordered that the army should sup, and take their rest for the night.

Darkness had closed over the tents of the Macedonians, when Alexander's veteran general, Parmenio, came to him, and proposed that they should make a night attack on the Persians. The King is said to have answered, that he scorned to such a victory, and that Alexander must conquer openly and fairly. Arrian justly remarks that Alexander's resolution was as wise as it was spirited. Besides the confusion and uncertainty which are inseparable from night engagements, the value of Alexander's victory would have been impaired, if gained under circumstances which might supply the enemy with any excuse for his defeat, and encourage him to renew the contest. It was necessary for Alexander not only to beat Darius, but to gain such a victory as should leave his rival without apology for defeat, and without hope of recovery.

The Persians, in fact, expected, and were prepared to meet a night attack. Such was the apprehension that Darius entertained of it, that he formed his troops at evening in order of battle, and kept them under arms all night. The effect of this was, that the morning found them jaded and dispirited, while it brought their adversaries all fresh and vigorous against them.

The written order of battle which Darius himself caused to be drawn up, fell into the hands of the Macedonians after the engagement, and Aristobulus copied it into his journal. We thus possess, through Arrian, unusually authentic information as to the composition and arrangement of the Persian Army. On the extreme left were the Bactrian, Daan, and Arachosian cavalry. Next to these Darius placed the troops from Persia proper, both horse and foot. Then came the Susians, and next to these the Cadusians. These forces made up the left wing. Darius's own station was in the centre. This was composed of the Indians, the Carians, the Mardian archers, and the division of Persians who were distinguished by the golden apples that formed knobs of their spears. Here also were stationed the body-guard of the Persian nobility.

Besides these, there were in the centre, formed in deep order, the Uxian and Babylonian troops, and the soldiers from the Red Sea. The brigade of Greek mercenaries, whom Darius had in his service, and who were alone considered fit to stand in the charge of the Macedonian *phalanx*, was drawn up on either side of the royal chariot. The right wing was composed of the Coelosyrians and Mesopotamians, the Medes, the Parthians, the Sacians, the Tapurians, Hyrcanians, Albanians, and Sacesinae. In advance of the line on the left wing were placed the Scythian cavalry, with a thousand of the Bactrian horse, and a hundred scythe-armed chariots. The elephants and fifty scythe-armed chariots were ranged in front of the centre; and fifty more chariots, with the Armenian and Cappadocian cavalry, were drawn up in advance of the right wing.

Thus arrayed, the great host of King Darius passed the night, that to many thousands of them was the last of their existence. The morning of the first of October, two thousand one hundred and eighty-two years ago, dawned slowly to their wearied watching, and they could hear the note of the Macedonian trumpet sounding to arms, and could see King Alexander's forces descend from their tents on the heights, and form in order of battle on the plain.[5]

There was deep need of skill, as well as of valour, on Alexander's side; and few battlefields have witnessed more consummate generalship than was now displayed by the Macedonian king. There were no natural barriers by which he could protect his flanks; and not only was he certain to be overlapped on either wing by the vast lines of the Per-

5. See Clinton's *Fasti Hellenici*. The battle was fought eleven days after an eclipse of the moon, which gives the means of fixing the precise date.

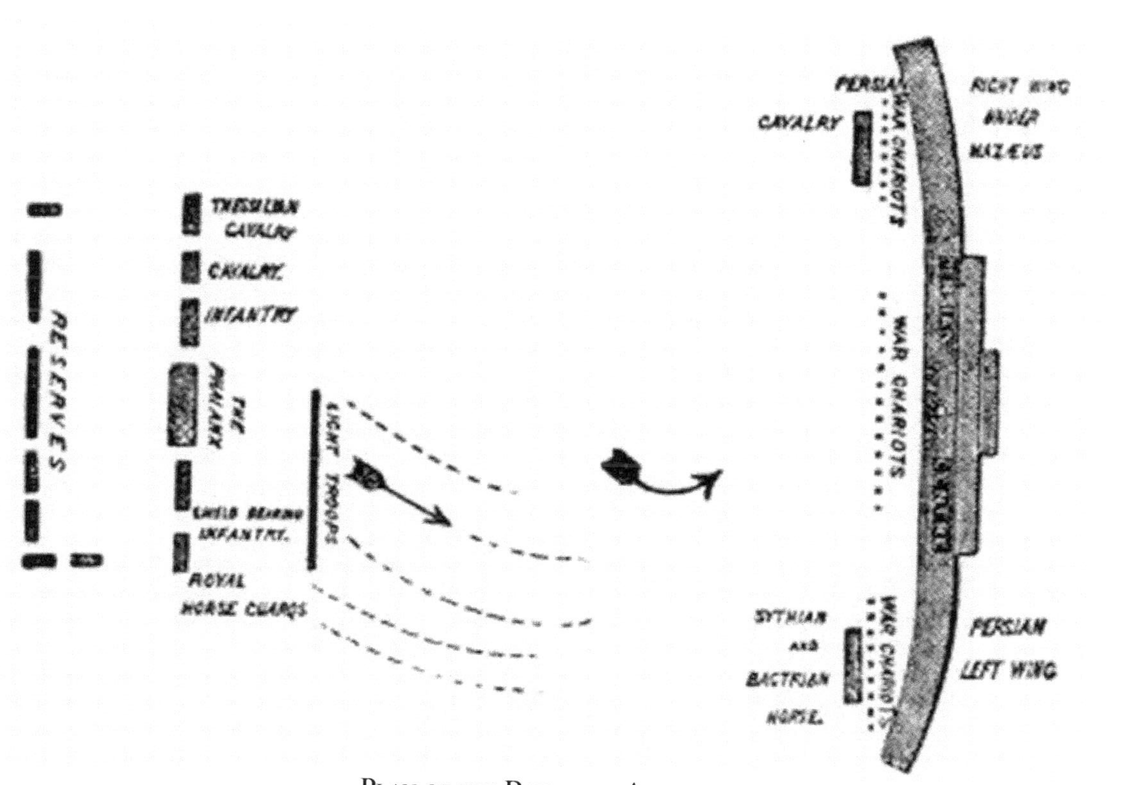

Plan of the Battle of Arbela

sian army, but there was imminent risk of their circling round him and charging him in the rear, while he advanced against their centre. He formed, therefore, a second or reserve line, which was to wheel round, if required, or to detach troops to either flank; as the enemy's movements might necessitate: and thus, with their whole army ready at any moment to be thrown into one vast hollow square, the Macedonians advanced in two lines against the enemy, Alexander himself leading on the right wing, and the renowned phalanx forming the centre, while Parmenio commanded on the left.

Such was the general nature of the disposition which Alexander made of his army. But we have in Arrian the details of the position of each brigade and regiment; and as we know that these details were taken from the journals of Macedonian generals, it is interesting to examine them, and to read the names and stations of King Alexander's generals and colonels in this the greatest of his battles.

The eight troops of the royal horse-guards formed the right of Alexander's line. Their captains were Cleitus (whose regiment was on the extreme right, the post of peculiar danger), Graucias, Ariston, Sopolis, Heracleides, Demetrias, Meleager, and Hegelochus. Philotas was general of the whole division. Then came the shield-bearing infantry: Nicanor was their general. Then came the *phalanx*, in six brigades. Coenus's brigade was on the right, and nearest to the shield-bearers; next to this stood the brigade of Perdiccas, then Meleager's, then Polysperchon's; and then the brigade of Amynias, but which was now commanded by Simmias, as Amynias had been sent to Macedonia to levy recruits. Then came the infantry of the left wing, under the command of Craterus. Next to Craterus's infantry were placed the cavalry regiments of the allies, with Eriguius for their general. The Messalian cavalry, commanded by Philippus, were next, and held the extreme left of the whole army. The whole left wing was entrusted to the command of Parmenio, who had round his person the Pharsalian troop of cavalry, which was the strongest and best amid all the Thessalian horse-regiments.

The centre of the second line was occupied by a body of *phalangite* infantry, formed of companies, which were drafted for this purpose from each of the brigades of their *phalanx*. The officers in command of this corps were ordered to be ready to face about, if the enemy should succeed in gaining the rear of the army. On the right of this reserve of infantry, in the second line, and behind the royal horse-guards, Alexander placed half the Agrian light-armed infantry under Attalus, and with them Brison's body of Macedonian archers, and Cleander's regiment of foot. He also placed in this part of his army Menidas's squadron of cavalry, and Aretes's and Ariston's light horse. Menidas was ordered to watch if the enemy's cavalry tried to turn the flank, and if they did so, to charge them before they wheeled completely round, and so take them in flank themselves.

A similar force was arranged on the left of the second line for the same purpose, The Thracian infantry of Sitalces was placed there, and Coeranus's regiment of the cavalry of the Greek allies, and Agathon's troops of the Odrysian irregular horse. The extreme left of the second line in this quarter was held by Andromachus's cavalry. A division of Thracian infantry was left in guard of the camp. In advance of the right wing and centre was scattered a number of light-armed troops, of javelin-men and bowmen, with the intention of warding off the charge of the armed chariots.[6]

Conspicuous by the brilliancy of his armour, and by the chosen band of officers who were round his person, Alexander took his own station, as his custom was, in the right wing, at the head of his cavalry: and when all the arrangements for the battle were complete, and his generals were fully instructed how to act in each probable emergency, he began to lead his men towards the enemy.

It was ever his custom to expose his life freely in battle, and to emulate the personal prowess of his great ancestor, Achilles. Perhaps in the bold enterprise of conquering Persia, it was politic for Alexander to raise his army's daring to the utmost by the example of his own heroic valour: and, in his subsequent campaigns, the love of the excitement, of "the rapture of the strife," may have made him, like Murat, continue from choice a custom which he commenced from duty. But he never suffered the ardour of the soldier to make him lose the coolness of the general; and at Arbela, in particular, he showed that he could act up to his favourite Homeric maxim.

Great reliance had been placed by the Persian king on the effects of the scythe-bearing chariots. It was designed to launch these against the Macedonian *phalanx*, and to follow them up by a heavy charge of cavalry, which it was hoped would find the ranks of the spearmen disordered by the rush of the chariots, and easily destroy this most

---

6. Kleber's arrangement of his troops at the Battle of Heliopolis, where, with ten thousand Europeans, he had to encounter eighty thousand Asiatics in an open plain, is worth comparing with Alexander's tactics at Arbela. See Thiers's *Histoire du Consulat*, &c. vol. ii. *livre* v.

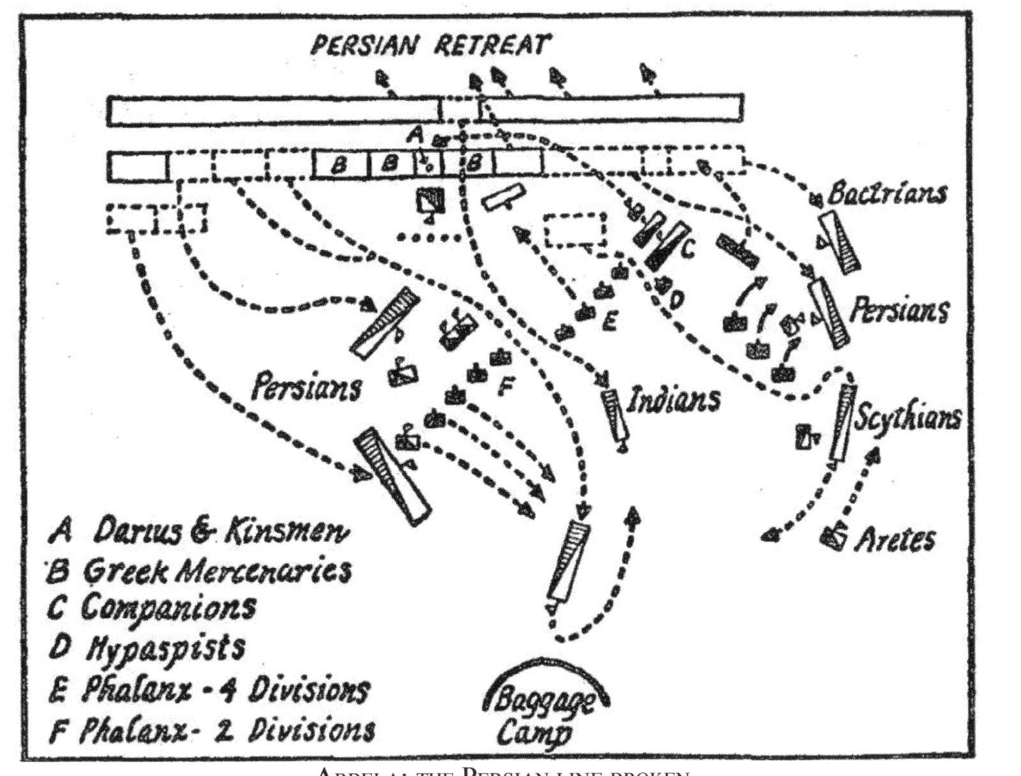

ARBELA; THE PERSIAN LINE BROKEN

formidable part of Alexander's force. In front, therefore, of the Persian centre, where Darius took his station, and which it was supposed the phalanx would attack, the ground had been carefully levelled and smoothed, so as to allow the chariots to charge over it with their full sweep and speed.

As the Macedonian Army approached the Persian, Alexander found that the front of his whole line barely equalled the front of the Persian centre, so that he was outflanked on his right by the entire left; wing of the enemy, and by their entire right wing on his left. His tactics were to assail some one point of the hostile army, and gain a decisive advantage; while he refused, as far as possible, the encounter along the rest of the line. He therefore inclined his order of march to the right so as to enable his right wing and centre to come into collision with the enemy on as favourable terms as possible though the manoeuvre might in some respects compromise his left.

The effect of this oblique movement was to bring the phalanx and his own wing nearly beyond the limits of the ground which the Persians had prepared for the operations of the chariots; and Darius, fearing to lose the benefit of this arm against the most important parts of the Macedonian force, ordered the Scythian and Bactrian cavalry, who were drawn up on his extreme left, to charge round upon Alexander's right wing, and check its further lateral progress. Against these assailants Alexander sent from his second line Menidas's cavalry. As these proved too few to make head against the enemy, he ordered Ariston also from the second line with his light horse, and Cleander with his foot, in support of Menidas.

The Bactrians and Scythians now began to give way, but Darius reinforced them by the mass of Bactrian cavalry from his main line, and an obstinate cavalry fight now took place. The Bactrians and Scythians were numerous, and were better armed than the horseman under Menidas and Ariston; and the loss at first was heaviest on the Macedonian side. But still the European cavalry stood the charge of the Asiatics, and at last, by their superior discipline, and by acting in squadrons that supported each other, instead of fighting in a confused mass like the barbarians, the Macedonians broke their adversaries, and drove them off the field. The best explanation of this may be found in Napoleon's account of the cavalry fights between the French and the Mamelukes:—

Two Mamelukes were able to make head against three French-

> men, because they were better armed, better mounted, and better trained; they had two pair of pistols, a blunderbuss, a carbine, a helmet with a vizor, and a coat of mail; they had several horses, and several attendants on foot. One hundred *cuirassiers*, however were not afraid of one hundred Mamelukes; three hundred could beat; an equal number, and one thousand could easily put to the rout fifteen hundred, so great is the influence of tactics, order, and evolutions! Leclerc and Lasalle presented their men to the Mamelukes in several lines. When the Arabs were on the point of overwhelming the first, the second came to its assistance on the right and left; the Mamelukes then halted and wheeled, in order to turn the wings of this new line; this moment was always seized upon to charge them, and they were uniformly broken.—Montholon's *History of the Captivity of Napoleon*, Iv.

Darius, now directed the scythe-armed chariots to be driven against Alexander's horse-guards and the *phalanx*; and these formidable vehicles were accordingly sent rattling across the plain, against the Macedonian line. When we remember the alarm which the war-chariots of the Britons created among Caesar's *legions*, we shall not be prone to deride this arm of ancient warfare as always useless. The object of the chariots was to create unsteadiness in the ranks against which they were driven, and squadrons of cavalry followed close upon them, to profit by such disorder. But the Asiatic chariots were rendered ineffective at Arbela by the light-armed troops whom Alexander had specially appointed for the service, and who, wounding the horses and drivers with their missile weapons, and running alongside so as to cut the traces or seize the reins, marred the intended charge; and the few chariots that reached the phalanx passed harmlessly through the intervals which the spearmen opened for them, and were easily captured in the rear.

A mass of the Asiatic cavalry was now, for the second time, collected against Alexander's extreme right, and moved round it, with the view of gaining the flank of his army. At the critical moment, Aretes, with his horsemen from Alexander's second line, dashed on the Persian squadrons when their own flanks were exposed by this evolution. While Alexander thus met and baffled all the flanking attacks of the enemy with troops brought up from his second line, he kept his own horse-guards and the rest of the front line of his wing fresh, and ready to take advantage of the first opportunity for striking a decisive blow. This soon came. A large body of horse, who were posted on the Persian left wing nearest to the centre, quitted their station, and rode off to help their comrades in the cavalry fight that still was going on at the extreme right of Alexander's wing against the detachments from his second line.

This made a huge gap in the Persian array, and into this space Alexander instantly dashed with his guard; and then pressing towards his left, he soon began to make havoc in the left flank of the Persian centre. The shield-bearing infantry now charged also among the reeling masses of the Asiatics; and five of the brigades of the phalanx, with the irresistible might of their *sarissas*, bore down the Greek mercenaries of Darius, and dug their way through the Persian centre. In the early part of the battle, Darius had showed skill and energy; and he now for some time encouraged his men, by voice and example, to keep firm. But the lances of Alexander's cavalry, and the pikes of the phalanx now gleamed nearer and nearer to him. His charioteer was struck down by a javelin at his side; and at last Darius's nerve failed him; and, descending from his chariot, he mounted on a fleet horse and galloped from the plain, regardless of the state of the battle in other parts of the field, where matters were going on much more favourably for his cause, and where his presence might have done much towards gaining a victory.

Alexander's operations with his right and centre had exposed his left to an immensely preponderating force of the enemy. Parmenio kept out of action as long as possible; but Mazaeus, who commanded the Persian right wing, advanced against him, completely outflanked him, and pressed him severely with reiterated charges by superior numbers. Seeing the distress of Parmenio's wing, Simmias, who commanded the sixth brigade of the *phalanx*, which was next to the left wing, did not advance with the other brigades in the great charge upon the Persian centre, but kept back to cover Parmenio's troops on their right flank; as otherwise they would have been completely surrounded and cut off from the rest of the Macedonian army. By so doing, Simmias had unavoidably opened a gap in the Macedonian left centre; and a large column of Indian and Persian horse, from the Persian right centre, had galloped forward through this interval, and right through the troops of the Macedonian second line.

Instead of then wheeling round upon Sarmenio, or upon the rear of Alexander's conquering wing, the Indian and Persian cavalry rode straight on to the Macedonian camp, overpowered the Thracians who were left in charge of it, and began to plunder. This was stopped by the *phalangite* troops of the second line, who, after the enemy's horsemen had rushed by them, faced about, countermarched upon the camp, killed many of the Indians and Persians in the act of plundering, and forced the rest to ride off again. Just at this crisis, Alexander had been recalled from his pursuit of Darius, by tidings of the distress of Parmenio, and of his inability to bear up any longer against the hot attacks of Mazaeus. Taking his horse-guards with him, Alexander rode towards the part of the field where his left wing was fighting; but on his way thither he encountered the Persian and Indian cavalry, on their return from his camp.

These men now saw that their only chance of safety was to cut their way through; and in one huge column they charged desperately upon the Macedonians. There was here a close hand-to-hand fight, which lasted some time, and sixty of the royal horse-guards fell, and three generals, who fought close to Alexander's side, were wounded. At length the Macedonian, discipline and valour again prevailed, and a large number of the Persian and Indian horsemen were cut down; some few only succeeded in breaking through and riding away. Relieved of these obstinate enemies, Alexander again formed his horse-guards, and led them towards Parmenio; but by this time that general also was victorious.

Probably the news of Darius's flight had reached Mazaeus, and had damped the ardour of the Persian right wing; while the tidings of their comrades' success must have proportionally encouraged the Macedonian forces under Parmenio. His Thessalian cavalry particularly distinguished themselves by their gallantry and persevering good conduct; and by the time that Alexander had ridden up to Parmenio, the whole Persian army was in full flight from the field.

It was of the deepest importance to Alexander to secure the person of Darius, and he now urged on the pursuit. The River Lycus was between the field of battle and the city of Arbela, whither the fugitives directed their course, and the passage of this river was even more destructive to the Persians than the swords and spears of the Macedonians had been in the engagement.[7]

The narrow bridge was soon choked up by the flying thousands who rushed towards it, and vast numbers of the Persians threw them-

---

7. I purposely omit any statement of the loss in the battle. There is a palpable error of the transcribers in the numbers which we find in our present manuscripts of Arrian; and Curtius is of no authority.

selves, or were hurried by others, into the rapid stream, and perished in its waters. Darius had crossed it, and had ridden on through Arbela without halting. Alexander reached that city on the next day, and made himself master of all Darius's treasure and stores; but the Persian king unfortunately for himself, had fled too fast for his conqueror: he had only escaped to perish by the treachery of his Bactrian satrap, Bessus.

A few days after the battle Alexander entered Babylon, "the oldest seat of earthly empire" then in existence, as its acknowledged lord and master. There were yet some campaigns of his brief and bright career to be accomplished. Central Asia was yet to witness the march of his phalanx. He was yet to effect that conquest of Affghanistan in which England since has failed. His generalship, as well as his valour, were yet to be signalised on the banks of the Hydaspes, and the field of Chillianwallah; and he was yet to precede the Queen of England in annexing the Punjaub to the dominions of an European sovereign. But the crisis of his career was reached; the great object of his mission was accomplished; and the ancient Persian empire, which once menaced all the nations of the earth with subjection, was irreparably crushed, when Alexander had won his crowning victory at Arbela.

CHAPTER 4

The Battle of the Metaurus, B.C. 207

About midway between Rimini and Ancona a little river falls into the Adriatic, after traversing one of those districts of Italy, in which a vain attempt has lately been made to revive, after long centuries of servitude and shame, the spirit of Italian nationality, and the energy of free institutions. That stream is still called the Metauro; and wakens by its name recollections of the resolute daring of ancient Rome, and of the slaughter that stained its current two thousand and sixty-three years ago, when the combined consular armies of Livius and Nero encountered and crushed near its banks the varied hosts which Hannibal's brother was leading from the Pyrenees, the Rhone, the Alps, and the Po, to aid the great Carthaginian in his stern struggle to annihilate the growing might of the Roman Republic, and make the Punic power supreme over all the nations of the world.

The Roman historian, Livy, who termed that struggle the most memorable of all wars that ever were carried on, wrote-in no spirit of exaggeration. For it is not in ancient but in modern history, that parallels for its incidents and its heroes are to be found. The similitude between the contest which Rome maintained against Hannibal, and that which England was for many years engaged in against Napoleon, has not passed unobserved by recent historians.

> Twice, has there been witnessed the struggle of the highest individual genius against the resources and institutions of a great nation; and in both cases the nation has been victorious. For seventeen years Hannibal strove against Rome; for sixteen years Napoleon Bonaparte strove against England; the efforts of the first ended in Zama, those of the second in Waterloo.—Arnold, Vol. iii; Alison—*Passim.*

One point, however, of the similitude between the two wars has scarcely been adequately dwelt on. That is, the remarkable parallel between the Roman general who finally defeated the great Carthaginian, and the English general who gave the last deadly overthrow to the French emperor. Scipio and Wellington both held for many years commands of high importance, but distant from the main theatres of warfare. The same country was the scene of the principal military career of each. It was in Spain that Scipio, like Wellington, successively encountered and overthrew nearly all the subordinate generals of the enemy, before being opposed to the chief champion and conqueror himself. Both Scipio and Wellington restored their countrymen's confidence in arms, when shaken by a series of reverses. And each of them closed a long and perilous war by a complete and overwhelming defeat of the chosen leader and the chosen veterans of the foe.

Nor is the parallel between them limited to their military characters and exploits. Scipio, like Wellington, became an important leader of the aristocratic party among his countrymen, and was exposed to the unmeasured invectives of the violent section of his political antagonists. When, early in the last reign, an infuriated mob assaulted the Duke of Wellington in the streets of the English capital on the anniversary of Waterloo, England was even more disgraced by that outrage, than Rome was by the factious accusations which demagogues brought against Scipio, but which he proudly repelled on the day of trial, by reminding the assembled people that it was the anniversary of the battle of Zama.

Happily, a wiser and a better spirit has now for years pervaded all classes of our community; and we shall be spared the ignominy of having worked out to the end the parallel of national ingratitude. Scipio died a voluntary exile from the malevolent turbulence of Rome. Englishmen of all ranks and politics have now long united in affectionate admiration of our modern Scipio: and even those who have most widely differed from the duke on legislative or administrative questions, forget what they deem the political errors of that time-honoured head, while they gratefully call to mind the laurels that have wreathed it.

Scipio at Zama trampled in the dust the power of Carthage; but that power had been already irreparably shattered in another field, where neither Scipio nor Hannibal commanded. When the Metaurus witnessed the defeat and death of Hasdrubal, it witnessed the ruin of the scheme by which alone Carthage could hope to organise decisive success,—the scheme of enveloping Rome at once from the north and the south of Italy by chosen armies, led by two sons of Hamilcar.[1] That battle was the determining crisis of the contest, not merely between Rome and Carthage, but between the two great families of the world, which then made Italy the arena of their oft-renewed contest for pre-eminence.

The French historian Michelet whose *Histoire Romaine* would have been invaluable, if the general industry and accuracy of the writer had in any degree equalled his originality and brilliancy, eloquently remarks: "It is not without reason that so universal and vivid a remembrance of the Punic wars has dwelt in the memories of men. They formed no mere struggle to determine the lot of two cities or two empires; but it was a strife on the event of which depended the fate of two races of mankind, whether the dominion of the world should belong to the Indo-Germanic or to the Semitic family of nations. Bear in mind, that the first of these comprises, besides the Indians and the Persians, the Greeks, the Romans, and the Germans. In the other are ranked the Jews and the Arabs, the Phoenicians and the Carthaginians.

On the one side is the genius of heroism, of art, and legislation: on the other is the spirit of industry, of commerce, of navigation. The two opposite races have everywhere come into contact, everywhere into hostility. In the primitive history of Persia and Chaldea, the heroes are perpetually engaged in combat with their industrious and perfidious, neighbours. The struggle is renewed between the Phoenicians and the Greeks on every coast of the Mediterranean. The Greek supplants the Phoenician in all his factories, all his colonies in the east: soon will the Roman come, and do likewise in the west. Alexander did far more against Tyre than Salmanasar or Nabuchodonosor had done. Not content with crushing her, he took care that she never should revive: for he founded Alexandria as her substitute, and changed for ever the track of commerce of the world. There remained Carthage—the great Carthage, and her mighty empire,—mighty in a far different degree than Phoenicia's had been. Rome annihilated it. Then occurred that which has no parallel in history,—an entire civilisation perished at one blow—vanished, like a falling star. The *Periplus* of Hanno, a few coins, a score of lines in Plautus, and, lo, all that remains of the Carthaginian world!

1. See Arnold, vol. 3.

Many generations must needs pass away before the struggle between the two races could be renewed; and the Arabs, that formidable rear-guard of the Semitic world, dashed forth from their deserts. The conflict between the two races then became the conflict of two religions. Fortunate was it that those daring Saracenic cavaliers encountered in the East the impregnable walls of Constantinople, in the West the chivalrous valour of Charles Martel and the sword of the Cid. The crusades were the natural reprisals for the Arab invasions, and form the last epoch of that great struggle between the two principal families of the human race.

It is difficult amid the glimmering light supplied by the allusions of the classical writers to gain a full idea of the character and institutions of Rome's great rival. But we can perceive how inferior Carthage was to her competitor in military resources; and how far less fitted than Rome she was to become the founder of centralized and centralizing dominion, that should endure for centuries, and fuse into imperial unity the narrow nationalities of the ancient races that dwelt around and near the shores of the Mediterranean Sea.

Carthage was originally neither the most ancient nor the most powerful of the numerous colonies which the Phoenicians planted on the coast of Northern Africa. But her advantageous position, the excellence of her constitution (of which, though ill-informed as to its details, we know that it commanded the admiration of Aristotle), and the commercial and political energy of her citizens, gave her the ascendancy over Hippo, Utica, Leptis, and her other sister Phoenician cities in those regions; and she finally seduced them to a condition of dependency, similar to that which the subject allies of Athens occupied relatively to that once imperial city. When Tyre and Sidon and the other cities of Phoenicia itself sank from independent republics into mere vassal states of the great Asiatic monarchies and obeyed by turns a Babylonian, a Persian, and a Macedonian master, their power and their traffic rapidly declined; and Carthage succeeded to the important maritime and commercial character which they had previously maintained.

The Carthaginians did not seek to compete with the Greeks on the north-eastern shores of the Mediterranean, or in the three inland seas which are connected with it; but they maintained an active intercourse with the Phoenicians, and through them with lower and

Central Asia; and they, and they alone, after the decline and fall of Tyre, navigated the waters of the Atlantic. They had the monopoly of all the commerce of the world that was carried on beyond the Straits of Gibraltar. We have yet extant (in a Greek translation) the narrative of the voyage of Hanno, one of their admirals, along the western coast of Africa as far as Sierra Leone. And in the Latin poem of Festus Avienus, frequent references are made to the records of the voyages of another celebrated Carthaginian admiral, Himilco, who had explored the north-western coast of Europe.

Our own islands are mentioned by Himilco as the lands of the Hiberni and the Albioni. It is indeed certain that the Carthaginians frequented the Cornish coast (as the Phoenicians had done before them) for the purpose of procuring tin; and there is every reason to believe that they sailed as far as the coasts of the Baltic for amber. When it is remembered that the mariner's compass was unknown in those ages, the boldness and skill of the seamen of Carthage, and the enterprise of her merchants, may be paralleled with any achievements that the history of modern navigation and commerce can supply.

In their Atlantic voyages along the African shores, the Carthaginians followed the double object of trade and colonization. The numerous settlements that were planted by them along the coast from Morocco to Senegal, provided for the needy members of the constantly-increasing population of a great commercial capital; and also strengthened the influence which Carthage exercised among the tribes of the African coast. Besides her fleets, her caravans gave her a large and lucrative trade with the native Africans; nor must we limit our belief of the extent of the Carthaginian trade with the tribes of Central and Western Africa, by the narrowness of the commercial intercourse which civilized nations of modern times have been able to create in those regions.

Although essentially a mercantile and seafaring people, the Carthaginians by no means neglected agriculture. On the contrary, the whole of their territory was cultivated like a garden. The fertility of the soil repaid the skill and toil bestowed on it; and every invader, from Agathocles to Scipio Æmilianus, was struck with admiration at the rich pasture-lands carefully irrigated, the abundant harvests, the luxuriant vineyards, the plantations of fig and olive-trees, the thriving villages, the populous towns, and the splendid villas of the wealthy Carthaginians, through which his march lay, as long as he was on Carthaginian ground.

The Carthaginians abandoned the Aegean and the Pontus to the Greeks, but they were by no means disposed to relinquish to those rivals the commerce and the dominion of the coasts of the Mediterranean westward of Italy. For centuries the Carthaginians strove to make themselves masters of the islands that lie between Italy and Spain. They acquired the Balearic islands, where the principal harbour, Port Mahon, still bears the name of the Carthaginian admiral. They succeeded in reducing the greater part of Sardinia; but Sicily could never be brought into their power. They repeatedly invaded that island, and nearly overran it; but the resistance which was opposed to them by the Syracusans under Gelon, Dionysius, Timoleon, and Agathocles, preserved the island from becoming Punic, though many of its cities remained under the Carthaginian rule, until Rome finally settled the question to whom Sicily was to belong, by conquering it for herself.

With so many elements of success, with almost unbounded wealth with commercial and maritime activity, with a fertile territory, with a capital city of almost impregnable strength, with a constitution that ensured for centuries the blessings of, social order, with an aristocracy singularly fertile in men of the highest genius, Carthage yet failed signally and calamitously in her contest for power with Rome. One of the immediate causes of this may seem to have been the want, of firmness among her citizens, which made them terminate the first Punic war by begging peace, sooner than endure any longer the hardships and burdens caused by a state of warfare, although their antagonists had suffered far more severely than themselves.

Another cause was the spirit of faction among their leading men, which prevented Hannibal in the second war from being properly reinforced and supported. But there were also more general causes why Carthage proved inferior to Rome. These were her position relatively to the mass of the inhabitants of the country which she ruled, and her habit of trusting to mercenary armies in her wars.

Our clearest information as to the different races of men in and about Carthage is derived from Diodorus Siculus. That historian enumerates four different races: first, he mentions the Phoenicians who dwelt in Carthage: next, he speaks of the Liby-Phoenicians; these, he tells us, dwelt in many of the maritime cities, and were connected by intermarriages with the Phoenicians, which was the cause of their compound name: thirdly, he mentions the Libyans, the bulk and the most ancient part of the population, hating the Carthaginians intensely, on account of the oppressiveness of their domination: lastly, he names the Numidians, the nomad tribes of the frontier.

It is evident, from this description, that the native Libyans were a subject class, without franchise or political rights; and, accordingly, we find no instance specified in history of a Libyan holding political office or military command. The half-castes, the Liby-Phoenicians, seem to have been sometimes sent out as colonists;[3] but it may be inferred, from what Diodorus says of their residence, that they had not the right of the citizenship of Carthage: and only a solitary case occurs of one of this race being entrusted with authority, and that, too, not emanating from the home government. This is the instance of the officer sent by Hannibal to Sicily, after the fall of Syracuse; whom Polybius calls Myttinus the Libyan, but whom, from the fuller account in Livy, we find to have been a Liby-Phoenician and it is expressly mentioned what indignation was felt by the Carthaginian commanders in the island that this half-caste should control their operations.

With respect to the composition of their armies, it is observable that, though thirsting for extended empire, and though some of the leading men became generals of the highest order, the Carthaginians, as a people, were anything but personally warlike. As long as they could hire mercenaries to fight for them, they had little appetite for the irksome training, and they grudged the loss of valuable time, which military service would have entailed on themselves.

As Michelet remarks:

> The life of an industrious merchant, of a Carthaginian, was too precious to be risked, as long as it was possible to substitute advantageously for it that of a barbarian from Spain or Gaul. Carthage knew, and could tell to a *drachma*, what the life of a man of each nation came to. A Greek was worth more than a Campanian, a Campanian worth more than a Gaul or a Spaniard. When once this tariff of blood was correctly made out, Carthage began a war as a mercantile speculation. She tried to make conquests in the hope of getting new mines to work, or to open fresh markets for her exports. In one venture she could afford to spend fifty thousand mercenaries, in another, rather more. If the returns were good, there was no regret felt for the capital that had been lavished in the investment; more money got more men, and all went on well.—*Histoire Romaine*, vol. ii.

Armies composed of foreign mercenaries have, in all ages, been

3. See the *Periplus* of Hanno.

as formidable to their employers as to the enemy against whom they were directed. We know of one occasion (between the first and second Punic wars) when Carthage was brought to the very brink of destruction by a revolt of her foreign troops. Other mutinies of the same kind must from time to time have occurred. Probably one of these was the cause of the comparative weakness of Carthage at the time of the Athenian expedition against Syracuse; so different from the energy with which she attacked Gelon half a century earlier, and Dionysius half a century later.

And even when we consider her armies with reference only to their efficiency in warfare, we perceive at once the inferiority of such bands of condottieri, brought together without any common bond of origin, tactics, or cause, to the *legions* of Rome, which at the time of the Punic wars were raised from the very flower of a hardy agricultural population trained in the strictest discipline, habituated to victory, and animated by the most resolute patriotism. And this shows also the transcendency of the genius of Hannibal, which could form such discordant materials into a compact organised force, and inspire them with the spirit of patient discipline and loyalty to their chief; so that they were true to him in his adverse as well as in his prosperous fortunes; and throughout the chequered series of his campaigns no panic rout ever disgraced a division under his command; no mutiny, or even attempt at mutiny, was ever known in his camp; and, finally, after fifteen years of Italian warfare, his men followed their old leader to Zama, "with no fear and little hope;"[4] and there, on that disastrous field, stood firm around him, his Old Guard, till Scipio's Numidian allies came up on their flank; when at last, surrounded and overpowered, the veteran battalions sealed their devotion to their general with their blood.

> But if Hannibal's genius may be likened to the Homeric god, who, in his hatred to the Trojans, rises from the deep to rally the fainting Greeks, and to lead them against the enemy, so the calm courage with which Hector met his more than human adversary in his country's cause, is no unworthy image of the unyielding magnanimity displayed by the aristocracy of Rome. As Hannibal utterly eclipses Carthage, so, on the contrary, Fabius, Marcellus, Claudius Nero, even Scipio himself,

4. We advanced to Waterloo as the Greeks did to Thermopylae; all of us without fear and most of us without hope.—Speech of General Foy.

> are as nothing when compared to the spirit, and wisdom, and power of Rome. The senate, which voted its thanks to its political enemy, Varro, after his disastrous defeat, 'because he had not despaired of the commonwealth,' and which disdained either to solicit, or to reprove, or to threaten, or in any way to notice the twelve colonies which had refused their customary supplies of men for the army, is far more to be honoured than the conqueror of Zama.
>
> This we should the more carefully bear in mind because our tendency is to admire individual greatness far more than national; and, as no single Roman will bear comparison to Hannibal, we are apt to murmur at the event of the contest, and to think that the victory was awarded to the least worthy of the combatants. On the contrary, never was the wisdom of God's Providence more manifest than in the issue of the struggle between Rome and Carthage. It was clearly for the good of man kind that Hannibal should be conquered: his triumph would have stopped the progress of the world. For great men can only act permanently by forming great nations; and no one man, even though it were Hannibal himself, can in one generation effect such a work. But where the nation has been merely enkindled for a while by a great man's spirit, the light passes away with him who communicated it; and the nation, when he is gone, is like a dead body, to which magic power had, for a moment, given unnatural life: when the charm has ceased, the body is cold and stiff as before.
>
> He who grieves over the battle of Zama should carry on his thoughts to a period thirty years later, when Hannibal must, in the course of nature, have been dead, and consider how the isolated Phoenician city of Carthage was fitted to receive and to consolidate the civilization of Greece, or by its laws and institutions to bind together barbarians of every race and language into an organised empire, and prepare them for becoming, when that empire was dissolved, the free members of the commonwealth of Christian Europe.—Arnold, vol. iii.

It was in the spring of 207 B.C. that Hasdrubal, after skilfully disentangling himself from the Roman forces in Spain, and, after a march conducted with great judgment and little loss, through the interior of Gaul and the passes of the Alps, appeared in the country that now is the north of Lombardy, at the head of troops which he had partly brought out of Spain, and partly levied among the Gauls and Ligurians on his way. At this time Hannibal with his unconquered, and seemingly unconquerable army, had been eleven years in Italy, executing with strenuous ferocity the vow of hatred to Rome which had been sworn by him while yet a child at the bidding of his father, Hamilcar; who, as he boasted, had trained up his three sons, Hannibal, Hasdrubal, and Mago, Like three lion's whelps, to prey upon the Romans. But Hannibal's latter campaigns had not been signalised by any such great victories as marked the first years of his invasion of Italy.

The stern spirit of Roman resolution, ever highest in disaster and danger, had neither bent nor despaired beneath the merciless blows which "the dire African" dealt her in rapid succession at Trebia, at Thrasymene, and at Cannae. Her population was thinned by repeated slaughter in the field; poverty and actual scarcity wore down the survivors, through the fearful ravages which Hannibal's cavalry spread through their corn-fields, their pasture-lands, and their vineyards; many of her allies went over to the invader's side; and new clouds of foreign war threatened her from Macedonia and Gaul. But Rome receded not. Rich and poor among her citizens vied with each other in devotion to their country.

The wealthy placed their stores, and all placed their lives at the state's disposal. And though Hannibal could not be driven out of Italy, though every year brought its sufferings and sacrifices, Rome felt that her constancy had not been exerted in vain. If she was weakened by the continual strife, so was Hannibal also; and it was clear that the unaided resources of his army were unequal to the task of her destruction. The single deer-hound could not pull down the quarry which he had so furiously assailed. Rome not only stood fiercely at bay, but had pressed back and gored her antagonist, that still, however, watched her in act to spring. She was weary, and bleeding at every pore; and there seemed to be little hope of her escape, if the other hound of old Hamilcar's race should come up in time to aid his brother in the death-grapple.

Hasdrubal had commanded the Carthaginian armies in Spain for some time, with varying but generally unpropitious fortune. He had not the full authority over the Punic forces in that country which his brother and his father had previously exercised. The faction at Carthage, which was at feud with his family, succeeded in fettering and interfering with his power; and other generals were from time to time sent into Spain, whose errors and misconduct caused the reverses that Hasdrubal met with. This is expressly attested by the Greek historian Polybius, who was the intimate friend of the younger Africanus, and drew his information respecting the second Punic war from the best possible authorities. Livy gives a long narrative of campaigns between the Roman commanders in Spain and Hasdrubal, which is so palpably deformed by fictions and exaggerations as to be hardly deserving of attention.[5]

It is clear that in the year 208 B.C., at least, Hasdrubal outmanoeuvred Publius Scipio, who held the command of the Roman forces in Spain; and whose object was to prevent him from passing the Pyrenees and marching upon Italy. Scipio expected that Hasdrubal would attempt the nearest route, along the coast of the Mediterranean; and he therefore carefully fortified and guarded the passes of the eastern Pyrenees. But Hasdrubal passed these mountains near their western extremity; and then, with a considerable force of Spanish infantry, with a small number of African troops, with some elephants and much treasure, he marched, not directly towards the coast of the Mediterranean, but in a north-eastern line towards the centre of Gaul. He halted for the winter in the territory of the Arverni, the modern Auvergne; and conciliated or purchased the good-will of the Gauls in that region so far, that he not only found friendly winter quarters among them, but great numbers of them enlisted under him, and on the approach of spring marched with him to invade Italy.

By thus entering Gaul at the south-west, and avoiding its southern maritime districts, Hasdrubal kept the Romans in complete ignorance of his precise operations and movements in that country; all that they knew was that Hasdrubal had baffled Scipio's attempts to detain him in Spain; that he had crossed the Pyrenees with soldiers, elephants, and money, and that he was raising fresh forces among the Gauls. The spring was sure to bring him into Italy; and then would come the real tempest of the war, when from the north and from the south the two Carthaginian armies, each under a son of the Thunderbolt, were to gather together around the seven hills of Rome.[6]

In this emergency the Romans looked among themselves earnestly and anxiously for leaders fit to meet the perils of the coming campaign.

---

5. See the excellent criticisms of Sir Walter Raleigh on this, in his *History of the World*. 6. Hamilcar was surnamed Barca, which means the Thunderbolt. Sultan Bajazet had the similar surname of Yilderim.

The senate recommended the people to elect, as one of their consuls, Caius Claudius Nero, a patrician of one of the families of the great Claudian house. Nero had served during the preceding years of the war, both against Hannibal in Italy, and against Hasdrubal in Spain; but it is remarkable that the histories, which we possess, record no successes as having been achieved by him either before or after his great campaign of the Metaurus. It proves much for the sagacity of the leading men of the senate, that they recognised in Nero the energy and spirit which were required at this crisis, and it is equally creditable to the patriotism of the people, that they followed the advice of the senate by electing a general who had no showy exploits to recommend him to their choice.

It was a matter of greater difficulty to find a second consul; the laws required that one consul should be a plebeian; and the plebeian nobility had been fearfully thinned by the events of the war. While the senators anxiously deliberated among themselves what fit colleague for Nero could be nominated at the coming *comitia*, and sorrowfully recalled the names of Marcellus, Gracchus, and other *plebeian* generals who were no more—one taciturn and moody old man sat in sullen apathy among the conscript fathers. This was Marcus Livius, who had been consul in the gear before the beginning of this war, and had then gained a victory over the Illyrians. After his consulship he had been impeached before the people on a charge of peculation and unfair division of the spoils among his soldiers: the verdict was unjustly given against him, and the sense of this wrong, and of the indignity thus put upon him, had rankled unceasingly in the bosom of Livius, so that for eight years after his trial he had lived in seclusion at his country seat, taking no part in any affairs of state.

Latterly the censors had compelled him to come to Rome and resume his place in the senate, where he used to sit gloomily apart, giving only a silent vote. At last an unjust accusation against one of his near kinsmen made him break silence; and he harangued the house in words of weight and sense, which drew attention to him, and taught the senators that a strong spirit dwelt beneath that unimposing exterior. Now, while they were debating on what noble of a plebeian house was fit to assume the perilous honours of the consulate, some of the elder of them looked on Marcus Livius, and remembered that in the very last triumph which had been celebrated in the streets of Rome this grim old man had sat in the car of victory; and that he had offered the last grand thanksgiving sacrifice for the success of the Roman arms that had bled before Capitoline Jove.

There had been no triumphs since Hannibal came into Italy.[7] The Illyrian campaign of Livius was the last that had been so honoured; perhaps it might be destined for him now to renew the long-interrupted series. The senators resolved that Livius should be put in nomination as consul with Nero; the people were willing to elect him; the only opposition came from himself. He taunted them with their inconsistency is honouring a man they had convicted of a base crime.

> If I am innocent, why did you place such a stain on me? If I am guilty, why am I more fit for a second consulship than I was for my first one?

The other senators remonstrated with him urging the example of the great Camillus, who, after an unjust condemnation on a similar charge, both served and saved his country. At last Livius ceased to object; and Caius Claudius Nero and Marcus Livius were chosen consuls of Rome.

A quarrel had long existed between the two consuls, and the senators strove to effect a reconciliation between them before the campaign. Here again Livius for a long time obstinately resisted the wish of his fellow-senators. He said it was best for the state that he and Nero should continue to hate one another. Each would do his duty better, when he knew that he was watched by an enemy in the person of his own colleague. At last the entreaties of the senators prevailed, and Livius consented to forego the feud, and to co-operate with Nero in preparing for the coming struggle.

As soon as the winter snows were thawed, Hasdrubal commenced his march from Auvergne to the Alps. He experienced none of the difficulties which his brother had met with from the mountain tribes. Hannibal's army had been the first body of regular troops that had ever traversed the regions; and, as wild animals assail a traveller, the natives rose against it instinctively, in imagined defence of their own habitations, which they supposed to be the objects of Carthaginian ambition. But the fame of the war, with which Italy had now been convulsed for eleven years, had penetrated into the Alpine passes; and the mountaineers understood that a mighty city, southward of the Alps, was to be attacked by the troops whom they saw marching among them.

They not only opposed no resistance to the passage of Hasdrubal,

7. Marcellus had been only allowed an ovation for the conquest of Syracuse.

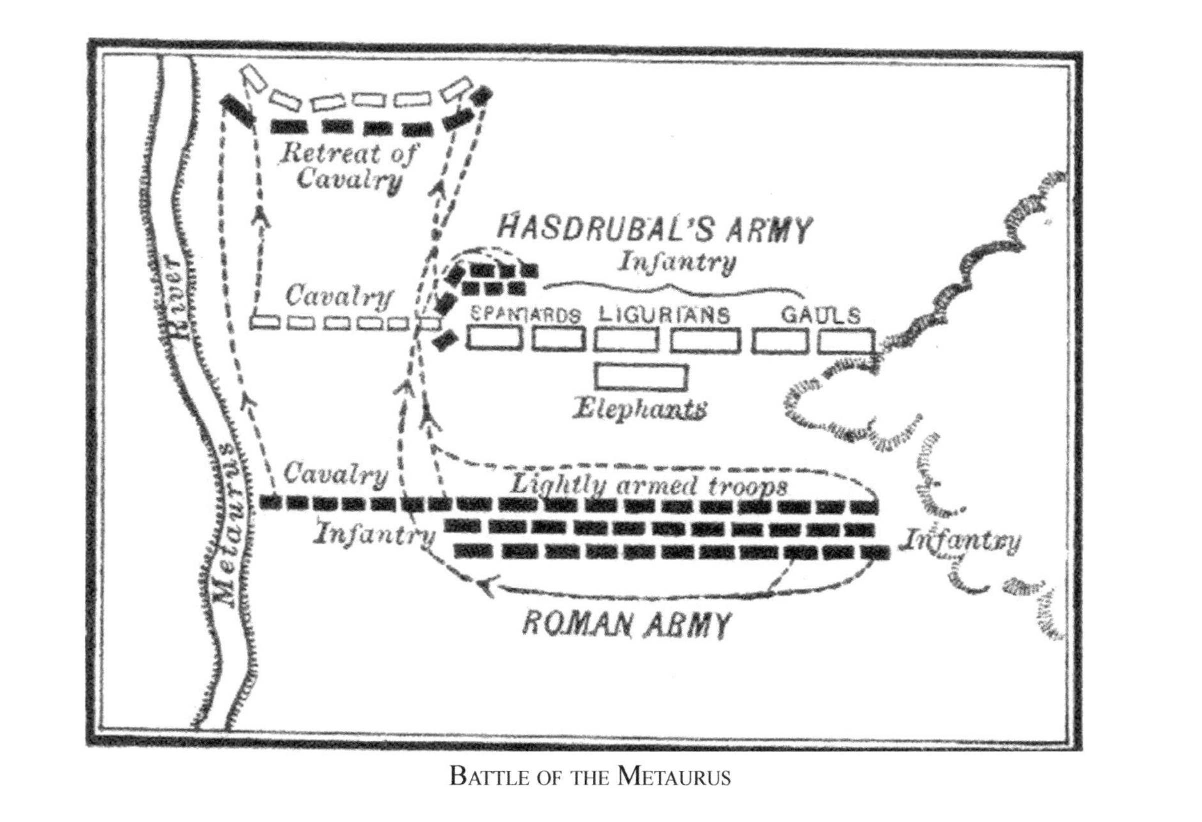

Battle of the Metaurus

but many of them, out of the love of enterprise and plunder, or allured by the high pay that he offered, took service with him; and thus he advanced upon Italy with an army that gathered strength at every league. It is said, also, that some of the most important engineering works which Hannibal had constructed, were found by Hasdrubal still in existence, and materially favoured the speed of his advance. He thus emerged into Italy from the Alpine valleys much sooner than had been anticipated. Many warriors of the Ligurian tribes joined him; and, crossing the river Po, he marched down its southern bank to the city of Placentia, which he wished to secure as a base for his future operations. Placentia resisted him as bravely as it had resisted Hannibal eleven years before; and for some time Hasdrubal was occupied with a fruitless siege before its walls.

Six armies were levied for the defence of Italy when the long-dreaded approach of Hasdrubal was announced. Seventy thousand Romans served in the fifteen legions of which, with an equal number of Italian allies, those armies and the garrisons were composed. Upwards of thirty thousand more Romans were serving in Sicily, Sardinia, and Spain. The whole number of Roman citizens of an age fit for military duty scarcely exceeded a hundred and thirty thousand. The census taken before the war had shown a total of two hundred and seventy thousand, which had been diminished by more than half during twelve years. These numbers are fearfully emphatic of the extremity to which Rome was reduced, and of her gigantic efforts in that great agony of her fate. Not merely men, but money and military stores, were drained to the utmost; and if the armies of that year should be swept off by a repetition of the slaughters of Thrasymene and Cannae, all felt that Rome would cease to exist. Even if the campaign were to be marked by no decisive success on either side, her ruin seemed certain.

In South Italy Hannibal had either detached Rome's allies from her, or had impoverished them by the ravages of his army. If Hasdrubal could have done the same in Upper Italy; if Etruria, Umbria, and Northern Latium had either revolted or been laid waste, Rome must have sunk beneath sheer starvation; for the hostile or desolated territory would have yielded no supplies of corn for her population; and money, to purchase it from abroad, there was none. Instant victory was a matter of life and death. Three of her six armies were ordered to the north, but the first of these was required to overawe the disaffected Etruscans. The second army of the north was pushed forward, under

Porcius, the praetor, to meet and keep in, check the advanced troops of Hasdrubal; while the third, the grand army of the north, which was to be under the immediate command of the consul Livius, who had the chief command in all North Italy, advanced more slowly in its support. There were similarly three armies in the south, under the orders of the other consul Claudius Nero.

The lot had decided that Livius was to be opposed to Hasdrubal, and that Nero should face Hannibal.

> And when all was ordered as themselves thought best, the two consuls went forth of the city; each his several way. The people of Rome were now quite otherwise affected, than they had been, when L. Æmilius Paulus and C. Tarentius Varro were sent against Hannibal. They did no longer take upon them to direct their generals, or bid them dispatch, and win the victory betimes; but rather they stood in fear, lest all diligence, wisdom, and valour should prove too little. For since, few years had passed, wherein some one of their generals had not been slain; and since it was manifest, that if either of these present consuls were defeated, or put to the worst, the two Carthaginians would forthwith join, and make short work with the other: it seemed a greater happiness than could be expected, that each of them should return home victor; and come off with honour from such mighty opposition as he was like to find.
> With extreme difficulty had Rome held up her head ever since the battle of Cannae; though it were so, that Hannibal alone, with little help from Carthage, had continued the war in Italy. But there was now arrived another son of Amilcar; and one that, in his present expedition, had seemed a man of more sufficiency than Hannibal himself. For, whereas in that long and dangerous march through barbarous nations, over great rivers and mountains, that were thought unpassable, Hannibal had lost a great part of his army; this Asdrubal, in the same places, had multiplied his numbers; and gathering the people that he found in the way, descended from the Alps like a rolling snow-ball, far greater than he came over the Pyrenees at his first setting out of Spain.
> These considerations, and the like, of which fear presented many unto them, caused the people of Rome to wait upon their consuls out of the town, like a pensive train of mourners;

> thinking upon Marcellus and Crispinus, upon whom, in the like sort, they had given attendance the last year, but saw neither of them return alive from a less dangerous war. Particularly old Q. Fabius gave his accustomed advice to M. Livius, that he should abstain from giving or taking battle, until he well understood the enemies' condition. But the consul made him a froward answer, and said, that he would fight the very first day, for that he thought it long till he should either recover his honour by victory, or, by seeing the overthrow of his own unjust citizens, satisfy himself with the joy of a great, though not an honest revenge. But his meaning was better than his words.—Sir Walter Raleigh.

Hannibal at this period occupied with his veteran but much reduced forces the extreme south of Italy. It had not been expected either by friend or foe, that Hasdrubal would effect his passage of the Alps so early in the year as actually occurred. And even when Hannibal learned that his brother was in Italy, and had advanced as far as Placentia, he was obliged to pause for further intelligence, before he himself commenced active operations, as he could not tell whether his brother might not be invited into Etruria, to aid the party there that was disaffected to Rome or whether he would march down by the Adriatic Sea. Hannibal led his troops out of their winter quarters in Bruttium, and marched northward as far as Canusium. Nero had his head-quarters near Venusia, with an army which he had increased to forty thousand foot and two thousand five hundred horse, by incorporating under his own command some of the legions which had been intended to set under other generals in the south.

There was another Roman Army twenty thousand strong, south of Hannibal, at Tarentum. The strength of that city secured this Roman force from any attack by Hannibal, and it was a serious matter to march northward and leave it in his rear, free to act against all his depots and allies in the friendly part of Italy, which for the last two or three campaigns had served him for a base of his operations. Moreover, Nero's army was so strong that Hannibal could not concentrate troops enough to assume the offensive against it without weakening his garrisons, and relinquishing, at least for a time, his grasp upon the southern provinces. To do this before he was certainly informed of his brother's operations would have been an useless sacrifice; as Nero could retreat before him upon the other Roman armies near the capital, and Hannibal knew by experience that a mere advance of his army upon the walls of Rome would have no effect on the fortunes of the war.

In the hope, probably, of inducing Nero to follow him, and of gaining an opportunity of outmanoeuvring the Roman consul and attacking him on his march, Hannibal moved into Lucania, and then back into Apulis;—he again marched down into Bruttium, and strengthened his army by a levy of recruits in that district. Nero followed him, but gave him no chance of assailing him at a disadvantage. Some partial encounters seem to have taken place; but the consul could not prevent Hannibal's junction with his Bruttian levies, nor could Hannibal gain an opportunity of surprising and crushing the consul. Hannibal returned to his former headquarters at Canusium, and halted there in expectation of further tidings of his brother's movements. Nero also resumed his former position in observation of the Carthaginian Army. [8]

Meanwhile, Hasdrubal had raised the siege of Placentia, and was advancing towards Ariminum on the Adriatic, and driving before him the Roman army under Porcina. Nor when the consul Livius had come up, and united the second and third armies of the north, could he make head against the invaders. The Romans still fell back before Hasdrubal, beyond Ariminum, beyond the Metaurus, and as far as the little town of Sena, to the southeast of that river. Hasdrubal was not unmindful of the necessity of acting in concert with his brother. He sent messengers to Hannibal to announce his own line of march and to propose that they should unite their armies in South Umbria, and

---

8. The annalists whom Livy copied, spoke of Nero's gaining repeated victories over Hannibal, and killing; and taking his men by tens of thousands. The falsehood of all this is self-evident. If Nero could thus always beat Hannibal, the Romans would not have been in such an agony of dread about Hasdrubal, as all writers describe. Indeed, we have the express testimony of Polybius that such statements as we read in Livy of Marcellus, Nero, and others gaining victories over Hannibal in Italy, must be all fabrications of Roman vanity. Polybius states that Hannibal was never defeated before the battle of Zama; and in another passage he mentions that after the defeats which Hannibal inflicted on the Romans in the early years of the war, they no longer dared face his army in a pitched battle on a fair field, and yet they resolutely maintained the war. He rightly explains this by referring to the superiority of Hannibal's cavalry the arm which gained him all his victories. By keeping within fortified lines, or close to the sides of the mountains when Hannibal approached them, the Romans rendered his cavalry ineffective; and a glance at the geography of Italy will show how an army can traverse the greater part of that country without venturing far from the high grounds.

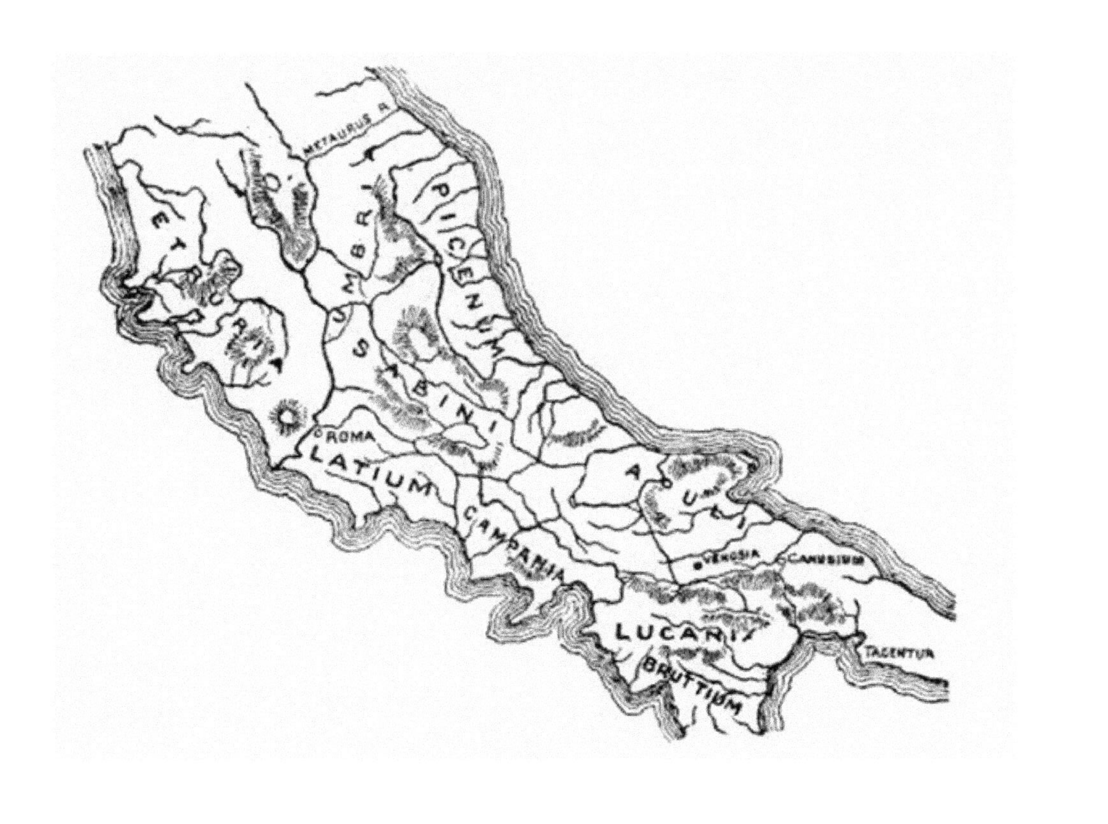
PICENUM
UMBRI
SABINI
LATIUM
ROMA
CAMPANIA
LUCANI
BRUTTIUM
TARENTUM
CANUSIUM
VENUSIA
METAURUS R.

then wheel round against Rome.

Those messengers traversed the greater part of Italy in safety; but, when close to the object of their mission, were captured by a Roman detachment; and Hasdrubal's letter, detailing his whole plan of the campaign, was laid, not in his brother's hands, but in those of the commander of the Roman armies of the south. Nero saw at once the full importance of the crisis. The two sons of Hamilcar were now within two hundred miles of each other, and if Rome were to be saved, the brothers must never meet alive. Nero instantly ordered seven thousand picked men, a thousand being cavalry, to hold themselves in readiness for a secret expedition against one of Hannibal's garrisons; and as soon as night had set in, he hurried forward on his bold enterprise: but he quickly left the southern road towards Lucania, and wheeling round, pressed northward with the utmost rapidity towards Picenum.

He had, during the preceding afternoon, sent messengers to Rome, who were to lay Hasdrubal's letters before the senate. There was a law forbidding a consul to make war or to march his army beyond the limits of the province assigned to him; but in such an emergency Nero did not wait for the permission of the senate to execute his project, but informed them that he was already on his march to join Livius against Hasdrubal. He advised them to send the two *legions* which formed the home garrison, on to Narnia, so as to defend that pass of the Flaminian road against Hasdrubal, in case he should march upon Rome before the consular armies could attack him. They were to supply the place of those two legions at Rome by a levy *en masse* in the city, and by ordering up the reserve legion from Capua.

These were his communications to the senate. He also sent horseman forward along his line of march, with orders to the local authorities to bring stores of; provisions and refreshments of every kind to the road-side, and to have relays of carriages ready for the conveyance of the wearied soldiers. Such were the precautions which he took for accelerating his march; and when he had advanced some little distance from his camp, he briefly informed his soldiers of the real object of their expedition. He told them that there never was a design more seemingly audacious, and more really safe. He said he was leading them to a certain victory, for his colleague had an army large enough to balance the enemy already, so that *their* swords would decisively turn the scale.

The very rumour that a fresh consul and a fresh army had come up, when heard on the battlefield (and he would take care that they should not be heard of before they were seen and felt) would settle the campaign. They would have all the credit of the victory, and of having dealt the final decisive blow, He appealed to the enthusiastic reception which they already met with on their line of march as a proof and an omen of their good fortune. And, indeed, their whole path was amidst the vows and prayers and praises of their countrymen. The entire population of the districts through which they passed, flocked to the road-side to see and bless the deliverers of their country. Food, drink, and refreshments of every kind were eagerly pressed on their acceptance. Each peasant thought a favour was conferred on him, if one of Nero's chosen band would accept aught at his hands. The soldiers caught the full spirit of their leader. Night and day they marched forwards, taking their hurried meals in the ranks and resting by relays in the waggons which the zeal of the country-people provided, and which followed in the rear of the column.

Meanwhile, at Rome, the news of Nero's expedition had caused the greatest excitement and alarm. All men felt the full audacity of the enterprise, but hesitated what epithet to apply to it. It was evident that Nero's conduct would be judged of by the event, that most unfair criterion, as the Roman historian, Livy, truly terms it—*Adparebat (quo nihil iniquius est) ex eventu famam habiturum.* People reasoned on the perilous state in which Nero had left the rest of his army, without a general, and deprived of the core of its strength, in the vicinity of the terrible Hannibal. They speculated on how long it would take Hannibal to pursue and overtake Nero himself, and his expeditionary force. They talked over the former disasters of the war, and the fall of both the consuls of the last year.

All these calamities had come on them while they had only one Carthaginian general and army to deal with in Italy. Now they had two Punic wars at one time. They had two Carthaginian armies; they had almost two Hannibals in Italy, Hasdrubal was sprung from the same father; trained up in the same hostility to Rome; equally practised in battle against its legions; and, if the comparative speed and success with which he had crossed the Alps was a fair test, he was even a better general than his brother. With fear for their interpreter of every rumour, they exaggerated the strength of their enemy's forces in every quarter, and criticised and distrusted their own.

Fortunately for Rome, while she was thus a prey to terror and anxiety, her consul's nerves were strong, and he resolutely urged on his march towards Sena, where his colleague, Livius, and the praetor

Portius were encamped; Hasdrubal's army being in position about half a mile to the north. Nero had sent couriers forward to apprise his colleague of his project and of his approach; and by the advice of Livius, Nero so timed his final march as to reach the camp at Sena by night. According to a previous arrangement, Nero's men were received silently into the tents of their comrades, each according to his rank. By these means there was no enlargement of the camp that could betray to Hasdrubal the accession of force which the Romans had received. This was considerable; as Nero's numbers had been increased on the march by the volunteers, who offered themselves in crowds, and from whom he selected the most promising men, and especially the veterans of former campaigns. A council of war was held on the morning after his arrival, in which some advised that time should be given for Nero's men to refresh themselves, after the fatigue of such a march. But Nero vehemently opposed all delay.

> The officer who is for giving time for my men here to rest themselves, is for giving time to Hannibal to attack my men, whom I have left in the camp in Apulia. He is for giving time to Hannibal and Hasdrubal to discover my march, and to manoeuvre for a junction with each other in Cisalpine Gaul at their leisure. We must fight instantly, while both the foe here and the foe in the south are ignorant of our movements. We must destroy this Hasdrubal, and I must be back In Apulia before Hannibal awakes from his torpor.—Livy, lib. xxvii. c. 45.

Nero's advice prevailed. It was resolved to fight directly; and before the consuls and *praetor* left the tent of Livius, the red ensign, which was the signal to prepare for immediate action, was hoisted, and the Romans forthwith drew up in battle array outside the camp.

Hasdrubal had been anxious to bring Livius and Porcius to battle, though he had not judged it expedient to attack them in their lines. And now, on hearing that the Romans offered battle, he also drew up his men, and advanced towards them. No spy or deserter had informed him of Nero's arrival; nor had he received any direct information that he had more than his old enemies to deal with. But as he rode forward to reconnoitre the Roman lines, he thought that their numbers seemed to have increased, and that the armour of some-of them was unusually dull and stained. He noticed also that the horses of some of the cavalry appeared to be rough and out of condition, as if they had just come from a succession of forced marches.

So also, though, owing to the precaution of Livius, the Roman camp showed no change of size, it had not escaped the quick ear of the Carthaginian general, that the trumpet, which gave the signal to the Roman legions, sounded that morning once oftener than usual, as if directing the troops of some additional superior officer. Hasdrubal, from his Spanish campaigns, was well acquainted with all the sounds and signals of Roman war; and from all that he heard and saw, he felt convinced that both the Roman consuls were before him. In doubt and difficulty as to what might have taken place between the armies of the south, and probably hoping that Hannibal also was approaching, Hasdrubal determined to avoid an encounter with the combined Roman forces, and to endeavour to retreat upon Insubrian Gaul, where he would be in a friendly country, and could endeavour to re-open his communications with his brother. He therefore led his troops back into their camp; and, as the Romans did not venture on an assault upon his entrenchments, and Hasdrubal did not choose to commence his retreat in their sight, the day passed away in inaction.

At the first watch of the night, Hasdrubal led his men silently out of their camp, and moved northwards towards the Metaurus, in the hope of placing that river between himself and the Romans before his retreat was discovered. His guides betrayed him; and having purposely led him away from the part of the river that was fordable, they made their escape in the dark, and left Hasdrubal and his army wandering in confusion along the steep bank, and seeking in vain for a spot where the stream could be safely crossed.

At last they halted; and when day dawned on them, Hasdrubal found that great numbers of his men, in their fatigue and impatience, had lost all discipline and subordination, and that many of his Gallic auxiliaries had got drunk, and were lying helpless in their quarters. The Roman cavalry was soon seen coming up in pursuit, followed at no great distance by the *legions*, which marched in readiness for an instant engagement. It was hopeless for Hasdrubal, to think of continuing his retreat before them. The prospect of immediate battle might recall the disordered part of his troops to a sense of duty, and revive the instinct of discipline. He therefore ordered his men to prepare for action instantly, and made the best arrangement of them that the nature of the ground would permit.

Heeren has well described the general appearance of a Carthaginian army. He says:

It was an assemblage of the most opposite races of the human species, from the farthest parts of the globe. Hordes of half-naked Gauls were ranged next to companies of white clothed Iberians, and savage Ligurians next to the far-travelled Nasamones and Lotophagi. Carthaginians and Phoenici-Africans formed the centre; while innumerable troops of Numidian horse-men, taken from all the tribes of the Desert, swarmed about on unsaddled horses, and formed the wings; the van was composed of Balearic slingers; and a line of colossal elephants, with their Ethiopian guides, formed, as it were, a chain of moving fortresses before the whole army. Such were the usual materials and arrangements of the hosts that fought for Carthage; but the troops under Hasdrubal were not in all respects thus constituted or thus stationed. He seems to have been especially deficient in cavalry, and he had few African troops, though some Carthaginians of high rank were with him.

His veteran Spanish infantry, armed with helmets and shields, and short cut-and-thrust swords, were the best part of his army. These, and his few Africans, he drew up on his right wing, under his own personal command. In the centre, he placed his Ligurian infantry, and on the left wing he placed or retained the Gauls, who were armed with long javelins and with huge broadswords and targets. The rugged nature of the ground in front and on the flank of this part of his line, made him hope that the Roman right wing would be unable to come to close quarters with these unserviceable barbarians, before he could make some impression with his Spanish veterans on the Roman left.

This was the only chance that he had of victory or safety, and he seems to have done everything that good generalship could do to secure it. He placed his elephants in advance of his centre and right wing. He had caused the driver of each of them to be provided with a sharp iron spike and a mallet; and had given orders that every beast that became unmanageable, and ran back upon his own ranks, should be instantly killed, by driving the spike into the vertebra at the junction of the head and the spine. Hasdrubal's elephants were ten in number. We have no trustworthy information as to the amount of his infantry, but it is quite clear that he was greatly outnumbered by the combined Roman forces.

The tactic of the Roman *legions* had not yet acquired the perfection which it received from the military genius of Marius,[9] and which we read of in the first chapter of Gibbon. We possess in that great work an account of the Roman legions at the end of the commonwealth, and during the early ages of the empire, which those alone can adequately admire, who have attempted a similar description. We have also, in the sixth and seventeenth books of Polybius, an elaborate discussion on the military system of the Romans in his time, which was not far distant from the time of the battle of the Metaurus. But the subject is beset with difficulties: and instead of entering into minute but inconclusive details, I would refer to Gibbon's first chapter, as serving for a general description of the Roman army in its period of perfection; and remark, that the training and armour which the whole legion received in the time of Augustus, was, two centuries earlier, only partially introduced.

Two divisions of troops, called *hastati* and *principes*, formed the bulk of each Roman *legion* in the second Punic war. Each of these divisions was twelve hundred strong. The *hastatus* and the *princeps legionary* bore a breast-plate or coat of mail, brazen greaves, and a brazen helmet, with a lofty, upright crest of scarlet or black feathers. He had a large oblong shield; and, as weapons of offence, two javelins, one of which was light and slender, but the other was a strong and massive weapon, with a shaft about four feet long, and an iron head of equal length. The sword was carried on the right thigh, and was a short cut-and thrust weapon, like that which was used by the Spaniards. Thus armed, the *hastati* formed the front division of the *legion*, and the *Principes* the second. Each division was drawn up about ten deep; a space of three feet being allowed between the files as well as the ranks, so as to give each legionary ample room for the use of his javelins, and of his sword and shield. The men in the second rank did not stand immediately behind those in the first rank, but the files were alternate, like the position of the men on a draught board. This was termed the quincunx order. Niebuhr considers that this arrangement enabled the *legion* to keep up a shower of javelins on the enemy for some considerable time. He says:

> When the first line had hurled its *pila*, it probably stepped back between those who stood behind it, who with two steps for-

9. Most probably during the period of his prolonged consulship, from B.C. 104 to B.C. 101, while he was training his army against the Cimbri and the Teutons.

ward restored the front nearly to its first position; a movement which, on account of the arrangement of the *quincunx*, could be executed without losing a moment. Thus one line succeeded the other in the front till it was time to draw the swords; nay, when it was found expedient, the lines which had already been in the front might repeat this change, since the stores of *pila* were surely not confined to the two which each soldier took with him into battle.

The same change must have taken place in fighting with the sword; which, when the same tactic was adopted on both sides, was anything but a confused *mêlée*; on the contrary, it was a series of single combats.

He adds, that a military man of experience had been consulted by him on the subject, and had given it as his opinion, "that the change of the lines as described above was by no means impracticable; and in the absence of the deafening noise of gunpowder, it cannot have had even any difficulty with trained troops."

The third division of the *legion* was six hundred strong, and acted as a reserve. It was always composed of veteran soldiers, who were called the *triarii*. Their arms were the same as those of the *principes* and *hastati*; except that each *triarian* carried a spear instead of javelins. The rest of the legion consisted of light armed troops, who acted as skirmishers. The cavalry of each *legion* was at this period about three hundred strong. The Italian allies, who were attached to the legion, seem to have been similarly armed and equipped, but their numerical proportion of cavalry was much larger.

Such was the nature of the forces that advanced on the Roman side to the battle of the Metaurus. Nero commanded the right wing, Livius the left, and the *praetor* Porcius had the command of the centre.

Both Romans and Carthaginians well understood how much depended upon the fortune of this day, and how little hope of safety there was for the vanquished. Only the Romans herein seemed to have had the better in conceit and opinion, that they were to fight with men desirous to have fled from them. And according to this presumption came Livius the consul, with a proud bravery, to give charge on the Spaniards and Africans, by whom he was so sharply entertained that victory seemed very doubtful. The Africans and Spaniards were stout soldiers, and well acquainted with the manner of the Roman fight. The Ligurians, also, were a hardy nation, and not accustomed to give ground; which they needed the less, or were able now to do, being placed in the midst. Livius, therefore, and Porcius found great opposition; and, with great slaughter on both sides, prevailed little or nothing.

Besides other difficulties, they were exceedingly troubled by the elephants, that brake their first ranks, and put them in such disorder, as the Roman ensigns were driven to fall back; all this while Claudius Nero, labouring in vain against a steep hill, was unable to come to blows with the Gauls that stood opposite him, but out of danger. This made Hasdrubal the more confident, who, seeing his own left wing safe, did the more boldly and fiercely make impression on the other side upon the left wing of the Romans.—*Historie of the World*, by Sir Walter Raleigh.

But at last Nero, who found that Hasdrubal refused his left wing, and who could not overcome the difficulties of the ground in the quarter assigned to him, decided the battle by another stroke of that military genius which had inspired his march. Wheeling a brigade of his best men round the rear of the rest of the Roman army, Nero fiercely charged the flank of the Spaniards and Africans. The charge was as successful as it was sudden. Rolled back in disorder upon each other, and overwhelmed by numbers, the Spaniards and Ligurians died, fighting gallantly to the last. The Gauls, who had taken little or no part in the strife of the day, were then surrounded, and butchered almost without resistance. Hasdrubal, after having, by the confession of his enemies, done all that a general could do, when he saw that the victory was irreparably lost, scorning to survive the gallant; host which he had led, and to gratify, as a captive, Roman cruelty and pride, spurred his horse into the midst of a Roman cohort; where, sword in hand, he met the death that was worthy of the son of Hamilcar and the brother of Hannibal.

Success the most complete had crowned Nero's enterprise. Returning as rapidly as he had advanced, he was again facing the inactive enemies in the south, before they even knew of his march. But he brought with him a ghastly trophy of what he had done. In the true spirit of that savage brutality which deformed the Roman national character, Nero ordered Hasdrubal's head to be flung into his brother's camp. Eleven years had passed since Hannibal had last gazed on those features. The sons of Hamilcar had then planned their system of warfare against Rome, which they had so nearly brought to successful accomplishment. Year after year had Hannibal been struggling in Italy, in the hope of one day hailing the arrival of him whom he had left in Spain; and of seeing his brother's eye flash with affection and pride at the junction of their irresistible hosts. He now saw that eye glazed in death and, in the agony of his heart, the great Carthaginian groaned aloud that he recognised his country's destiny.

Rome was almost delirious with joy:[10] so agonising had been the suspense with which the battle's verdict on that great issue of a nation's life and death had been awaited; so overpowering was the sudden reaction to the consciousness of security, and to the full glow of glory and success. From the time when it had been known at Rome that the armies were in presence of each other, the people had never ceased to throng the forum, the Conscript Fathers had been in permanent sitting at the senate house. Ever and anon a fearful whisper crept among the crowd of a second Cannae won by a second Hannibal. Then came truer rumours that the day was Rome's; but the people were sick at heart, and heeded them not. The shrines were thronged with trembling women, who seemed to weary heaven with prayers to shield them from the brutal Gaul and the savage African. Presently the reports of good fortune assumed a more definite form.

It was said that two Narnian horseman had ridden from the east into the Roman camp of observation in Umbria, and had brought tidings of the utter slaughter of the foe. Such news seemed too good to be true, Men tortured their neighbours and themselves by demonstrating its improbability and by ingeniously criticising its evidence. Soon, however, a letter came from Lucius Manlius Acidinus, who commanded in Umbria, and who announced the arrival of the Narnian horsemen in his camp, and the intelligence which they brought thither.

The letter was first laid before the senate, and then before the assembly of the people. The excitement grew more and more vehement. The letter was read and re-read aloud to thousands. It confirmed the previous rumour. But even this was insufficient to allay the feverish anxiety that thrilled through every breast in Rome. The letter might be a forgery: the Narnian horseman might be traitors or impostors. "We must see officers from the army that fought, or hear despatches

10. See the splendid description in Livy, *lib.* xxvii.

from the consuls themselves, and then only will we believe."

Such was the public sentiment, though some of more hopeful nature already permitted themselves a foretaste of joy. At length came news that officers who really had been in the battle were near at hand. Forthwith the whole city poured forth to meet them, each person coveting to be the first to receive with his own eyes and ears convincing proofs of the reality of such a deliverance. One vast throng of human beings filled the road from Rome to the Milvian bridge. The three officers, Lucius Veturius Pollio, Publius Licinius Vasus, and Quintus Caecilius Metellus came riding on, making their way slowly through the living sea around them, As they advanced, each told the successive waves of eager questioners that Rome was victorious.

> We have destroyed Hasdrubal and his army, our *legions* are safe, and our consuls are unhurt.

Each happy listener, who caught the welcome sounds from their lips, retired to communicate his own joy to others, and became himself the centre of an anxious and inquiring group.

When the officers had, with much difficulty, reached the senate house, and the crowd was with still greater difficulty put back from entering and mingling with the Conscript Fathers, the despatches of Livius and Nero were produced and read aloud. From the senate house the officers proceeded to the public assembly, where the despatches were read again; and then the senior officer, Lucius Veturius, gave in his own words a fuller detail of how went the fight. When he had done speaking to the people, an universal shout of rapture rent the air. The vast assembly then separated: some hastening to the temples to find in devotion a vent for the overflowing excitement of their hearts; others seeking their homes to gladden their wives and children with the good news, and to feast their own eyes with the sight of the loved ones, who now, at last, were safe from outrage and slaughter.

The senate ordained a thanksgiving of three days for the great deliverance which had been vouchsafed to Rome; and throughout that period the temples were incessantly crowded with exulting worshippers; and the matrons, with their children round them, in their gayest attire, and with joyous aspects and voices, offered grateful praises to the immortal gods, as if all apprehension of evil were over, and the war were already ended.

With the revival of confidence came also the revival of activity in traffic and commerce, and in all the busy intercourse of daily life.

A numbing load was taken off each heart and brain, and once more men bought and sold, and formed their plans freely, as had been done before the dire Carthaginians came into Italy. Hannibal was, certainly, still in the land; but all felt that his power to destroy was broken, and that the crisis of the war-fever was past. The Metaurus, indeed, had not only determined the event of the strife between Rome and Carthage, but it had ensured to Rome two centuries more of almost unchanged conquest.

Hannibal did actually, with almost superhuman skill, retain his hold on Southern Italy for a few years longer, but the imperial city, and her allies, were no longer in danger from his arms; and, after Hannibal's downfall, the great military republic of the ancient world met in her career of conquest no other worthy competitor. Byron has termed Nero's march "unequalled," and, in the magnitude of its consequences, it is so. Viewed only as a military exploit, it remains unparalleled save by Marlborough's bold march from Flanders to the Danube, in the campaign of Blenheim, and perhaps also by the Archduke Charles's lateral march in 1796, by which he overwhelmed the French under Jourdain, and then, driving Moreau through the Black Forest and across the Rhine, for a while freed Germany from her invaders.

CHAPTER 5

Victory of Arminius Over the Roman Legions Under Varus, A.D. 9.

To a truly illustrious Frenchman, whose reverses as a minister can never obscure his achievements in the world of letters, we are indebted for the most profound and most eloquent estimate that we possess of the importance of the Germanic element in European civilization, and of the extent to which the human race is indebted to those brave warriors, who long were the unconquered antagonists, and finally became the conquerors, of Imperial Rome.

Twenty-three eventful years have passed away since M. Guizot delivered from the chair of modern history at Paris his course of lectures on the History of Civilization in Europe. During those years the spirit of earnest inquiry into the germs and early developments of existing institutions has become more and more active and universal; and the merited celebrity of M. Guizot's work has proportionally increased. Its admirable analysis of the complex political and social organizations of which the modern civilized world is made up, must have led thousands to trace with keener interest the great crises of times past, by which the characteristics of the present were determined.

The narrative of one of these great crises, of the epoch A.D. 9, when Germany took up arms for her independence against Roman invasion, has for us this special attraction—that it forms part of our own national history. Had Arminius been supine or unsuccessful, our Germanic ancestors would have been enslaved or exterminated in their original seats along the Eyder and the Elbe; this island would never have borne the name of England, and "we, this great English nation, whose race and language are now over-running the earth, from one end of it to the other," (Arnold's *Lectures on Modern History*) would have been utterly cut off from existence.

Arnold may, indeed, go too far in holding that we are wholly unconnected in race with the Romans and Britons who inhabited this country before the coming over of the Saxons; that, "nationally speaking, the history of Caesar's invasion has no more to do with us than the natural history of the animals which then inhabited our forests." There seems ample evidence to prove that the Romanized Celts, whom our Teutonic forefathers found here, influenced materially the character of our nation. But the main stream of our people was and is Germanic. Our language alone decisively proves this. Arminius is far more truly one of our national heroes than Caractacus: and it was our own primeval fatherland that the brave German rescued, when he slaughtered the Roman legions eighteen centuries ago in the marshy glens between the Lippe and the Ems.

Dark and disheartening, even to heroic spirits, must have seemed the prospects of Germany when Arminius planned the general rising of his countrymen against Rome. Half the land was occupied by Roman garrisons; and, what was worse, many of the Germans seemed patiently acquiescent in their state of bondage. The braver portion, whose patriotism could be relied on, was ill-armed and undisciplined; while the enemy's troops consisted of veterans in the highest state of equipment and training, familiarized with victory, and commanded by officers of proved skill and valour. The resources of Rome seemed boundless; her tenacity of purpose was believed to be invincible. There was no hope of foreign sympathy or aid; for:

> The self-governing powers that had filled the old world, had bent one after another before the rising power of Rome, and had vanished. The earth seemed left void of independent nations.—Ranke.

The (German) chieftain knew well the gigantic power of the oppressor. Arminius was no rude savage, fighting out of mere animal instinct, or in ignorance of the might of his adversary. He was familiar with the Roman language and civilization; he had served in the Roman armies; he had been admitted to the Roman citizenship, and raised to the dignity of the equestrian order. It was part of the subtle policy of Rome to confer rank and privileges on the youth of the leading families in the nations which she wished to enslave.

Among other young German chieftains, Arminius and his brother, who were the heads of the noblest house in the tribe of the Cherusci,

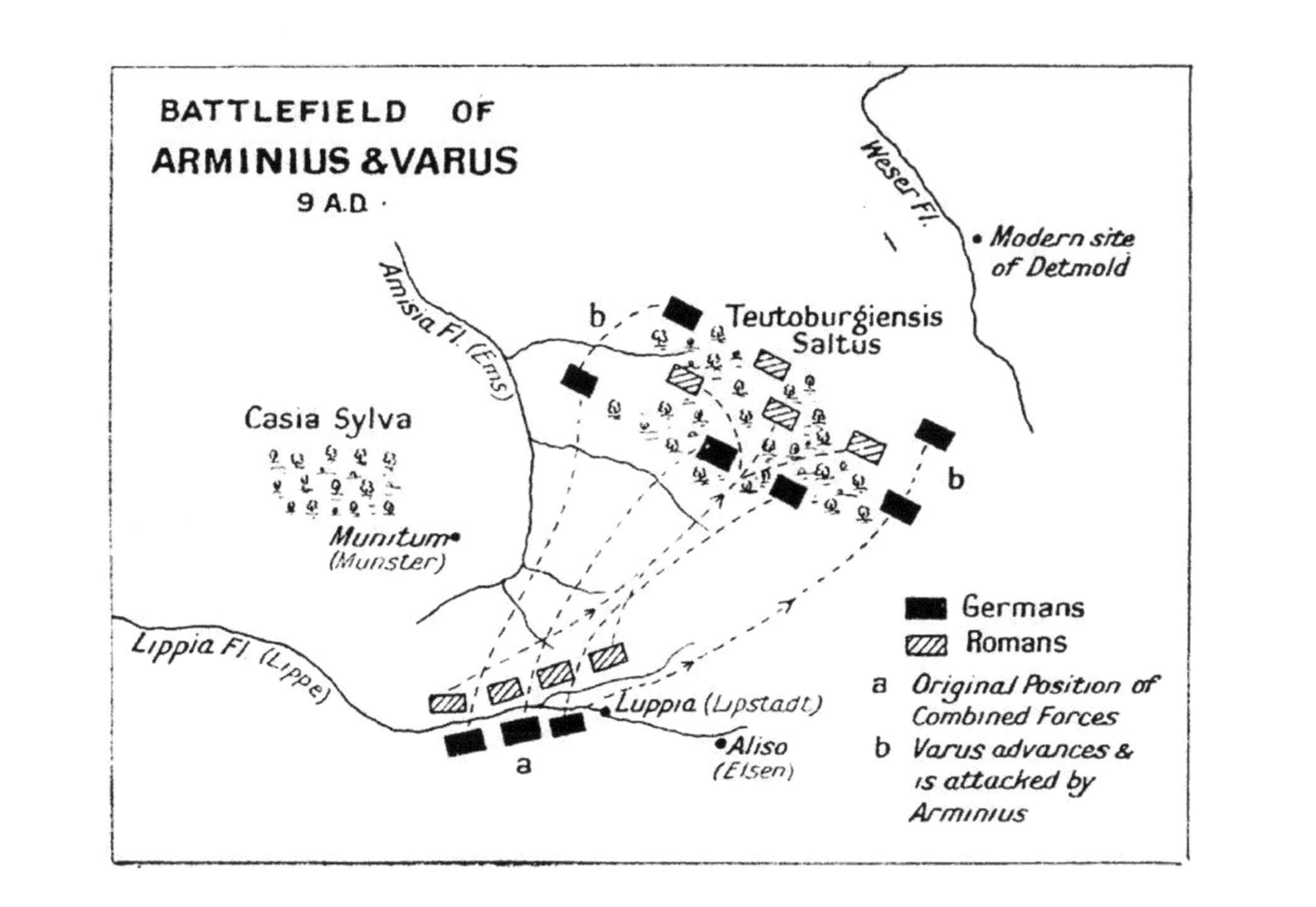

BATTLEFIELD OF
ARMINIUS & VARUS
9 A.D.
Weser Fl.
Modern site
of Detmold
Amisia Fl. (Ems)
Teutoburgiensis
Saltus
b
Casia Sylva
Munitum
(Munster)
b
Germans
Romans
Lippia Fl. (Lippe)
Luppia (Lipstadt)
Aliso
(Elsen)
a
a Original Position of
Combined Forces
b Varus advances &
is attacked by
Arminius

had been selected as fit objects for the exercise of this insidious system. Roman refinements and dignities succeeded in denationalizing the brother, who assumed the Roman name of Flavius, and adhered to Rome throughout all her wars against his country. Arminius remained unbought by honours or wealth, uncorrupted by refinement or luxury. He aspired to and obtained from Roman enmity a higher title than ever could have been given him by Roman favour. It is in the page of Rome's greatest historian, that his name has come down to us with the proud addition of "*Liberator haud dubiè Germaniae*." (Tacitus, Annals, ii.)

Often must the young chieftain, while meditating the exploit which has thus immortalised him, have anxiously revolved in his mind the fate of the many great men who had been crushed in the attempt which he was about to renew,—the attempt to stay the chariot-wheels of triumphant Rome. Could he hope to succeed where Hannibal and Mithridates had perished? What had been the doom of Viriathus? and what warning against vain valour was written on the desolate site where Numantia once had fourished? Nor was a caution wanting in scenes nearer home and in more recent times. The Gauls had fruitlessly struggled for eight years against Caesar; and the valiant Vercingetorix, who in the last year of the war had roused all his countrymen to insurrection, who had cut off Roman detachments, and brought Caesar himself to the extreme of peril at Alesia—he, too, had finally succumbed, had been led captive in Caesar's triumph, and had then been butchered in cold blood in a Roman dungeon.

It was true that Rome was no longer the great military republic which for so many ages had shattered the kingdoms of the world. Her system of government was changed; and, after a century of revolution and civil war, she had placed herself under the despotism of a single ruler. But the discipline of her troops was yet unimpaired, and her warlike spirit seemed unabated. The first wars of the empire had been signalised by conquests as valuable as any gained by the republic in a corresponding period. It is a great fallacy, though apparently sanctioned by great authorities, to suppose that the foreign policy pursued by Augustus was pacific.

He certainly recommended such a policy to his successors, either from timidity, or from jealousy of their fame outshining his own; but he himself, until Arminius broke his spirit, had followed a very different course. Besides his Spanish wars, his generals, in a series of principally aggressive campaigns, had extended the Roman frontier from the Alps to the Danube; and had reduced into subjection the large and important countries that now form the territories of all Austria south of that river, and of East Switzerland, Lower Wirtemberg, Bavaria, the Valteline, and the Tyrol. While the progress of the Roman arms thus pressed the Germans from the south, still more formidable inroads had been made by the Imperial legions in the west.

Roman armies, moving from the province of Gaul, established a chain of fortresses along the right as well as the left bank of the Rhine, and, in a series of victorious campaigns, advanced their eagles as far as the Elbe; which now seemed added to the list of vassal rivers, to the Nile, the Rhine, the Rhone, the Danube, the Tagus, the Seine, and many more, that acknowledged the supremacy of the Tiber. Roman fleets also, sailing from the harbours of Gaul along the German coasts, and up the estuaries, co-operated with the land-forces of the empire; and seemed to display, even more decisively than her armies, her overwhelming superiority over the rude Germanic tribes. Throughout the territory thus invaded, the Romans had, with their usual military skill, established chains of fortified posts; and a powerful army of occupation was kept on foot, ready to move instantly on any spot where a popular outbreak might be attempted.

Vast however, and admirably organised as the fabric of Roman power appeared on the frontiers and in the provinces, there was rottenness at the core. In Rome's unceasing hostilities with foreign foes, and, still more, in her long series of desolating civil wars, the free middle classes of Italy had almost wholly disappeared. Above the position which they had occupied, an oligarchy of wealth had reared itself: beneath that position a degraded mass of poverty and misery was fermenting. Slaves, the chance sweepings of every conquered country, shoals of Africans, Sardinians, Asiatics, Illyrians, and others, made up the bulk of the population of the Italian peninsula. The foulest profligacy of manners was general in all ranks.

In universal weariness of revolution and civil war, and in consciousness of being too debased for self-government, the nation had submitted itself to the absolute authority of Augustus. Adulation was now the chief function the senate: and the gifts of genius and accomplishments of art were devoted to the elaboration of eloquently false panegyrics upon the prince and his favourite courtiers. With bitter indignation must the German chieftain have beheld all this, and contrasted with it the rough worth of his own countrymen;—their bravery, their fidelity to their word, their manly independence of spirit their love of their national free institutions, and their loathing of every pollution and meanness. Above all, he must have thought of the domestic virtues that hallowed a German home; of the respect there shown to the female character, and of the pure affection by which that respect was repaid. His soul must have burned within him at the contemplation of such a race yielding to these debased Italians.

Still, to persuade the Germans to combine, in spite of their frequent feuds among themselves, in one sudden outbreak against Rome; to keep the scheme concealed from the Romans until the hour for action had arrived; and then, without possessing a single walled town, without military stores, without training, to teach his insurgent countrymen to defeat veteran armies, and storm fortifications, seemed so perilous an enterprise, that probably Arminius would have receded from it, had not a stronger feeling even than patriotism urged him on. Among the Germans of high rank who had most readily submitted to the invaders, and become zealous partisans of Roman authority, was a chieftain named Segestes. His daughter, Thusnelda, was pre-eminent among the noble maidens of Germany. Arminius had sought her hand in marriage; but Segestes, who probably discerned the young chief's disaffection to Rome, forbade his suit, and strove to preclude all communication between him and his daughter.

Thusnelda, however, sympathised far more with the heroic spirit of her lover, than with the time serving policy of her father. An elopement baffled the precautions of Segestes; who, disappointed in his hope of preventing the marriage, accused Arminius, before the Roman governor, of having carried off his daughter, and of planning treason against Rome. Thus assailed, and dreading to see his bride torn from him by the officials of the foreign oppressor, Arminius delayed no longer, but bent all his energies to organise and execute a general insurrection of the great mass of his countrymen, who hitherto had submitted in sullen inertness to the Roman dominion.

A change of governors had recently taken place, which, while it materially favoured the ultimate success of the insurgents, served, by the immediate aggravation of the Roman oppressions which it produced, to make the native population more universally eager to take arms. Tiberius, who was afterwards emperor, had lately been recalled from the command in Germany, and sent into Pannonia to put down a dangerous revolt which had broken out against the Romans in that province. The German patriots were thus delivered from the stern supervision of one of the most auspicious of mankind, and were also relieved from having to contend against the high military talents of a veteran commander, who thoroughly understood their national character, and the nature of the country, which he himself had principally subdued.

In the room of Tiberius, Augustus sent into Germany Quintilius Varus, who had lately returned from the proconsulate of Syria. Varus was a true representative of the higher classes of the Romans; among whom a general taste for literature, a keen susceptibility to all intellectual gratifications, a minute acquaintance with the principles and practice of their own national jurisprudence, a careful training in the schools of the rhetoricians, and a fondness for either partaking in or watching the intellectual strife of forensic oratory, had become generally diffused; without, however, having humanized the old Roman spirit of cruel indifference for human feelings and human sufferings, and without acting as the least check on unprincipled avarice and ambition, or on habitual and gross profligacy. Accustomed to govern the depraved and debased natives of Syria, a country where courage in man, and virtue in woman, had for centuries been unknown, Varus thought that he might gratify his licentious and rapacious passions with equal impunity among the high-minded sons and pure-spirited daughters of Germany.

When the general of an army sets the example of outrages of this description, he is soon faithfully imitated by his officers, and surpassed by his still more brutal soldiery. The Romans now habitually indulged in those violations of the sanctity of the domestic shrine, and those insults upon honour and modesty, by which far less gallant spirits than those of our Teutonic ancestors have often been maddened into insurrection.

Arminius found among the other German chiefs many who sympathised with him in his indignation at their country's debasement, and many whom private wrongs had stung yet more deeply. There was little difficulty in collecting bold leaders for an attack on the oppressors, and little fear of the population not rising readily at those leaders' call. But to declare open war against Rome, and to encounter Varus's army in a pitched battle, would have been merely rushing upon certain destruction. Varus had three legions under him, a force which, after allowing for detachments, cannot be estimated at less than fourteen thousand Roman infantry. He had also eight or nine hundred Roman cavalry, and at least an equal number of horse and foot sent from the allied states, or raised among those provincials who had not received the Roman franchise.

It was not merely the number, but the quality of this force that made it formidable; and however contemptible Varus might be as a general, Arminius well knew how admirably the Roman armies were organised and officered, and how perfectly the *legionaries* understood every manoeuvre and every duty which the varying emergencies of a stricken field might require. Stratagem was, therefore, indispensable; and it was necessary to blind Varus to his schemes until a favourable opportunity should arrive for striking a decisive blow.

For this purpose the German confederates frequented the head-quarters of Varus, which seem to have been near the centre of the modern country of Westphalia, where the Roman general conducted himself with all the arrogant security of the governor of a perfectly submissive province. There Varus gratified at once his vanity, his rhetorical taste, and his avarice, by holding courts, to which he summoned the Germans for the settlement of all their disputes, while a bar of Roman advocates attended to argue the cases before the tribunal of the proconsul; who did not omit the opportunity of exacting court-fees and accepting bribes. Varus trusted implicitly to the respect which the Germans pretended to pay to his abilities as a judge, and to the interest which they affected to take in the forensic eloquence of their conquerors.

Meanwhile a succession of heavy rains rendered the country more difficult for the operations of regular troops; and Arminius, seeing that the infatuation of Varus was complete, secretly directed the tribes near the Weser and the Ems to take up arms in open revolt against the Romans. This was represented to Varus as an occasion which required his prompt attendance at the spot; but he was kept in studied ignorance of its being part of a concerted national rising; and he still looked on Arminius as his submissive vassal, whose aid he might rely on in facilitating the march of his troops against the rebels, and in extinguishing the local disturbance. He therefore set his army in motion, and marched eastward in a line parallel to the course of the Lippe. For some distance his route lay along a level plain; but on arriving at the tract between the curve of the upper part of that stream and the sources of the Ems, the country assumes a very different character; and here, in the territory of the modern little principality of Lippe, it was that Arminius had fixed the scene of his enterprise.

A woody and hilly region intervenes between the heads of the two rivers, and forms the watershed of their streams. This region still retains the name (*Teutoberger wald—Teutobergiensis saltus*) which it bore in the days of Arminius. The nature of the ground has probably also remained unaltered. The eastern part of it, round Detmoldt, the present capital of the principality of Lippe, is described by a modern German scholar, Dr. Plate, as being:

> A table-land intersected by numerous deep and narrow valleys, which in some places form small plains, surrounded by steep mountains and rocks, and only accessible by narrow defiles. All the valleys are traversed by rapid streams, shallow in the dry season, but subject to sudden swellings in autumn and winter. The vast forests which cover the summits and slopes of the hills consist chiefly of oak; there is little underwood, and both men and horse would move with ease in the forests if the ground were not broken by gulleys, or rendered impracticable by fallen trees.

This is the district to which Varus is supposed to have marched; and Dr. Plate adds, that "the names of several localities on and near that spot seem to indicate that a great battle had once been fought there. We find the names '*das Winnefeld*' (the field of victory), '*die Knochenbahn*' (the bone-lane), '*die Knochenleke*' (the bone-brook), '*der Mordkessel*' (the kettle of slaughter), and others."

Contrary to the usual strict principles of Roman discipline, Varus had suffered his army to be accompanied and impeded by an immense train of baggage-waggons, and by a rabble of camp followers; as if his troops had been merely changing their quarters in a friendly country. When the long array quitted the firm level ground, and began to wind its way among the woods, the marshes, and the ravines, the difficulties of the march, even without the intervention of an armed foe, became fearfully apparent. In many places the soil, sodden with rain, was impracticable for cavalry and even for infantry, until trees had been felled, and a rude causeway formed through the morass.

The duties of the engineer were familiar to all who served in the Roman armies. But the crowd and confusion of the columns embarrassed the working parties of the soldiery, and in the midst of their toil and disorder the word was suddenly passed through their ranks that the rear-guard was attacked by the barbarians. Varus resolved on pressing forward; but a heavy discharge of missiles from the woods on either flank taught him how serious was the peril, and he saw the best men falling round him without the opportunity of retaliation; for his light-armed auxiliaries, who were principally of Germanic race, now rapidly deserted, and it was impossible to deploy the *legionaries* on such broken ground for a charge against the enemy. Choosing one of the most open and firm spots which they could force their way to, the Romans halted for the night; and, faithful to their national discipline and tactics, formed their camp amid the harassing attacks of the rapidly thronging foes, with the elaborate toil and systematic skill, the traces of which are impressed permanently on the soil of so many European countries, attesting the presence in the olden time of the imperial eagles.

On the morrow the Romans renewed their march; the veteran officers who served under Varus now probably directing the operations, and hoping to find the Germans drawn up to meet them; in which case they relied on their own superior discipline and tactics for such a victory as should reassure the supremacy of Rome. But Arminius was far too sage a commander to lead on his followers, with their unwieldy broadswords and inefficient defensive armour, against the Roman *legionaries*, fully armed with helmet, *cuirass*, greaves, and shield; who were skilled to commence the conflict with a murderous volley of heavy javelins, hurled upon the foe when a few yards distant, and then, with their short cut-and-thrust swords, to hew their way through all opposition; preserving the utmost steadiness and coolness, and obeying each word of command. In the midst of strife and slaughter with the same precision and alertness as if upon parade.

Arminius suffered the Romans to march out from their camp, to form first in line for action, and then in column for marching, without the show of opposition. For some distance Varus was allowed to move on, only harassed by slight skirmishes, but struggling with difficulty through the broken ground; the toil and distress of his men being aggravated by heavy torrents of rain, which burst upon the devoted legions as if the angry gods of Germany were pouring out the vials of their wrath upon the invaders.

After some little time their van approached a ridge of high woody ground, which is one of the off-shoots of the great Hercynian forest, and is situate between the modern villages of Driburg and Bielefeld. Arminius had caused barricades of hewn trees to be formed here, so as to add to the natural difficulties of the passage. Fatigue and discouragement now began to betray themselves in the Roman ranks. Their line became less steady; baggage-waggons were abandoned from the impossibility of forcing them along; and, as this happened, many soldiers left their ranks and crowded round the waggons to secure the most valuable portions of their property; each was busy about his own affairs, and purposely slow in hearing the word of command from his officers. Arminius now gave the signal for a general attack.

The fierce shouts of the Germans pealed through the gloom of the forests, and in thronging multitudes they assailed the flanks of the invaders, pouring in clouds of darts on the encumbered *legionaries*, as they struggled up the glens or floundered in the morasses, and watching every opportunity of charging through the intervals of the disjointed column, and so cutting off the communication between its several brigades. Arminius, with a chosen band of personal retainers round him, cheered on his countrymen by voice and example. He and his men aimed their weapons particularly at the horses of the Roman cavalry. The wounded animals, slipping about in the mire and their own blood, threw their riders, and plunged among the ranks of the legions, disordering all round them. Varus now ordered the troops to be countermarched, in the hope of reaching the nearest Roman garrison on the Lippe.[1]

But retreat now was as impracticable as advance; and the falling back of the Romans only augmented the courage of their assailants, and caused fiercer and more frequent charges on the flanks of the disheartened army. The Roman officer who commanded the cavalry, Numonius Vala, rode off with his squadrons, in the vain hope of escaping by thus abandoning his comrades. Unable to keep together, or force their way across the woods and swamps, the horsemen were overpowered in detail and slaughtered to the last man. The Roman infantry still held together and resisted, but more through the instinct of discipline and bravery than from any hope of success or escape.

Varus, after being severely wounded in a charge of the Germans against his part of the column, committed suicide to avoid falling into the hands of those whom he had exasperated by his oppressions. One of the lieutenant-generals of the army fell fighting; the other surrendered to the enemy. But mercy to a fallen foe had never been a Roman virtue, and those among her legions who now laid down their arms in hope of quarter, drank deep of the cup of suffering, which Rome had held to the lips of many a brave but unfortunate enemy. The infuriated Germans slaughtered their oppressors with deliberate ferocity;

1. The circumstances of the early part of the battle which Arminius fought with Caecina six years afterwards, evidently resembled those of his battle with Varus, and the result was very near being the same.

and those prisoners who were not hewn to pieces on the spot, were only preserved to perish by a more cruel death in cold blood.

The bulk of the Roman Army fought steadily and stubbornly, frequently repelling the masses of the assailants, but gradually losing the compactness of their array, and becoming weaker and weaker beneath the incessant shower of darts and the reiterated assaults of the vigorous and unencumbered Germans.

At last, in a series of desperate attacks the column was pierced through and through, two of the eagles captured, and the Roman host, which on the yester morning had marched forth in such pride and might, now broken up into confused fragments, either fell fighting beneath the overpowering numbers of the enemy, or perished in the swamps and woods in unavailing efforts at flight. Few, very few, ever saw again the left bank of the Rhine.

One body of brave veterans, arraying themselves in a ring on a little mound, beat off every charge of the Germans, and prolonged their honourable resistance to the close of that dreadful day. The traces of a feeble attempt at forming a ditch and mound attested in after years the spot where the last of the Romans passed their night of suffering and despair. But on the morrow this remnant also, worn out with hunger, wounds, and toil, was charged by the victorious Germans, and either massacred on the spot, or offered up in fearful rites at the alters of the deities of the old mythology of the North.

A gorge in the mountain ridge, through which runs the modern road between Paderborn and Pyrmont, leads from the spot where the heat of the battle raged, to the Extersteine, a cluster of bold and grotesque rocks of sandstone; near which is a small sheet of water, overshadowed by a grove of aged trees. According to local tradition, this was one of the sacred groves of the ancient Germans, and it was here that the Roman captives were slain in sacrifice by the victorious warriors of Arminius.

Never was victory more decisive, never was the liberation of an oppressed people more instantaneous and complete. Throughout Germany the Roman garrisons were assailed and cut off; and, within a few weeks after Varus had fallen, the German soil was freed from the foot of an invader.

At Rome, the tidings of the battle was received with an agony of terror, the descriptions of which we should deem exaggerated, did they not come from Roman historians themselves. These passages in the Roman writers not only tell emphatically how great was the awe which the Romans felt of the prowess of the Germans, if their various tribes could be brought to reunite for a common purpose, but also they reveal bow weakened and debased the population of Italy had become.[2] Dion Cassius says:

> Then Augustus, when he heard the calamity of Varus, rent his garments, and was in great affliction for the troops he had lost, and for terror respecting the Germans and the Gauls. And his chief alarm was, that he expected them to push on against Italy and Rome: and there remained no Roman youth fit for military duty, that were worth speaking of, and the allied populations that were at all serviceable had been wasted away. Yet he prepared for the emergency as well as his means allowed; and when none of the citizens of military age were willing to enlist he made them cast lots, and punished by confiscation of goods and disfranchisement every fifth man among those under thirty-five, and every tenth man of those above that age. At last, when he found that not even thus; could he make many come forward, he put some of them to death. So he made a conscription of discharged veterans and emancipated slaves, and collecting as large a force as he could, sent it, under Tiberius, with all speed into Germany.—Lib. lvi. sec. 23.

Dion mentions, also, a number of terrific portents that were believed to have occurred at the time; and the narration of which is not immaterial, as it shows the state of the public mind, when such things were so believed in, and so interpreted. The summits of the Alps were said to have fallen, and three columns of fire to have blazed up from them. In the Campus Martius, the temple of the War-God, from whom the founder of Rome had sprung, was struck by a thunderbolt. The nightly heavens glowed several times, as if on fire. Many comets blazed forth together; and fiery meteors shaped like spears, had shot from the northern quarter of the sky, down into the Roman camps. It was said, too, that a statue of Victory, which had stood at a place on the frontier, pointing the way towards Germany, had of its own accord turned round, and now pointed to Italy.

These and other prodigies were believed by the multitude to ac-

---

2. It is clear that the Romans followed the policy of fomenting dissension and wars of the Germans among themselves. See the thirty-third section of the "*Germania*" of Tacitus, where he mentions the destruction of the Bructeri by the neighbouring tribes.

company the slaughter of Varus's *legions*, and to manifest the anger of the gods against Rome, Augustus himself was not free from superstition; but on this occasion no supernatural terrors were needed to increase the alarm and grief that he felt; and which made him, even for months after the news of the battle had arrived, often beat his head against the wall, and exclaim, "Quintilius Varus, give me back my *legions*!" We learn this from his biographer, Suetonius; and, indeed, every ancient writer who alludes to the overthrow of Varus, attests the importance of the blow against the Roman power, and the bitterness with which it was felt.

The Germans did not pursue their victory beyond their own territory. But that victory secured at once and for ever the independence of the Teutonic race. Rome sent, indeed, her legions again into Germany, to parade a temporary superiority; but all hopes of permanent conquest were abandoned by Augustus and his successors.

The blow which Arminius had struck never was forgotten, Roman fear disguised itself under the specious title of moderation; and the Rhine became the acknowledged boundary of the two nations until the fifth century of our era, when the Germans became the assailants, and carved with their conquering swords the provinces of Imperial Rome into the kingdoms of modern Europe.

Arminius.

I have said above that the great Cheruscan is more truly one of our national heroes than Caractacus is. It may be added that an Englishman is entitled to claim a closer degree of relationship with Arminius than can be claimed by any German of modern Germany. The proof of this depends on the proof of four facts: first, that the Cherusci were Old Saxons, or Saxons of the interior of Germany; secondly, that the Anglo-Saxons, or Saxons of the coast of Germany, were more closely akin than other German tribes were to the Cheruscan Saxons; thirdly, that the Old Saxons were almost exterminated by Charlemagne; fourthly, that the Anglo-Saxons are our immediate ancestors. The last of these may be assumed as an axiom in English history. The proofs of the other three are partly philological, and partly historical. I have not space to go into them here. It may be, however, here remarked that the present Saxons of Germany are of the High Germanic division of the German race, whereas both the Anglo-Saxon and Old Saxon were of the Low Germanic.

Being thus the nearest heirs of the glory of Arminius, we may fairly devote more attention to his career than, in such a work as the present, could be allowed to any individual leader, and it is interesting to trace how far his fame survived during the middle ages, both among the Germans of the Continent and among ourselves.

It seems probable that the jealousy with which Maraboduus, the king of the Suevi and Marcomanni, regarded Arminius, and which ultimately broke out into open hostilities between those German tribes and the Cherusci, prevented Arminius from leading the confederate Germans to attack Italy after his first victory. Perhaps he may have had the rare moderation of being content with the liberation of his country, without seeking to retaliate on her former oppressors. When Tiberius marched into Germany in the year 10, Arminius was too cautious to attack him on ground favourable to the legions, and Tiberius was too skilful, to entangle his troops in difficult parts of the country. His march and counter-march were as unresisted as they were unproductive.

A few years later, when a dangerous revolt of the Roman legions near the frontier caused their generals to find them active employment by leading them into the interior of Germany, we find Arminius again energetic in his country's defence. The old quarrel between him and his father-in-law, Segestes, had broken out afresh. Segestes now called in the aid of the Roman general, Germanicus, to whom he surrendered himself; and by his contrivance his daughter Thusnelda, the wife of Arminius, also came into the hands of the Romans, being far advanced in pregnancy.

She showed, as Tacitus relates, more of the spirit of her husband than of her father, a spirit that could not be subdued into tears or supplications. She was sent to Ravenna, and there gave birth to a son, whose life we find, from an allusion in Tacitus, to have been eventful and unhappy; but the part of the great historian's work which narrated his fate has perished, and we only know from another quarter that the son of Arminius was, at the age of four years, led captive in a triumphal pageant along the streets of Rome.

The high spirit of Arminius was goaded almost into frenzy by these bereavements. The fate of his wife, thus torn from him, and of his babe doomed to bondage even before its birth, inflamed the eloquent invectives with which he roused his countrymen against the home traitors, and against their invaders, who thus made war upon women and children. Germanicus had marched his army to the place where Varus had perished, and had there paid funeral honours to the ghastly relics of his predecessor's *legions* that he found heaped around him.[3] Arminius lured him to advance a little further into the country, and then assailed him, and fought a battle, which, by the Roman accounts, was a drawn one. The effect of it was to make Germanicus resolve on retreating to the Rhine. He himself, with part of his troops, embarked in some vessels on the Ems, and returned by that river, and then by sea; but part of his forces were entrusted to a Roman general, named Caecina, to lead them back by land to the Rhine. Arminius followed this division on its march, and fought several battles with it, in which he inflicted heavy loss on the Romans, captured the greater part of their baggage, and would have destroyed them completely, had not his skilful system of operations been finally thwarted by the haste of Inguiomerus, a confederate German chief who insisted on assaulting the Romans in their camp, instead of waiting till they were entangled in the difficulties of the country, and assailing their columns on the march.

In the following year the Romans were inactive; but in the year afterwards Germanicus led a fresh invasion. He placed his army on ship-board, and sailed to the mouth of the Ems, where he disembarked, and marched to the Weser, where he encamped, probably in the neighbourhood of Minden. Arminius had collected his army on the other side of the river; and a scene occurred, which is powerfully told by Tacitus, and which is the subject of a beautiful poem by Praed. It has been already mentioned that the brother of Arminius, like himself, had been trained up, while young, to serve in the Roman armies; but, unlike Arminius, he not only refused to quit the Roman service for that of his country, but fought against his country with the *legions* of Germanicus. He had assumed the Roman name of Flavius, and had gained considerable distinction in the Roman service, in which he had lost an eye from a wound in battle.

When the Roman outposts approached the River Weser, Arminius called out to them from the opposite bank, and expressed a wish to see his brother. Flavius stepped forward, and Arminius ordered his own followers to retire, and requested that the archers should be removed from the Roman bank of the river. This was done: and the brothers, who apparently had not seen each other for some years, began a conversation from the opposite sides of the stream, in which Arminius

3. In the Museum of Rhenish antiquities at Bonn there is a Roman sepulchral monument, the inscription on which records that it was erected to the memory of M. Coelius, who fell *Bello Variano*.

questioned his brother respecting the loss of his eye, and what battle it had been lost in, and what reward he had received for his wound. Flavius told him how the eye was destroyed, and mentioned the increased pay that he had on account of its loss, and showed the collar and other military decorations that had been given him.

Arminius mocked at these as badges of slavery; and then each began to try to win the other over; Flavius boasting the power of Rome, and her generosity to the submissive; Arminius appealing to him in the name of their country's gods, of the mother that had borne them, and by the holy names of fatherland and freedom, not to prefer being the betrayer to being the champion of his country. They soon proceeded to mutual taunts and menaces, and Flavius called aloud for his horse and his arms, that he might dash across the river and attack his brother; nor would he have been checked from doing so, had not the Roman general, Stertinius, run up to him, and forcibly detained him. Arminius stood on the other bank, threatening the renegade, and defying him to battle.

I shall not be thought to need apology for quoting here the stanzas in which Praed has described this scene—a scene among the most affecting, as well as the most striking, that history supplies. It makes us reflect on the desolate position of Arminius, with his wife and child captives in the enemy's hands, and with his brother a renegade in arms against him. The great liberator of our German race stood there, with every source of human happiness denied him, except the consciousness of doing his duty to his country.

On the day after the Romans had reached the Weser, Germanicus led his army across that river, and a partial encounter took place, in which Arminius was successful. But on the succeeding day a general action was fought, in which Arminius was severely wounded, and the German infantry routed with heavy loss. The horsemen of the two armies encountered without either party gaining the advantage. But the Roman army remained master of the ground, and claimed a complete victory. Germanicus erected a trophy in the field, with a vaunting inscription, that the nations between the Rhine and the Elbe had been thoroughly conquered by his army. But that army speedily made a final retreat to the left bank of the Rhine; nor was the effect of their campaign more durable than their trophy.

The sarcasm with which Tacitus speaks of certain other triumphs of Roman generals over Germans, may apply to the pageant which Germanicus celebrated on his return to Rome from his command of the Roman army of the Rhine. The Germans were "*triumphati potius quam victi.*"

After the Romans had abandoned their attempts on Germany, we find Arminius engaged in hostilities with Maroboduus, the king of the Suevi and Marcomanni who was endeavouring to bring the other German tribes into a state of dependency on him. Arminius was at the head of the Germans who took up arms against this home invader of their liberties. After some minor engagements, a pitched battle was fought between the two confederacies, *A.D.* 16, in which the loss on each side was equal; but Maroboduus confessed the ascendency of his antagonist by avoiding a renewal of the engagement, and by imploring the intervention of the Romans in his defence. The younger Drusus then commanded the Roman *legions* in the province of Illyricum, and by his mediation a peace was concluded between Arminius and Maroboduus, by the terms of which it is evident that the latter must have renounced his ambitious schemes against the freedom of the other German tribes.

Arminius did not long survive this second war of independence, which he successfully waged for his country. He was assassinated in the thirty-seventh year of his age, by some of his own kinsmen, who conspired against him. Tacitus says that this happened while he was engaged in a civil war, which had been caused by his attempts to make himself king over his countrymen. It is far more probable (as one of the best biographers of Arminius has observed) that Tacitus misunderstood an attempt of Arminius to extend his influence as elective war-chieftain of the Cherusci, and other tribes, for an attempt to obtain the royal dignity. When we remember that his father-in-law and his brother were renegades, we can well understand that a party among his kinsmen may have been bitterly hostile to him, and have opposed his authority with the tribe by open violence, and when that seemed ineffectual, by secret assassination.

Arminius left a name, which the historians of the nation against which he combated so long and so gloriously have delighted to honour. It is from the most indisputable source, from the lips of enemies, that we know his exploits. His country men made history, but did not write it. But his memory lived among them in the lays of their bards, who recorded

The deeds he did, the fields he won, The freedom he restored.

Tacitus, many years after the death of Arminius, says of him, "*Can-*

itur adhuc barbaras apud gentes." As time passed on, the gratitude of ancient Germany to her great deliverer grew into adoration, and divine honours were paid for centuries to Arminius by every tribe of the Low Germanic division of the Teutonic races. The Irmin-sul, or the column of Herman, near Eresburg, the modern Stadtberg, was the chosen object of worship to the descendants of the Cherusci, the Old Saxons, and in defence of which they fought most desperately against Charlemagne and his christianised Franks.

> Irmin, in the cloudy Olympus of Teutonic belief, appears as a king and a warrior; and the pillar, the 'Irmin-sul,' bearing the statue, and considered as the symbol of the deity, was the Palladium of the Saxon nation, until the temple of Eresburg was destroyed by Charlemagne, and the column itself transferred to the monastery of Corbey, where, perhaps, a portion of the rude rock idol yet remains, covered by the ornaments of the Gothic era.—Palgrave on the English Commonwealth, vol. ii.

Traces of the worship of Arminius are to be found among our Anglo-Saxon ancestors, after their settlement in this island. One of the four great highways was held to be under the protection of the deity, and was called the "Irmin-street." The name Arminius is, of course, the mere Latinized form of "Herman," the name by which the hero and the deity were known by every man of Low German blood, on either side of the German Sea. It means, etymologically, the "Warman," the "man of hosts." No other explanation of the worship of the "Irmin-sul," and of the name of the "Irmin-street," is so satisfactory as that which connects them with the deified Arminius. We know for certain of the existence of other columns of an analogous character. Thus, there was the Roland-seule in North Germany; there was a Thor-seule in Sweden, and (what is more important) there was an Athelstan-seule in Saxon England.

There is at the present moment a song respecting the Irmin-sul current in the bishopric of Minden, one version of which might seem only to refer to Charlemagne having pulled down the Irmin-sul:—

But there is another version, which probably is the oldest, and which clearly refers to the great Arminius:—

About ten centuries and a half after the demolition of the Irminsul, and nearly eighteen after the death of Arminius, the modern Germans conceived the idea of rendering tardy homage to their great hero; and, accordingly some eight or ten years ago, a general subscription was organised in Germany, for the purpose of erecting on the Osning—a conical mountain, which forms the highest summit of the Teutoberger Wald, and is eighteen hundred feet above the level of the sea—a colossal bronze statue of Arminius. The statue was designed by Bandel. The hero was to stand uplifting a sword in his right hand, and looking towards the Rhine. The height of the statue was to be eighty feet from the base to the point of the sword, and was to stand on a circular Gothic temple, ninety feet high, and supported by oak trees as columns.

The mountain, where it was to be erected, is wild and stern, and overlooks the scene of the battle. It was calculated that the statue would be clearly visible at a distance of sixty miles. The temple is nearly finished, and the statue itself has been cast at the copper works at Lemgo. But there, through want of funds to set it up, it has lain for some years, in disjointed fragments, exposed to the mutilating homage of relic-seeking travellers. The idea of honouring a hero who belongs to *all* Germany, is not one which the present rulers of that divided country have any wish to encourage; and the statue may long continue to lie there, and present too true a type of the condition of Germany herself.

Surely this is an occasion in which Englishmen might well prove, by acts as well as words, that we also rank Arminius among our heroes.

The Catapult and the Balista

By Ralph Payne-Gallwey

Since my recent work on the crossbow and ancient projectile weapons was issued. I have obtained additional information concerning the catapult and *balista* of the Greeks and Romans. I now, therefore, print a revised account of the construction of these two engines. Their history and effects in warfare I have already dealt with.

R. P. G.

Thirkleby Park,
Thirsk:
Jan. 1907.

Introductory Notes on Ancient Projectile Engines

Of ancient Greek authors who have left us accounts of these engines. Heron (284-221 B.C.) and Philo (about 200 B.C.) are the most trustworthy.

Both these mechanicians give plans and dimensions with an accuracy that enables us to reconstruct the machines, if not with exactitude at any rate with sufficient correctness for practical application.

Though in the books of Athensus, Biton, Apollodorus, Diodorus, Procopius, Polybius and Josephus we find incomplete descriptions, these authors, especially Josephus, frequently allude to the effects of the engines in warfare; and scanty as is the knowledge they impart, it is useful and explanatory when read in conjunction with the writings of Heron and Philo.

Among the Roman historians and military engineers, Vitruvius and Ammianus are the best authorities.

Vitruvius copied his descriptions from the Greek writers, which shows us that the Romans adopted the engines from the Greeks.

Of all the old authors who have described the engines, we have but copies of the original writings. It is, therefore, natural that we should come across many phrases and drawings which are evidently incorrect, as a result of repeated transcription, and which we know to be at fault though we cannot actually prove them to be so.

With few exceptions, all the authors named simply present us with their own ideas when they are in doubt respecting the mechanical details and performances of the engines they wish to describe.

All such spurious information is, of course, more detrimental than helpful to our elucidation of their construction and capabilities.

It frequently happens that in a mediaeval picture of one of these machines some important mechanical detail is omitted, or, from the difficulty of portraying it correctly, is purposely concealed by figures of soldiers, an omission that may be supplied by reference to other representations of the same weapon.

It is, indeed, impossible to find a complete working plan of any one of these old weapons, a perfect design being only obtainable by consulting many ancient authorities, and, it may be said, piecing together the details of construction they individually give.

We have no direct evidence as to when the engines for throwing projectiles were invented.

It does not appear that King Shalmaneser II. of Assyria (859-825 B.C.) had any, for none are depicted on the bronze doors of the palace of Baliwat, now in the British Museum, on which his campaigns are represented, though his other weapons of attack and defence are clearly shown.

The earliest allusion is the one in the Bible, where we read of Uzziah, who reigned from B.C. 808-9 to B.C. 756-7. 'Uzziah made in Jerusalem engines invented by cunning men, to be on the towers and upon the bulwarks, to shoot arrows and great stones withal.' (2 Chronicles xxvi. 15.)

Diodorus tells us that the engines were first seen about 400 B.C., and that when Dionysius of Syracuse organised his great expedition against the Carthaginians (397 B.C.) there was a genius among the experts collected from all over the world, and that this man designed the engines that cast stones and javelins.

From the reign of Dionysius and for many subsequent centuries, or till near the close of the fourteenth, projectile-throwing engines are constantly mentioned by military historians.

But it was not till the reign of Philip of Macedon (360-336 B.C.) and that of his son Alexander the Great (336-323 B.C.) that their improvement was carefully attended to and their value in warfare fully recognised.

As before stated, the Romans adopted the engines from the Greeks.

Vitruvius and other historians tell us this, and even copy their descriptions of them from the Greek authors, though too often with palpable inaccuracy.

To ascertain the power and mechanism of these ancient engines a very close study of all the old authors who wrote about them is essential, with a view to extracting here and there useful facts amid what are generally verbose and confused references.

There is no doubt that the engines made and used by the Romans after their conquest of Greece (B.C. 146), in the course of two or three centuries became inferior to the original machines previously constructed by the Greek artificers.

Their efficiency chiefly suffered because the art of manufacturing their important parts was gradually neglected and allowed to become lost.

For instance, how to make the skein of sinew that bestowed the very life and existence on every projectile-casting engine of the ancients.

The tendons of which the sinew was composed, the animals from which it was taken, and the manner in which it was prepared, we can never learn now.

Every kind of sinew, or hair or rope, with which I have experimented, either breaks or loses its elasticity in a comparatively short time, if great pressure is applied. It has then to be renewed at no small outlay of expense and trouble. Rope skeins, with which we are obliged to fit our models, cannot possibly equal in strength, and above all in elasticity, skeins of animal sinew or even of hair.

The formation of the arm or arms of an engine, whether it is a catapult with its single upright arm or a *balista* with its pair of lateral ones, is another difficulty which cannot now be overcome, for we have no idea how these arms were made to sustain the great strain they had to endure.

We know that the arm of a large engine was composed of several spars of wood and lengths of thick sinew fitted longitudinally, and then bound round with broad strips of raw hide which would afterwards set nearly as hard and tight as a sheath of metal.

We know this, but we do not know the secret of making a light and flexible arm of sufficient strength to bear such a strain as was formerly applied to it in a catapult or a *balista*.

Certainly, by shaping an arm of great thickness we can produce one that will not fracture, but substance implies weight, and undue weight prevents the arm from acting with the speed requisite to cast its projectile with good effect.

A heavy and ponderous arm of solid wood cannot, of course, rival in lightness and effectiveness a composite one of wood, sinew and hide.

The former is necessarily inert and slow in its action of slinging a stone, while the latter would, in comparison, be as quick and lively as a steel spring.

When the art of producing the perfected machines of the Greeks was lost, they were replaced by less effective contrivances.

If the knowledge of constructing the great catapult of the ancients in its original perfection had been retained, such a clumsy engine as the medieval trebuchet would never have gained popularity. The trebuchet derived its power from the gravity of an immense weight at one end of its pivoted arm tipping up the other end, to which a sling was attached for throwing a stone.

As regards range, there could be no comparison between the efficiency of a *trebuchet*, however large, as worked merely by a counterpoise, and that of an engine deriving its power from the elasticity of an immense coil of tightly twisted sinew.

It is certain that if the latter kind of engine had survived in its perfect state the introduction of cannon would have been considerably delayed, for the effects in warfare of the early cannon were for a long period decidedly inferior to those of the best projectile engines of the ancients.

Notwithstanding many difficulties, I have succeeded in reconstructing, though of course on a considerably smaller scale, the chief projectile-throwing engines of the ancients, and with a success that enables them to compare favourably, as regards their range, with the Greek and Roman weapons they represent.

Still, my engines are by no means perfect in their mechanism, and are, besides, always liable to give way under the strain of working.

One reason of this is that all modern engines of the kind require to be worked to their utmost capacity, *i.e.* to the verge of their breaking point, to obtain from them results that at all equal those of their prototypes.

A marked difference between the ancient engines and their modern imitations, however excellent the latter may be, is, that the former did their work easily, and well within their strength, and thus without any excessive strain which might cause their collapse after a short length of service.[1]

The oft-disputed question as to the distance to which catapults

---

1. Again, though my largest catapult will throw a stone to a great distance it cannot throw one of nearly the weight n should be able to do, considering the size of its frame, skein of cord and mechanism. In this respect it is decidedly inferior to the ancient engine.

and *balistas* shot their projectiles can be solved with approximate accuracy by comparing their performances—as given by ancient military writers—with the results obtainable from modern reproductions.

While treating of this matter we should carefully consider the position and surroundings of the engines when engaged in a siege, and especially the work for which they were designed.

As an example, archers, with the advantage of being stationed on high towers and battlements, would be well able to shoot arrows from 270 to 280 yards. For this reason it was necessary for the safe manipulation of the attacking engines that they should be placed at about 300 yards from the outer walls of any fortress they were assailing.

As a catapult or a *balista* was required not only to cast its missile among the soldiers on the ramparts of a fortified place, but also to send it clear over the walls amid the houses and people within the defences, it is evident that the engines must have had a range of from 400 to 500 yards, or more, to be as serviceable and destructive as they undoubtedly were.

Josephus tells us that at the siege of Jerusalem, *A.D.* 70 (*Wars of the Jews*, Book V. Chapter VI.), stones weighing a talent (57! lbs. avoirdupois) were thrown by the catapults to a distance of two or more '*stades*.'

This statement may be taken as trustworthy, for Josephus relates what he personally witnessed and his comments are those of a commander of high rank and intelligence.

Two or more '*stades*,' or let us say 2 to 2¼ '*stades*,' represent 400 to 450 yards. Remarkable and conclusive testimony confirming the truth of what we read in Josephus is the fact that my largest catapult—though doubtless much smaller and less powerful than those referred to by the historian—throws a stone ball of 8 lbs. in weight to a range of from 450 to nearly 500 yards.

It is easy to realise that the ancients, with their great and perfect engines fitted with skeins of sinew, could cast a far heavier stone than one of 8 lbs., and to a longer distance than 500 yards.

Agesistratus,[2] a Greek writer who flourished B.C. 200, and who wrote a treatise on making arms for war, estimated that some of the engines shot from 3½ to 4 '*stades*' (700 to 800 yards).

Though such a very long flight as this appears almost incredible, I can adduce no sound reason for doubting its possibility. From recent experiments I am confident I could now build an engine of a size and

2. The writings of Agesistratus are non-extant but are quoted by Atheneeus.

Fig. 1.—Sketch plan of a catapult for slinging stones, its arms being partly wound down.

power to accomplish such a feat if light missiles were used, and if its cost were not a consideration.

The Catapult (With A Sling)

The mediaeval catapult was. usually fitted with an arm that had a hollow or cup at its upper end in which was placed the stone it projected.[3] I find, however, that the original and more perfect form of this engine, as employed by the Greeks and ancient Romans, had a sling, made of rope and leather, attached to its arm.[3] (Fig. 1 opposite page.)

The addition of a sling to the arm of a catapult increases its power by at least a third. For example, the catapult will throw a round stone 8 lbs. in weight, from 350 to 360 yards, but the same engine with the advantage of a sling to its arm will cast the 8-lb. stone from 450 to 460 yards, and when its skein is twisted to its limit of tension to nearly 500 yards.

If the upper end of the arm of a catapult is shaped into a cup to receive the stone, the arm is, of necessity, large and heavy at this part.

If, on the other hand, the arm is equipped with a sling, as shown in fig. 1, it can be tapered from its butt-end upwards, and is then much lighter and recoils with far more speed than an arm that has an enlarged extremity for holding its missile.

When the arm is fitted with a sling, it is practically lengthened by as much as the length of the sling attached to it, and this, too, without any appreciable increase in its weight.

The longer the arm of a catapult, the longer is its sweep through the air, and thus the farther will it cast its projectile, provided it is not of undue weight.

The difference in this respect is as between the range of a short sling and that of a long one, when both are used by a schoolboy for slinging pebbles.

---

3. In mediaeval times catapults which had not slings cast great stones, but only to a short distance in comparison with the earlier weapons of the same kind that were equipped with slings. I can find no allusions or pictures to show that during this period any engine was used with a sling except the *trebuchet*, a post-Roman invention. All evidence goes to prove that the secret of making the skein and other important parts of a catapult was in a great measure lost within a couple of centuries after the Romans copied the weapon from their conquered enemies the Greeks, with the result that the trebuchet was introduced for throwing stones. The catapult was gradually superseded as the art of its construction was neglected, and its efficiency in sieges was therefrom decreased. The catapults of the fifth and sixth centuries were very inferior to those described by Josephus as being used at the sieges of Jerusalem and Jotapata (*A.D.* 70, *A.D.* 67).

The increase of power conferred by the addition of a sling to the arm of a catapult is surprising.

A small model I constructed for throwing a stone ball, 1 lb. in weight, will attain a distance of 200 yards when used with an arm that has a cup for holding the ball, though when a sling is fitted to the arm the range of the engine is at once increased to 300 yards.

The, only historian who distinctly tells us that the catapult of the Greeks and Romans had a sling to its arm, is Ammianus Marcellinus. This author flourished about 380 *A.D.*, and a closer study of his writings, and of those of his contemporaries, led me to carry out experiments with catapults and *balistas* which I had not contemplated when my work dealing with the projectile engines of the ancients was published.

Ammianus writes of the catapult[4]:

> In the middle of the ropes (*i.e. in the middle of the twisted skein formed of ropes of sinew or hair*), rises a wooden arm like a chariot pole . . . to the top of the arm hangs a sling . . . when battle is commenced a round stone is set in the sling . . . four soldiers on each side of the engine wind the arm down till it is almost level with the ground . . . when the arm is set free it springs up and hurls forth from its sling the stone, which is certain to crush whatever it strikes. This engine was formerly called the "scorpion," because it has its sting erect, (*the upright and tapering arm of a catapult, with the iron pin on its top for the loop of the sling, is here fancifully likened to the erected tail of an angry scorpion with its sting protruding*), but later ages have given it the name of Onager, or wild ass, for when wild asses are chased they kick the stones behind them.

FIG. 2.—CATAPULT (WITH A SLING), SEE OPPOSITE PAGE.

A. The arm at rest, ready to be wound down by the rope attached to it and also to the wooden roller of the windlass. The stone may be seen in the sling.

The upper end of the pulley rope is hitched by a metal slip-hook (fig. 1) to a ring-bolt secured to the arm just below the sling.

B. The position of the arm when fully wound down by means of the windlass and rope. See also EE, fig. 3.

C. The position of the arm at the moment the stone D leaves the sling, which it does at an angle of about 45 degrees.

---

4. *Roman History*, Book XXIII., Chapter IV.

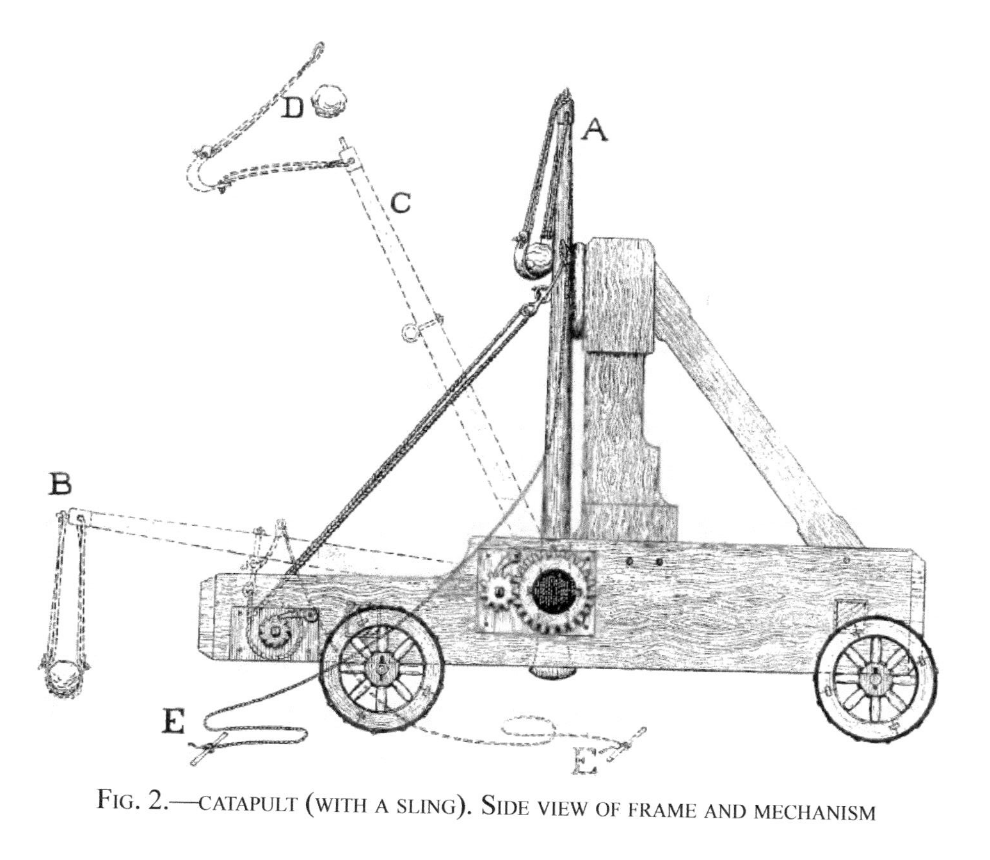

FIG. 2.—CATAPULT (WITH A SLING). SIDE VIEW OF FRAME AND MECHANISM

E. By pulling the cord E the arm B Is at once released from the slip-hook and, taking an upward sweep of 90 degrees, returns to its original position at A.

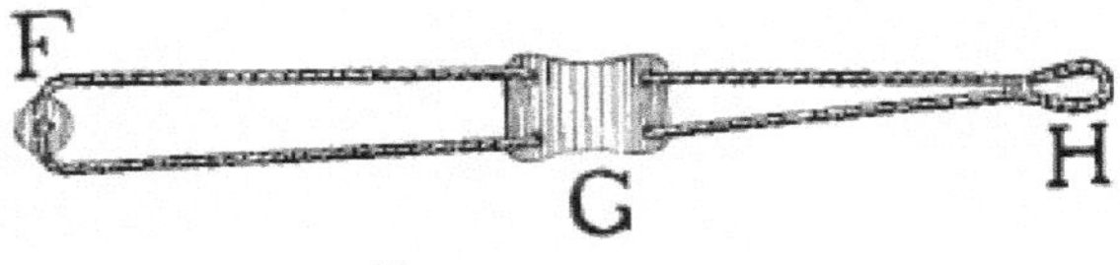

THE SLING OPEN

F. Its fixed end which passes through a hole near the top of the arm.
G. The leather pocket for the stone.

H. The loop which is hitched over the iron pin at the top of the arm when the stone is in position in the sling, as shown at A and B, fig. 2.

I. I. II. II. The side-pieces.

III. IV. The large cross-pieces.

V. The small cross-piece.

The ends of the cross-piece beams are stepped into the side-pieces.

AA. The skein of twisted cord.

BB. The large winding wheels. The skein is stretched between these wheels, its ends passing through the sides of the frame, and then through the wheels and over their cross-bars. (Fig. 6.)

By turning with a long spanner (fig. 1) the squared ends of the spindles DD, the pinion wheels CC rotate the large wheels BB and cause the latter to twist the skein A A, between the halves of which the arm EE is placed.

FF. The wooden roller which winds down the arm EE. (Fig. 1)

The roller is revolved by four men (two on each side of the engine) who fit long spanners on the squared ends of the iron spindle GG.

This spindle passes through the centre of the roller and through the sides of the frame.

The small cogged wheels, with their checks, which are fitted to the ends of the spindle GG, prevent the roller from reversing as the arm is being wound down. (Fig. 1.)

HH. The hollows in the sides of the frame which receive the lower tenons of the two uprights. Between the tops of these uprights the cross-beam is fixed against which the arm of the catapult strikes when it is released. (Fig. 1)

KK. The hollows for the lower tenons of the two sloping supports

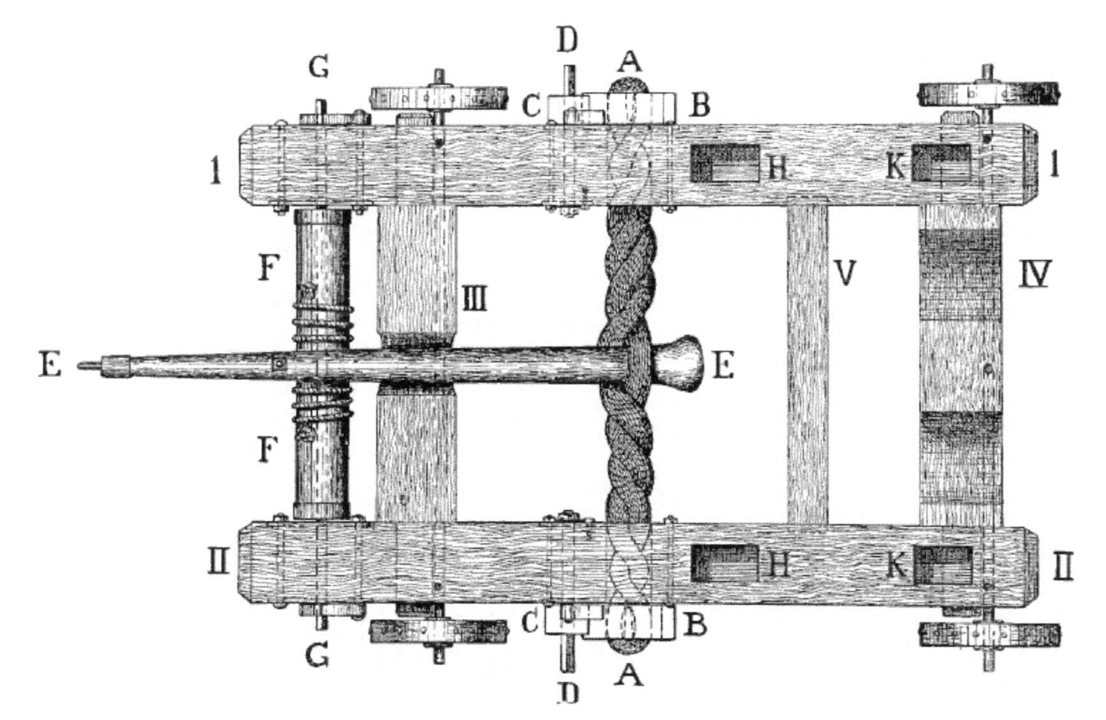

Fig. 3—Catapult (with a sling). Surface view of frame and mechanism.
The arm EE is here shown wound down to its full extent. (Compare with B, fig. 2.)

which prevent the uprights, and the cross-beam between them, from giving way when the arm recoils. (Fig. 1)

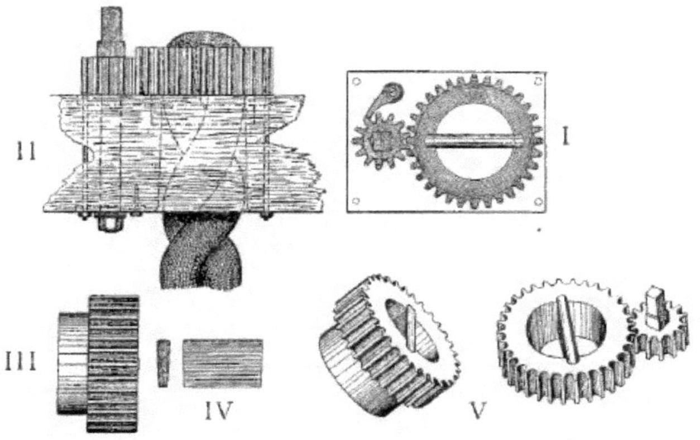

FIG. 4.— ONE OF THE PAIR OF WINCHES OF A CATAPULT.

I. Surface view of one of the winches and of the thick iron plate in which the socket of the large winding wheel of the winch revolves.

II. View of a winch (from above) as fitted into one of the sides of the frame of the catapult. One end of the twisted skein may be seen turned round the cross-bar of the large wheel.

III. Side view of the large wheel of a winch.

IV. The cross-bar of one of the large wheels. These pieces fit like wedges into tapering slots cut down the barrels, or inside surfaces, of their respective wheels.

V. Perspective view of the wheels of a winch.

The winches are the vital parts of the catapult, as they generate its projectile power.

They are employed to twist tightly the skein of cord between which the butt-end of the arm of the engine is placed.

The cord composing the skein is stretched to and fro across and through the sides of the catapult, and alternately through the insides of the large wheels and over their cross-bars; as shown in fig. 3.

FIG. 5.—THE IRON SLIP-HOOK.

This simple contrivance not only pulled down the arm of a catapult but was also the means of setting it free. However great the strain on the slip-hook, it will, if properly shaped, easily effect the release of the arm.

The trajectory of the missile can be regulated by this form of release, as the longer the distance the arm is pulled

FIG. 5.

down the higher the angle at which the projectile is thrown.

On the other hand, the shorter the distance the arm is drawn back, the lower the trajectory of its missile.

The slip-hook will release the arm of the engine at any moment, whether it is fully or only partially wound down by the windlass.

The slip-hook of the large catapult shown in fig. 1, has a handle *i.e.* lever, 10 inches long, the point of the hook, which passes through the eye-bolt secured to the arm, being 1 in. in diameter.

FIG. 6.—THE SKEIN OF CORD.

A. The skein as first wound over the cross-bars of the large wheels (shown in section) of the winches.

B. The skein with the butt-end of the arm (shown in section) placed between its halves.

C. The skein as it appears when tightly twisted up by the W | inches. Compare with A A, fig. 3.

Cord of Italian hemp, about ¼ in. thick, is excellent for small catapults. For large ones, horsehair rope, ½ in. thick, is the best and most

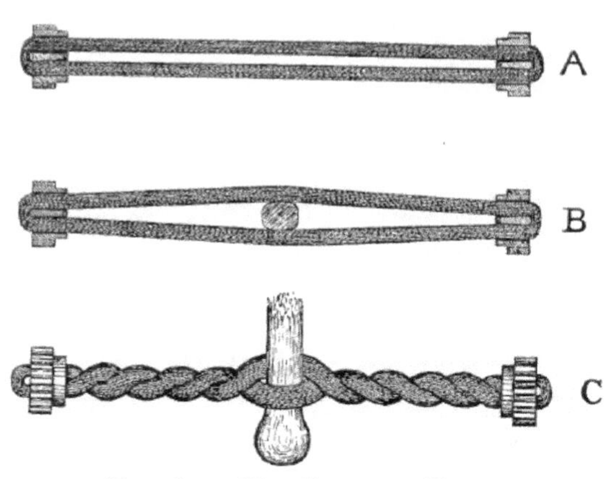

FIG, 6. — THE SKEIN OF CORD.

elastic. Whatever is used, the material of the skein must be thoroughly soaked in neat's-foot oil for some days previously, or it is sure to fray and cut under the friction of being very tightly twisted. Oil will also preserve the skein from damp and decay for many years.

How to Work the Catapult

There is little to write under this heading; as the plans, details of construction and illustrations will, I trust, elucidate its management.

The skein should never remain in a tightly twisted condition, but should be untwisted when the engine is not in use.

Previous to using the catapult its winches should be turned with the long spanner, fig. 1, first the winch on one side of the engine and then the one on the other side of it, and each to exactly the same amount.

Small numerals painted on the surfaces of the large wheels, near their edges, will show how much they have been revolved; in this way their rotation can be easily arranged to correspond.

As the skein of cord is being twisted by the very powerful winches, the arm will gradually press with increasing force against the cross-beam between the uprights. The arm should be so tightly pressed against the fender, or cushion of straw, attached to the centre of this beam, that it cannot be pulled back the least distance by hand. .

If the skein of my largest catapult is fully tightened up by the winches, three strong men are unable to draw the arm back with a rope even an inch from the cross-beam, though the windlass has to pull it down from six to seven feet when the engine is made ready for action.

When the skein is as tight as it should be, attach the slip-hook to the ring-bolt in the arm and place the stone in the sling suspended from the top of the arm.

The arm can now be drawn down by means of long spanners fitted to the windlass. Directly the arm is as low as it should be, or as is desired, it should be instantly released by pulling the cord fastened to the lever of the slip-hook.

The least delay in doing this, and the resulting continuation of the immense strain on the arm, may cause it to fracture when it would not otherwise have done so.

The plans I have given are those of my largest engine, which, ponderous as it seems—(it weighs two tons)— is, however, less than half the size of the catapult used by the ancients for throwing stones of from forty to fifty pounds in weight.

As the plans are accurately drawn to scale, the engine can easily be reproduced in a smaller size.

An interesting model can be constructed that has an arm 3 feet in length, and a skein of cord about 4 inches in diameter. It can be worked by one man and will throw a stone, the size of an orange, to a range of 300 yards.

The sling, when suspended with the stone in position, should be one third the length of the arm, as shown in fig. 2.

If the sling is shortened, the ball will be thrown at a high elevation. If the sling is lengthened, the ball will travel at a lower angle and with much more velocity.

The Balista

This engine is here shown ready for discharge with its bow-string drawn to its full extent by the windlass.

The heavy iron-tipped arrow rests in the shallow wooden trough which travels along the stock.

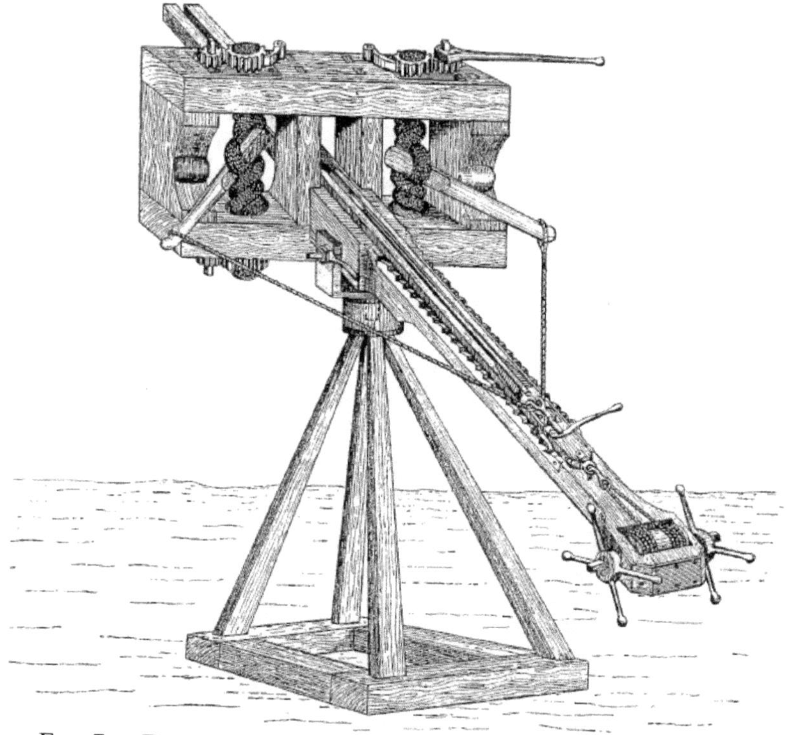

Fig. 7.—Balista for discharging heavy Arrows or Javelins.

The trough has a strip of wood, in the form of a keel, fixed beneath it. This keel travels to or fro in a dovetailed slot cut along the upper surface of the stock for the greater part of its length. (F, fig. 8.)

The arrow is laid in the trough before the bow-string is stretched. (A, B, fig. 8.)

The *balista* is made ready for use by turning the windlass. The windlass pulls back the sliding trough, and the arrow resting in it, along the stock of the engine, till the bow-string is at its proper tension for discharging the projectile. (Fig. 7.)

As the trough and the arrow are drawn back together, the arrow can be safely laid in position before the engine is prepared for action.

The catch for holding the bow-string, and the trigger for releasing it, are fixed to the solid after-end of the wooden trough. (Fig. 8.)

The two ratchets at the sides of the after-end of the trough travel over and engage, as they pass along, the metal cogs fixed on either side of the stock. (Fig. 8) When the bow-string has been released and the arrow discharged, the ratchets are lifted clear of the cogs on the stock of the engine. This allows the trough to be slid forward to its first position as shown in A, B, fig. 8. It is then ready to be drawn back again for the next shot.

By this arrangement the trough can be securely retained, in transit, at any point between the one it started from and the one it attains when drawn back to its full extent by the windlass.

As the lock and trigger of the *balista* are fitted to the after-end of the sliding trough (G, fig. 8), it will be realised that the arrow could be discharged at any moment required in warfare, whether the bow-string was fully or only partially stretched.

In this respect the *balista* differed from the crossbow, which it somewhat resembled, as in a crossbow the bow-string cannot be set free by the trigger at an intermediate point, but only when it is drawn to the lock of the weapon.

It will be seen that the *balista* derives its power from two arms; each with its separate skein of cord and pair of winches.

These parts of the *balista* are the same in their action and mechanism as those of the catapult.

FIG. 8. THE MECHANISM OF THE STOCK OF AN ARROW-THROWING BALISTA.

A. Side view of the stock, with the arrow laid in the sliding trough before the bow-string is stretched.

B. Surface view of the stock, with the arrow laid in the sliding-trough before the bow-string is stretched.

C. Section of the fore-end of the stock, and of the trough which slides in and along it.

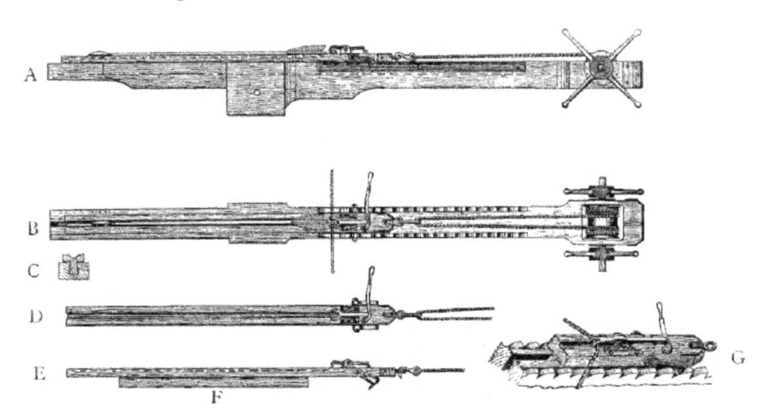

FIG. 8.—THE MECHANISM OF THE STOCK OF AN ARROW-THROWING BALISTA.

D. Surface view of the trough, with the trigger and catch for the bow-string.

E. Side view, showing the keel (F) which slides along the slot cut in the surface of the stock as the trough is drawn back by the windlass.

G. Enlarged view of the solid end of the trough. This sketch shows the catch for the bow-string, the trigger which sets it free, the ratchets which engage the cogs on the sides of the stock, and the slot cut in the stock for the dove-tailed keel of the trough to travel in.

Balistas were constructed of different sizes for the various purposes of siege and field warfare. The smallest of these engines was not larger than a heavy crossbow, though it more

The small *balistas* were chiefly used for shooting through loopholes and from battlemented walls at an enemy assaulting with scaling ladders and movable towers. The largest had arms of 3 ft. to 4 ft. in length, and skeins of twisted sinew of 6 in. to 8 in. in diameter.

Judging from models I have made and carefully experimented with, it is certain that the more powerful *balistas* of the ancients could cast arrows, or rather feathered javelins, of from 5 to 6 lbs. weight, to a range of from 450 to 500 yards.

It will be seen that this engine is almost identical in construction with the one last described. (Fig. 7.)

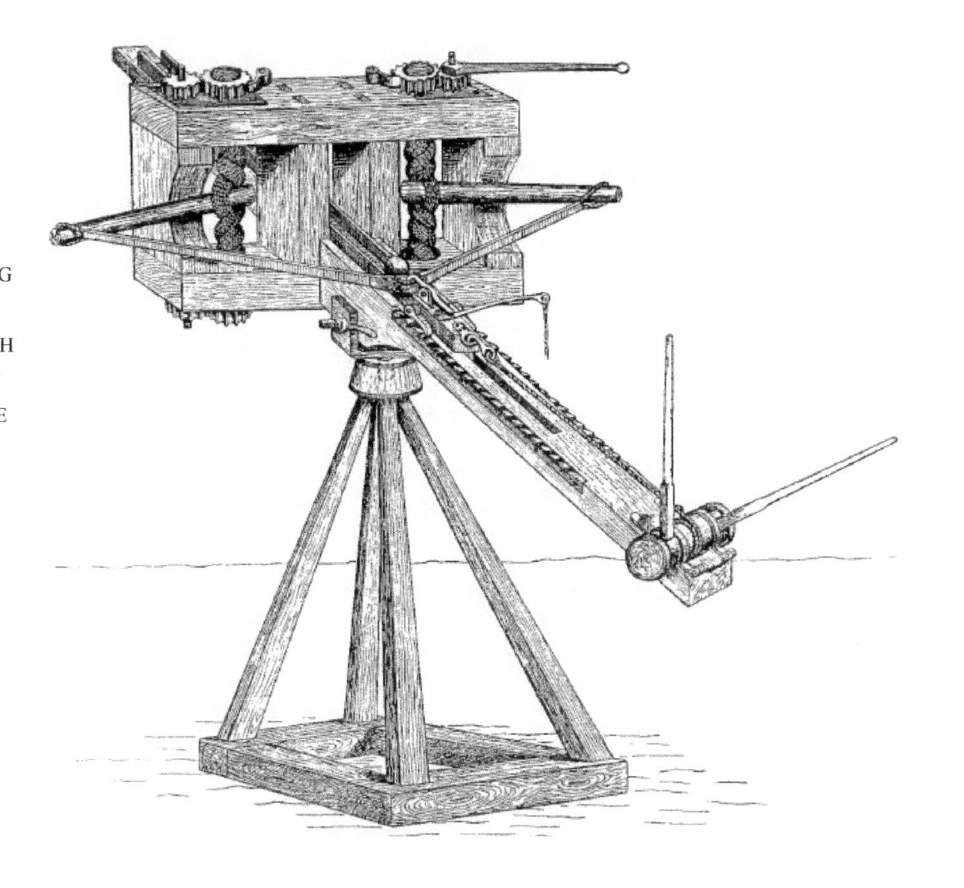

Fig. 9.—Balista for throwing Stone Balls.
This engine is here shown with its bow-string only slightly drawn along its stock by the windlass.

The difference is that it propelled a stone ball instead of a large arrow. The ball was driven along a square wooden trough, one-third of the diameter of the ball being enclosed by the sides of the trough so as to keep the missile in a true direction after the bow-string was released. The bow-string was in the form of a broad band, with an enlargement at its centre against which the ball rested.

The description given of the mechanism and management of the engine for throwing arrows can be applied to the construction and manipulation of this form of *balista*, which was also made of large and small dimensions.

Small engines, with arms about 2 ft. in length and skeins of cord about 4 in. in diameter, such as those I have built for experiment, will send a stone ball, 1 lb. in weight, from 300 to 350 yards.

There is little doubt that the large stone-throwing *balista* of the Greeks, and Romans was able to project a circular stone, of 6 to 8 lbs. weight, to a distance of from 450 to 500 yards.

The balls used by the ancients in their catapults and *balistas* were often formed of heavy pebbles inclosed in baked clay, the reason being that balls made in this way shattered on falling and hence could not be shot back by the engines of the enemy. The *balistas* for throwing arrows, and those employed for casting stones, were fitted with axles and wheels when constructed for use in field warfare.

A. Surface view, with the stone in position.

B. Side view, with the stone in position.

C. Front view of the stone as it rests in the trough against the enlarged centre of the bow-string.

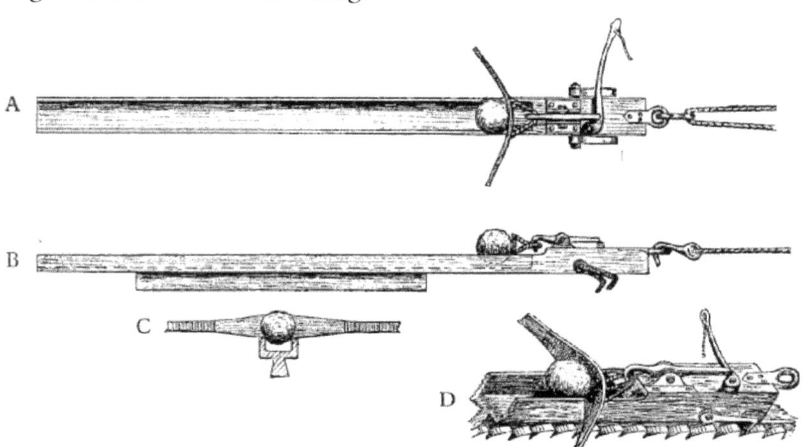

FIG. 10.—THE SLIDING TROUGH OF THE STONE-THROWING BALISTA.

D. Enlarged view of the solid end of the sliding trough. This sketch shows the ball in position against the bow-string; the catch holding the loop of the bow-string, and the pivoted trigger which, when pulled, releases the catch. One of the pair of ratchets which engage the cogs on the sides of the stock, as the trough is drawn back by the windlass to make ready the engine, is also shown. The trough has a keel to it, and slides to or fro along the stock in the same manner as in the arrow-throwing *balista*. (Fig. 7.)

Compare with figs. 7 & 8 for further explanation of details.

Lightning Source UK Ltd.
Milton Keynes UK
UKHW012011150922
408946UK00009B/181/J